The Vanished Imam

Musa al Sadr

The Vanished Imam

MUSA AL SADR AND THE SHIA OF LEBANON

Fouad Ajami

I.B.TAURIS & C^O L^{TD}

Publishers

LONDON

Published by I.B.Tauris & Co. Ltd.
3 Henrietta Street, Covent Garden
London WC2E 8PW

Printed in the United States of America

British Library Cataloguing in Publication Data

Ajami, Fouad
   The vanished Imam : Musa al Sadr and the Shia of Lebanon.
   1. Sadr, Musa al   2. Shiites——Biography
   3. Imam——Biography
   I. Title
   297'.82'0924   BP80.S/

ISBN 1-85043-025-X

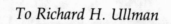

To Richard H. Ullman

Contents

[7]

A Note on Sources and Purpose

In writing this book I have used three kinds of material, which call for a few words of explanation.

I drew on American diplomatic cables and consular reports obtained under the Freedom of Information Act, covering the years 1965–1978. Much has been said, and appropriately so, about the folly of American policies in Lebanon and in other realms. But the diplomatic cables, sent by professionals from the field, were unusually thorough and reliable, stripped of any great illusions and doctrines. The diplomatic reports may not have been read back home; there is ample evidence that American policies toward Lebanon were not burdened by the knowledge and wisdom imparted in them. Rather like messages in a bottle, the reports tell us of the clear-sightedness of those who sent them; it is not their fault that the messages were not received on the other shore. For all the frustrations of acquiring this material, I found that the results vindicated the effort.

The second body of material consists of long interviews and discussions with many people who knew the Shia cleric at the center of this tale. The Shia of Lebanon, like similar disadvantaged populations in other parts of the Third World, are a people without much written and documented history. The oral material corrected some of this shortfall. A number of individuals gave freely of their time—and memory.

Sayyid Hussein Husseini, elected speaker of Parliament in 1984, was one of Musa al Sadr's early friends and companions in Lebanon; he sparked my interest in Musa al Sadr. In the fall of 1983, over a period of several weeks, he answered my queries about the cleric and provided his own perspective on the role that Musa al Sadr played in the change in the Shia situation.

Muhammad Mattar, a lawyer and historian, had the advantage of having been a "participant observer" in the politics of Shia Lebanon for more than a decade. Few know the recent history of Beirut and the dilemma of the Shia there as intimately as he. He was generous with what he knew of Musa al Sadr.

Nabih Berri, since 1980 leader of Amal, the militia established by Musa al Sadr, gave a brief reminiscence of the cleric.

Hamid al Sadr, the son of Musa al Sadr, was willing to talk to me at some length about his father. I brought to the subject the curiosity of an author. For Sayyid Hamid, the story was much more difficult and painful. I am grateful to him for his assistance, and for helping me overcome the feeling of an intruder stepping into sensitive territory.

Mamduh Abdallah, member of the Lebanese Parliament (1964– 1972) and of the Higher Shia Council (1969–1972), knew the world of the Shia before the political upheaval of recent years. He told of Musa al Sadr's early years in Lebanon.

Ali Ghandour, of Amman, Jordan, whose background is in southern Lebanon, shared with me some of Musa al Sadr's letters and helped untangle some of the events that surrounded his disappearance.

Jamil Marwah, a young journalist and editor, was in a position to know a good deal about Musa al Sadr. Mr. Marwah's father, Kamel (assassinated in 1966), who founded *Al Hayat*, one of Beirut's leading dailies, was a supporter and a friend of Musa al Sadr, and his son inherited his father's journalistic sense and his affection for the cleric. For over a year, he was uncommonly generous in answering my questions.

Muhammad Hammoud, a Shia businessman, had his own perspective on Musa al Sadr, and a reservoir of vivid recollections of Beirut and the Shia of Beirut.

Hassan Hashem, active in Amal since its inception, untangled for me some of the politics of the mid-1970s and told of his own political background.

Sayyid Hassan Husseini, son of Shia politician Sayyid Hussein Husseini, grew up in a political home and retained much of what he saw. He was both perceptive and generous.

Ahmad al Chalabi, a banker and a man with a keen sense of Arab politics, taught me a good deal about Musa al Sadr and the world of the Shia of Iraq.

[10]

Hussein Hijazi of southern Lebanon, a political activist, had a knack for retelling the traditional history of Shia Lebanon.

The Egyptian journalist Mohamed Heikal provided what information he had about Musa al Sadr and recalled the latter's relations with Cairo. Adel Rida and Sami Mansour, two other Egyptian journalists who wrote on Musa al Sadr, gave me their versions of what they thought the cleric was up to in Lebanon.

The gifted Arab writer Adonis (Ali Ahmad Said) advised me that I should capture the nonpolitical side of Musa al Sadr, that I should offer a portrait of him as a man. And toward that end, he related his own perception of Musa al Sadr, whom he knew, and his sense of his legacy.

Thomas Carolan, an American political officer in Beirut in the mid-1970s, reported on Musa al Sadr with frequency and depth. He was both candid and helpful with what he knew.

I have used my own discretion in attributing statements to individuals in the text.

A third unique source of information was supplied by the Shia journal *Al Irfan*. *Al Irfan* was founded in the coastal town of Sidon, in southern Lebanon, by a Shia writer, Ahmad Arif al Zayn, in 1909. To the extent that there is some kind of written record of Shia life in Lebanon, it is in the pages of *Al Irfan*. Quaint at times, depressing at others, run on a shoestring budget, *Al Irfan* is indispensable for understanding the history of Lebanon's Shia.

A word about intellectual detours: I myself saw Musa al Sadr only once, in the winter of 1963, when he visited my classroom. I was a few months short of eighteen and in my final year at a predominantly (Sunni) Muslim school in Beirut. He himself was new in the country, anxious to make himself known, a young man then, in his mid-thirties. He had arrived in Lebanon in 1959 from his birthplace in Iran.

As I was a Shia *assimilé*, from a background in the rural south, anxious to pass undetected in the modern world of Beirut, I showed no interest in the cleric. My school then was devoutly Pan-Arabist, the Egyptian Gamal Abdul Nasser its hero. Anything Persian, anything Shia, was anathema to me at the time. My great-grandfather had come from Iran to Lebanon in the mid-nineteenth century. That was part of some buried past, unexplored. It was given away in my last name, *Ajami*, which in Arabic meant "the Persian." The Arab-*Ajam* divide was very deep. And a Shia mullah wearing the black turban of a *sayyid* (a descendant of the Prophet) and speaking Persianized Arabic was a threat to something unresolved in my identity.

There was something special about him. He cut a striking figure. His looks—he was a very tall man—his aura, and the neatness of his clerical attire marked him as someone different from older Shia clerics who now and then came into my house in Beirut, or to my grandparents' home in a southern Lebanese village.

But this was Beirut in the early 1960s. One could not see a Shia cleric going very far in a city where the culture and the ways of the West were ascendant.

A year later, I left Lebanon for America. The cleric went on to fame and power. He became Shia Lebanon's leading figure and in 1978 he disappeared in Libya, only to become the object of a great cult. Two decades after I left, I became intensely curious about the man and decided to put together the puzzle of his career in Lebanon. Much had changed in Lebanon and, more important, in the nature of what was taken to be "modernity" and in the balance between the secular and worldly on the one hand and the religious on the other. By then I saw the cleric who had appeared in my classroom many years ago as standing at the crossroads of so many issues—across the Arab-Persian divide, across that split between the "modern" and the "traditional," the worldly and the sacred. There was something very concrete about him which I try to describe. But there was, too, something symbolic, something in his triumph and his disappearance, in the range of things men—detractors and devoted followers—read into him, in the history he embodied, which was even more relentless and more compelling. Now and then, a man, through no act of premeditation on his own part, serves as some kind of refractor: Standing at some remove from him, we see many lights converge on him; and then we see him illuminating the landscape around him.

I have incurred some debts along the way, and it is my pleasure to say something about them. The generosity of the MacArthur Foundation gave me the time to pursue this project. Walter Lippincott, Jr., my editor, has been unfailingly supportive, as he was a few years ago, when I wrote an earlier book. I have again drawn on his friendship and keen professional and literary sense. Kay Scheuer did a superb job editing the manuscript; her graceful touch always left me with the decent illusion that her many corrections were what I intended all along. Michelle Saltmarsh saw me through this entire effort: she did much of the library research, and her sturdiness was vital to the enterprise of telling such a sorrowful tale.

A final word about a special friend: Richard H. Ullman. Only I

A Note on Sources and Purpose

know the extent of my debt to him, and how important his friendship and support have been over the last decade. Fidelity is a special term; time and again, he has given evidence that fidelity is alive and well. It is to him that this book is dedicated; with all he has given, the deal is close to an act of banditry on my part.

Fouad Ajami

New York, New York

[13]

For the Nonspecialist Reader

So that the nonspecialist may easily follow the tale, while explanations in the text are kept to a minimum, this section offers a guide to relevant terms and dates.

GLOSSARY

abaya: gown.
ahl al bayt: the Prophet's family, descended through his daughter Fatima.
alim: religious scholar; its plural is ulama.
Ashura: literally, the tenth day of the month of Muharram; the date of Hussein's death at Kerbala.
Ayatollah: literally, "sign of God," a leading mujtahid.
fatwa: binding religious opinion.
ghaiba: concealment, absence; the occultation of the twelfth Imam.
hadith: the record of what the Prophet Muhammad said and did in his lifetime.
hasab: merit inherited from one's ancestors.
iqta: feudalism.
ijtihad: use of reason to interpret the intent of the law.
Imam: prayer leader in the Sunni tradition. In the Shia doctrine there are twelve Imams. Politics of the 1970s and 1980s have expanded the use of the term beyond its original meaning to include religious-political leaders such as Ayatollah Khomeini in Iran and Musa al Sadr in Lebanon.
khutba: sermon in a mosque after prayer.
al mahdi al Muntazar: the Awaited Imam, the twelfth Imam, vanished.
marja (model): an authoritative religious scholar to whose opinion laymen and lesser religious scholars defer. There is an element of selection and peer acceptance in the process whereby a marja emerges. The term marja is an abbreviation of the longer marja al Taqlid (literally meaning "model of imitation").

[15]

mufti: a religious judge or authority.
mujtahid: one who exercises ijtihad, one who has completed the study of Islamic jurisprudence.
mullah: cleric.
nasab: genealogy.
rujuh: return; along with ghaiba (absence) a central theme of the Shia belief in the "Hidden Imam."
sayyid: descendant of the Prophet through his daughter Fatima; noted families throughout the Muslim world claim sayyid status.
Taqiyya (dissimulation): a Shia doctrine that authorizes concealment of one's belief in an environment hostile to that belief.
taqlid: imitation; following a more learned individual.
tatruf: extremism.
ulama: religious leaders.
Umma: Muslim community.
Wilayat al Faqih: Ayatollah Ruhollah Khomeini's notion that a *faqih*, a jurist, has the right to govern.
zaim: political patron, a "big man." Lebanese term; another similar Ottoman title, bey, lingers in Lebanon. The plural is zuama.

THE TWELVE IMAMS

1. Ali (fourth caliph, first Imam); reigned 656–661

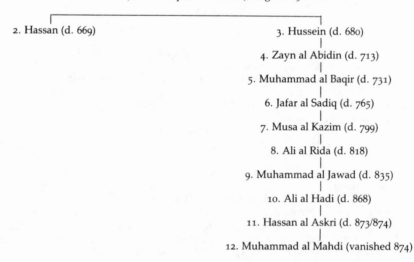

2. Hassan (d. 669)

3. Hussein (d. 680)

4. Zayn al Abidin (d. 713)

5. Muhammad al Baqir (d. 731)

6. Jafar al Sadiq (d. 765)

7. Musa al Kazim (d. 799)

8. Ali al Rida (d. 818)

9. Muhammad al Jawad (d. 835)

10. Ali al Hadi (d. 868)

11. Hassan al Askri (d. 873/874)

12. Muhammad al Mahdi (vanished 874)

ISLAMIC DATES OF RELEVANCE

A.D. 632	Death of the Prophet Muhammad; his daughter Fatima survives him.
632–656	The Rule of the Three Guided Caliphs (successors to the Prophet); the passing over of Ali, the Prophet's cousin and son-in-law, three times in a row for the Caliphate.

656–661	The murder of the third caliph, Uthman; a contested reign of Ali, the first Imam, who finally succeeds to the Caliphate; a civil war erupts between the partisans (literally the *Shia*) of Ali and those opposed to him. The power of Ali is in the Muslim province of Iraq, that of his opponents in Damascus. Ali is murdered. His oldest son, Hassan, abdicates in favor of Muawiyah, the governor of Damascus. Muawiyah lays the foundations of hereditary rule. The Umayyad empire is established with its seat of power in Damascus.
680	A great divide in Muslim history. The Prophet's grandson Imam Hussein, the third Imam, is killed in Kerbala, Iraq, by the troops of the Umayyad caliph Yazid. This gives the Shia of Ali and his line their martyr and endows Shiism with its sense of persecution and righteousness. Shiism assumes the role of the "pious opposition."
750	Collapse of the Damascus-based Umayyad dynasty, its replacement by the Abbasid dynasty. Early Shia hopes that this is a more favorable regime are thwarted.
765	Death of the sixth Imam, Jafar al Sadiq, who gives Shiism much of its jurisprudence and scholarly and legal content.
775–785	Abbasids gradually align with Sunni ulama.
873–874	The "occultation" of the twelfth Imam who, according to the millenarian expectation, is to return at the "end of time" and fill the earth with justice.
934–1055	A period dubbed the "Shia Century." Shia dynasties rise to power in some of the central lands of the Muslim world.
1055–1092	The reestablishment of a Sunni-based international Muslim order.
Early 1500s	The establishment of Shiism as state religion in Iran by the Safavid dynasty. Much of the rest of the Muslim world falls under the Sunni Ottoman state. Shiism identified with Persia and its thought and civilization.
1920s	What historian Bernard Lewis calls the "Sunni ascendancy" is established in the newly independent polity of Iraq, a country with a Shia majority.
1925	Reza Khan declares himself monarch of Iran. Proceeds with a "revolution from above" and undermines the Shia clergy.
1978–1979	The clerical revolution in Iran. The end of the Pahlavi dynasty.

SOME LEBANESE DATES OF RELEVANCE

1920	Ottoman sovereignty over Lebanon replaced by French mandate. The French establish Greater Lebanon by appending to Mount Lebanon, the heartland of the country, the (predominantly Sunni) coastal cities of Tripoli, Beirut, and Sidon and the predominantly Shia south and the Bekaa Valley in the East.

[17]

May 1926	Lebanese constitutional republic established under French mandatory control.
June 1941	Lebanon formally declared independent.
1943	Lebanese National Pact; Lebanese-French clashes.
1946	French evacuate Lebanon.
1958	First civil war in Lebanon between a pro-American regime and its Muslim and Druze antagonists.
1958–1964	The presidency of General Fuad Shihab; moderate, reform regime.
1959	Musa al Sadr arrives in Lebanon.
1964–1970	The presidency of Charles Helou, a weak, ineffective leader. Country subjected to the tremors of the Arab-Israeli war of June 1967.
1968	Israeli raid on Beirut airport. Beginning of conflict in Lebanon over Palestinian issue.
1969	Creation of Higher Shia Council.
November 1969	Cairo Agreement between Lebanese government and the PLO.
1970	Beginning of Suleiman Franjiyya's administration; PLO transfers its main base from Jordan to Lebanon.
May 1973	Confrontation between Lebanese army and PLO.
1973	Clash between tobacco planters and Lebanese security forces.
April 1975	Beginning of second civil war in Lebanon.
January 1976	Indirect Syrian intervention in the civil war.
February 1976	Syrian effort to formulate a political compromise in Lebanon.
June 1976	Syria invades in force; Palestinians mount a strong opposition.
1977	Kamal Junblatt, Druze chieftain and leftist leader, assassinated.
March 1978	Israel carries out Operation Litani in southern Lebanon.
August 31, 1978	Musa al Sadr disappears on visit to Libya.
June 1982	Israel invades Lebanon. Shatters Palestinian sanctuary.
August 1982	Bashir Gemayyel elected to the presidency of Lebanon. PLO evacuates Beirut.
September 1982	Bashir Gemayyel assassinated. Amin Gemayyel, Bashir's older brother, elected to the presidency.
Fall 1982–Winter 1984	An American attempt to shore up a pro-Western regime in Lebanon. Attempt all but abandoned after a suicide attack on U.S. Marine headquarters in October 1983 takes the lives of 241 Marines.
1983–1985	Growing Shia militancy in Beirut against the regime of President Amin Gemayyel, in the south against Israel.
May 1985	Palestinian-Shia fighting in Greater Beirut.

The Vanished Imam

I don't know why he should always have appeared to me symbolic. Perhaps this is the real cause of my interest in his fate.

Joseph Conrad, *Lord Jim*

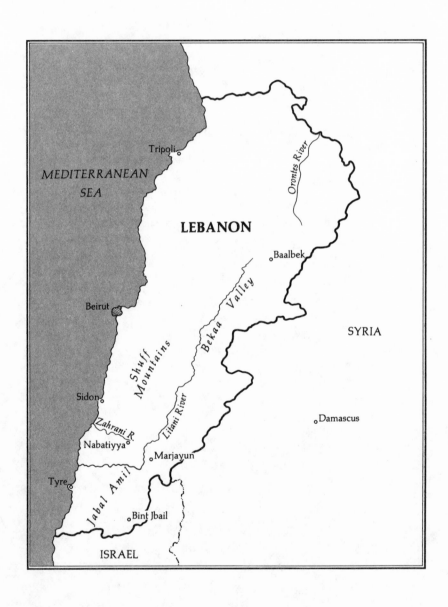

MEDITERRANEAN
SEA

Tripoli

Orontes River

LEBANON

Baalbek

Beirut

Bekaa Valley

SYRIA

Shuff Mountains

Sidon

Litani River

Damascus

Zahrani R.

Nabatiyya

Marjayun

Tyre

Jabal Amil

Bint Jbail

ISRAEL

Prologue: The Disappearance of Imam Musa al Sadr

In the summer of 1978, the tale of Sayyid Musa al Sadr, or Imam Musa al Sadr as he was known to his followers in Lebanon, came to a fitting Shia end: The cleric born in Qom, Iran, who had turned up in Lebanon in 1959 disappeared in Libya while on a visit to Libya's ruler, Colonel Muamar al Qaddafi. Musa al Sadr, a politically active and controversial cleric, had arrived in Libya on August 25; he was last seen on August 31, in a Tripoli hotel. He was on his way to a meeting with Colonel Qaddafi, he told a group of Lebanese who ran into him. He and two companions—a cleric and a journalist—were never heard from again. Musa al Sadr had come to Lebanon as a young man, thirty-one years of age. He was in his fiftieth year when he made his fateful trip to Libya. The Libyans claimed that he had left for Italy August 31 on an Alitalia flight. The Italian evidence belied the Libyan claim. Only his baggage arrived in Rome, checked into the Holiday Inn by two Libyans—one of them dressed in clerical attire —posing as Musa al Sadr and his lay companion.

Hard-headed men were sure that Musa al Sadr had been murdered by Qaddafi. But the cleric's faithful followers were left sitting under his posters, repeating his words, awaiting his "return." In the aftermath of his disappearance, Shia politics in Lebanon was in many ways a fight over the realm and the inheritance of a vanished Imam.

Reality imitated and served a Shia myth in Libya in that summer of 1978. In the Shia doctrine, the twelfth of the Imams (the successors to the Prophet through his daughter Fatima) vanished to the eyes of ordinary men in 873–874, to return at some future date and fill the earth with justice. This is the doctrine of the *Ghaiba,* the concealment of the

[21]

Hidden Imam. It came out of the early ordeals of Shiism, an embattled minority faith in the realm of Islam.

All eleven preceding Imams, so the Shia traditions maintained, had fallen in battle or had been poisoned or had died in prison at the hands of unjust usurpers of power. At its core Shia history was a tale of dispossession. The story of the martyrdom, *al maqatil*, of the Imams, related how the virtuous successors of the Prophet were denied the rule and the inheritance that should have been theirs. The Prophet had founded a state: it was both a religious and a political kingdom. He died in A.D. 632, some two decades after he received the revelation. In the scramble for his inheritance, the partisans, the *shia*, of the Prophet's family, maintained that legitimate succession belonged to the Prophet's cousin and son-in-law Ali and after him to the Prophet's descendants.

But the political kingdom was not to be Ali's or his descendants'; he was passed over for succession three times in a row. Under the rule of the first three caliphs (successors to the Prophet), Abu Bakr, Umar, and Uthman, Islam outgrew its Arabian birthplace, spilling into Syria, Iraq, Iran, and Egypt. It had become an affair of wealth and power. For the *shia* of Ali, however, history had become usurpation; the worldly had triumphed over the theocratic ideal. The caliphate finally came Ali's way a quarter century after the death of the Prophet. But it came during a time of discord in the Muslim polity. After a brief and contested reign Ali was murdered, and his son and designated successor, Hassan, abdicated in favor of Muawiyah, the governor of the Muslim province in Syria, a man of Banu Umayya—the Umayyad —whose leader had been an enemy of the Prophet. The Umayyads imposed on the Muslim community a system of hereditary rule. A century later, they were overthrown by another dynasty, the Abbasids, which manipulated the popular veneration of the Prophet's family to its own advantage. The Abbasids rose in rebellion in the name of *ahl al bayt* (the Prophet's family), but once triumphant they, too, ruled by the sword.

Against this worldly tale of dynastic triumph, the *Shia* of Ali and of his descendants and the dispossessed in the realm of Islam put forth an idea of an Imam (a religious and political leader) as the true inheritor of the Prophet's authority. The Imamate was transmitted through *nass*, special designation, from one legitimate Imam to his successor. In the eyes of these fervent partisans, the Imams, descendants of the Prophet through his daughter Fatima, were the bearers of Islam's message and truth. One Imam after another was eliminated, so the tradition maintained. And then, some two centuries after the assassi-

[22]

nation of the first Imam, the twelfth Imam, an infant, vanished lest he be harmed by the ruler. After his disappearance, the twelfth Imam made his will known through four of his deputies, during a period identified as *al Ghaiba al Sughra*, the lesser occultation, the lesser darkness. Then came the major occultation after the passing of the last of the four deputies in 939; *al Ghaiba al Kubra*, a period of greater darkness. History became usurpation. The deeds of men faltered, men awaited the return *rujuh*, of the Hidden Imam. In this messianic view, which shares its essential salvationism with Jewish and Christian eschatology, the Hidden Imam returns as a great avenger, a *mahdi*, a savior.[1] For this belief born of adversity and political dispossession, the Shia borrowed the authority of the Prophet Muhammad. A *hadith* (a tradition, a saying) attributed to the Prophet held out the promise of the Mahdi's return; "If there were to remain in the life of the world but one day, God would prolong that day until He sends in it a man from my community and my household. His name will be the same as my name. He will fill the earth with equity and justice as it was filled with oppression and tyranny."[2]

Shiism, politically vanquished early on in the history of Islam, had submitted to the harsh balance of force. There remained the consolation of a "blissful millennium" and the anticipation of an extraordinary individual who would bring it about. The promise to the faithful was "a blissful millennium, a culminating age when the world as we have known it will be put right. . . . Very shortly, the wicked great of this world would be humbled or destroyed, and the lowly, or those of them who had proved capable of maintaining the true faith and the loyalty, would be exalted to share the good things of this world."[3]

Musa al Sadr's tale merged with the millenarian sensibility of his people. The millenarian expectation of an extraordinary man who brings history to its appointed consummation, who appears when it is God's will for him to do so, was there for Musa al Sadr in a natural way. No one had to lean on the history or squeeze it too hard, or say that this modern tale was a playing out of an old belief. The pious would have been scandalized; there was no need to do this. The mil-

[1]Norman Cohn's classic work *The Pursuit of the Millennium* (New York, Oxford University Press, 1970), sketches the themes of millenarianism. The territory he covers is Western Europe between the eleventh and sixteenth century. But the sensibility he depicts is a universal one.

[2]Muhammad Husayn Tabataba'i, *Shi'ite Islam* (Albany: State University of New York Press, 1975), p. 211.

[3]Marshall Hodgson, *The Venture of Islam*, vol. I (Chicago: University of Chicago Press, 1974), pp. 373–374.

lenarian expectation worked in the aftermath of the cleric's disappearance just as it had when Sayyid Musa al Sadr was proclaimed Imam Musa al Sadr. Sayyids are a class that claim descent from the Prophet Muhammad. Sayyids inhabited the breadth of the Muslim world, the title had some prerogatives, a claim of a special place in the Prophet's eyes. But the title of Imam was a very special one. Strictly speaking, there were in the Shia doctrine only twelve Imams—Ali, and the eleven designated Imams who followed him, over a period of some two centuries, with the last one going into occultation. When Musa al Sadr "emerged" as Imam a mere decade after he had come to Lebanon, he had not claimed the title for himself. Nor had he been raised to the status of one of these twelve special, divinely ordained individuals; that would have been heresy. As with Khomeini in the late 1970s, the title of Imam was insinuated by followers and "accepted" by the designated cleric. In both cases, the designation, loaded with messianic expectation, emerged in the political arena. In Lebanon in the late 1960s, as in Iran ten years later, a cleric was set apart from other clerics and accorded a title with great evocative power and prestige. Both cases represented a break with Shia orthodoxy. Both cases represented the triumph of political activism over religious restraint.

If the beginning of Musa al Sadr's ascendancy fitted in with the ambiguity of the Shia symbolism—its mixture of things said and unsaid, its belief in an extraordinary individual to lead and redeem men—so did the disappearance in Libya. Musa al Sadr, his followers continued to say, will occupy the office he held (he was chairman of the Higher Shia Council which he himself had helped create in 1969, a mere decade after his arrival in Lebanon from his birthplace in Qom) until he reaches his sixty-fifth birthday in 1993. The ambiguity of the tale was a source of much of its power. The disorder in Lebanon—a civil war that broke out in 1975 with no end in sight, a Syrian drive into the country in 1976, an Israeli invasion in March 1978, and more disorder and ruin to come, a terrible war fought in the summer of 1982 between Israel and the Palestinians—made the time appropriate for a great millenarian myth. The people of the historically quiescent Shia community of Lebanon that Musa al Sadr had led and had tried to transform needed courage to stake out a claim to that fractured country. And the tale of Musa al Sadr served a multitude of needs. Like a chameleon, he was different things to different people. The patricians among his followers saw him as a man of moderate politics, a reformer. For others, Musa al Sadr was to become a great avenger, his tale and memory a warrant for daring deeds and uncompromising politics. His legacy was there to be claimed by men of means and caution and by young suicide drivers.

The legacy was enhanced when Iran erupted several months after Musa al Sadr's disappearance. Ayatollah Ruhollah Khomeini, a cleric leading men, an "armed Imam," brought down the monarchy in Iran. The men and women of Shia Lebanon had become part of a large upheaval. The Iranian revolution raised high the once timidly advanced and embarrassing symbols of Shia Islam. Shiism, for centuries a faith of lament and submission, had become a movement of exaltation and rebellion. The men of religion, mullahs like Musa al Sadr in his Iranian birthplace, had now instituted a rule of their own, *Wilayat al Faqih*, the rule of the jurist. The cleric who had come from Qom to Lebanon two decades earlier had broken with the dominant Shia clerical tradition of quietism and political withdrawal. And now, in Iran, the sole Shia state in the realm of Islam, clerics like him were summoning men to arms.

A Shia tradition attributed to the seventh Imam, Musa Ibn Jafar (d. 799), had prophesied the appearance in Qom of a man of faith who would lead a rebellion: "A man will come out from Qom and he will summon people to the right path. There will rally to him people resembling pieces of iron, not to be shaken by violent winds, unsparing and relying upon God."[4] The eighth-century saying was repeated in Iran as a tribute to the old cleric, Ayatollah Ruhollah Khomeini, who had returned in early 1979 from a fifteen-year exile to institute a "reign of virtue" and to proclaim an Islamic republic ruled by the clergy. But for the men and women in Shia Lebanon, the eighth-century saying applied to Musa al Sadr, the younger mullah they had known and embraced and whose return they claimed to anticipate.

Then in April 1980, a revered figure of Shia Iraq, Ayatollah Muhammad Baqir al Sadr, Sayyid Musa's cousin and brother-in-law (husband of his sister Fatima), a scholar of great prestige, was executed by Iraq's ruler, Saddam Hussein. That, too, spilled into Shia Lebanon, feeding the Shia theme of embattled righteousness and the revered aura of Musa al Sadr. Shia history is at its core martyrology: the death by poisoning or in battle of righteous Imams and leaders at the hands of cruel usurpers. Saddam Hussein, a merciless ruler from the Sunni minority of Iraq, was an embodiment of cruel authority, and Muhammad Baqir al Sadr, a literate man of sensitive temperament, as good a figure as the imagination could come up with for the role of martyr. Two years younger than Sayyid Musa, Muhammad Baqir al Sadr was the more scholarly of the two cousins. He was executed at age fifty. Sayyid Musa himself had disappeared when he was in his fiftieth

---

[4]Muhammad Jawad Maghniyya, *Khomeini wa al Dawla al Islamiyya* (Khomeini and the Islamic State) (Beirut: Dar al Ilm, 1979), pp. 38–39.

year. Muhammad Baqir al Sadr had written widely on matters of Islamic economics and modern philosophy. His books were bibles of Islamic modernists, Sunni and Shia alike, throughout the Muslim world. He wrote from a tradition nearly two centuries old: that of attempting to reconcile the traditions and strictures of Islam with the ideas and practices—and the threat—of the West. He had not been excessively political. But the Iranian upheaval in 1979 had widened the Sunni-Shia chasm in the Arab world. Across the border from Iraq, the Iranian revolution trumpeted its intention to export its ways; there were receptive men in Iraq. The regime of Saddam Hussein, at its base a minority Sunni regime of officers and state functionaries, was in a rule-or-die situation. Muhammad Baqir al Sadr was in the way; he was to be made an example of. He was, wrote one scholar of modern Iraq, Iraq's "most enlightened Shia legist and inspired much devotion among the people. Moreover, without any encouragement from him, more and more Shiis began to look up to him for political leadership and Iran's Arabic radio broadcasts repeatedly referred to him as the 'Khumayni of Iraq.' In the eyes of the government he loomed as a rival pole of attraction and a symbol of approaching danger."[5]

This was the Arab world during a particularly grim era. The subtlety had gone out of its politics. Rivals were murdered. Muhammad Baqir al Sadr and his sister were executed. The Shia laments and the literature of martyrology found contemporary enactments. Muhammad Baqir al Sadr's life had come to a grim end. Men mourned him—and vowed revenge. The story of his cousin, Sayyid Musa, was left unresolved; it was the more gripping tale.

In the summer of 1984, on the sixth anniversary of Musa al Sadr's disappearance, young men claiming him as their Imam shut down West Beirut, the Muslim half of the city divided by war. The deed was part expression of fidelity to the man who had worked amid the Shia of Lebanon for two decades, part demonstration of their new place and power in the ruined city; and, no doubt, there were those who believed, who wanted to believe, that the tall, handsome mullah would appear among them again, would be set free by his Libyan captors.

The mystery of Musa al Sadr's disappearance, with the rumors of his turning up now and then in Iran or Damascus, of being spotted praying in the Libyan desert with his companions, was of a piece with

[5]Hanna Batatu, "Iraq's Underground Shia Movements: Characteristics, Causes, and Prospects," *Middle East Journal*, 35 (Autumn 1981), 590.

the man's puzzle. Mystery trailed Musa al Sadr from the time he arrived in Lebanon; the Libyan episode only served to perpetuate the aura of a man who kept his own secrets, and about whom some of his own devoted followers continued to wonder. Musa al Sadr, a man with his own style and a man who knew how to get and hold attention, made his own entry into the world of Shia Lebanon. History arranged his fitting departure — or, shall we say, his fitting absence. He disappeared, leaving people to make of him what they wanted and what they needed.

Some remember Musa al Sadr as a man of simple needs, going about the country, they are fond of saying, in a small Volkswagen. Others recall a more narcissistic figure, a man overshadowing his followers, vain about his looks, theatrical and dramatic in appearance — tousled hair showing from underneath his turban in marked contrast to the austerity and "modesty" of a clerical look — and, naturally, they recall a more elegant and larger car. He presented himself for several years as a promoter of the Palestinian cause in Lebanon, yet many of his heirs and close companions suspect that the Libyans were doing what the Palestine Liberation Organization leaders had wanted done. In the early 1960s there were Christians in Lebanon who said that Musa al Sadr had the features and the aura of Christ; a decade later many of the same Christians, concerned about the Shia militia he had armed in the mid-1970s, dubbed him the Rasputin of Lebanon. His Pan-Arab critics had him arrive in Lebanon an agent of SAVAK, the Shah's intelligence, and had him disappear in 1978 a victim of foul play by the same dreaded SAVAK. He was both a rebel and a man who courted kings and men of wealth. An Egyptian Marxist who met him and distrusted him "right away" said of him that he was an "American pragmatist." An American diplomat in Beirut who knew him and reported on him with considerable insight said of him that he was a "crafty Persian." He was a cleric, and the son of an ayatollah at that, yet when he "thought aloud" among his more religiously skeptical followers, he was critical of the shackles and taboos of religion. For some he was a part of Shia Lebanon's drive for respectability, a man who said that Lebanon was *al Watan Nihai*, the final homeland, of the Shia; for others he was an ambitious, driven mullah who found a temporary haven in Lebanon but really wanted to make his mark in Iran.

Musa al Sadr's story now belongs to his followers in Lebanon; to the Shia community that embraced him. The story has become a piece of that community's history, reflecting its sense of being set apart from other men, its sense of righteousness and dispossession. The

[27]

story is not told here to pin down, once and for all, the "real" Sayyid Musa al Sadr or Imam Musa al Sadr. It is told to depict what men in need of help can make of a stranger's appearance and, then, of his absence.

[1]

The Intimate Stranger:
Sayyid Musa of Qom

The traffic between Iran and Shia Lebanon that brought Sayyid Musa to Lebanon is more than four centuries old. Ever since the Safavid dynasty imposed Shiism as a state religion in Iran in the sixteenth century, the traffic took ambitious Shia divines, mullahs, from the impoverished world of *Jabal Amil* (the mountain of Amil, a largely barren piece of land north of Galilee, today's southern Lebanon) to the large realm of Iran where clerics were needed to spread the Shia faith.[1] A latecomer to Shiism, Iran had become one of the two great centers in the Shia world (Iraq being the other). Imposed by the sword by a new dynasty, Shiism had to be transmitted and taught, men had to be instructed in the faith. The books and traditions of Shiism had been elaborated in the Arab heartland of Islam. The sixth of the twelve Shia Imams, Imam Jafar al Sadiq (d. 757), had laid the foundations of a Shia jurisprudence. These books and traditions were unknown in the Safavid realm; a zealous dynasty wanting to impose the Shia faith needed Shia divines to combat the strictures of the Sunni faith and to keep in check extreme sectarian Shia tendencies which venerated the Imams to a degree that placed the sectarians, *al Ghulat*, beyond the limits of Islam itself. The Shia divines invited into the Safavid realm were to steer a middle course between the dominant Sunni synthesis on the one hand and the excesses of popular religion on the other. The religious professionals who came to the

[1]Muhsin al Amin, *Khitat Jabal Amil* (A History of Jabal Amil) (Beirut: Matbat al Insaf, 1961); Muhammad Mekki, *Al Hayat al Fikriyya wa al Adabiyya fi Jabal Amil* (Intellectual and Literary Life in Jabal Amil) (Beirut: Dar al Andalus, 1963).

Safavid realm made ideal allies for the rulers: they were strangers; they needed and courted royal patronage.

There is a tale of nostalgia, timeless in so many ways, that Baha al Din al Amili (1546–1622), a Shia cleric who rose to great fame and distinction in the Persian city of Isfahan, told about the impoverished world he had left behind in Jabal Amil:

> Our fathers and grandfathers in Jabal Amil were devoted to knowledge, worship, and austerity and were men of standing and dignity. It was told about my grandfather Shams al Din that once upon a time heavy snow fell in our land and my grandfather had nothing to feed his family and children. My grandfather turned to my grandmother and asked her to quiet the children down so that he could pray to God to provide them with food. My grandmother took some snow to the *tanoor* (oven) and said this is the bread that we will bake. . . . Then out of the snow she made round loaves. This went on while my grandfather was busy praying. An hour later they had several loaves of our bread. When my grandfather saw this, he thanked God, Praise be to Him. . . . This is the way we were in Jabal Amil. All this was taken away from us when we came to the country of the *Ajam* (Persia).[2]

Baha al Din had been taken to Persia as a child. His father, Abdel Hussein Amili (d. 1576–1577) had fled to Persia when the (Sunni) Ottomans who governed the greater entity of Syria, of which Jabal Amil was then a remote corner, had executed his master on charges of heresy. In Persia, Baha al Din was to become one of the luminaries of his time. He studied theology, mathematics, and medicine and excelled as a writer and as a scholar. He caught the eye of the ruler, Shah Abbas, and became one of his confidants. In Isfahan, then the preeminent city of the Safavid realm, Baha al Din rose to the position of *Shaykh al Islam*, the highest religious dignitary in the city.

Persia had given Baha al Din the best that a scholar and a mullah with ambitions could have hoped for. But there remained in al Amili the theme passed onto him by his father—the marginality of the place his father fled. There was something of the wanderer in Baha al Din, a restlessness that led him to leave Persia and spend years of his life in Egypt, Syria, and other parts of the Muslim world. In a remarkable two-volume work, *Al Kashkul* (Beggar's Bowl), which offered a melange of his travels and views, he complained that it had been his fate to know kings and their courts.[3] He lamented that had it not

---

[2]Ali Marwah, *Tarikh Jibah* (The History of Jibah) (Beirut, 1967), p. 72.
[3]A modern edition of this work was published in Cairo in 1961, edited by Taher el Zawi: Baha al Din al Amili, *Al Kashkul* (Beggar's Bowl) (Cairo: Dar Ihya al Kutb, 1961).

been for the passage of his father to the country of *Ajam*, he would have been spared the patronage and the company of kings. Baha al Din's father had served the Safavid ruler Shah Tahmasp and had been appointed *Shaykh al Islam* in Khurasan, in northeastern Iran. There was more to Baha al Din's lament than the ingratitude of a man unable to appreciate what a new world had extended to him: there was also the romance with political and social marginality. In Jabal Amil one's hands were clean, poverty gave a sense of nobility and detachment. In Isfahan, power took away the outsider's badge of distinction and questioned the right of someone to lament cruelty and violations. Yet Baha al Din was too steeped in his father's tradition, the tradition of Jabal Amil, to come to terms with his new station. The dominant Shia tradition counseled distance from political power. At best one extended the state grudging acquiescence. Shia Iran challenged that response. A Shia state, or a state that claimed Shiism as a state religion, raised some fundamental problems for the Shia divines. Some of the religious scholars who came to the new realm were given considerable wealth and power. The dissonance between a tradition of political marginality and the new power was not easy to resolve; hence the lament of Baha al Din al Amili.

Coming as he did to Lebanon from Qom in 1959, Sayyid Musa al Sadr reversed the "normal" direction of the traffic. He came from a great center of the Shia world to a backwater. Musa al Sadr arrived in Lebanon with a Farsi accent and a Farsi way of speaking Arabic. Strictly speaking, he was an outsider; he had no Lebanese nationality; he came with an Iranian wife and an Iranian passport. He stood astride the great Arab-Persian divide—a chasm as old as Islam's triumph over Persia in the seventh century. But, by criteria much older than the nation-state, Musa al Sadr belonged. Far beyond Lebanon was a larger Shia world in Iraq and Iran. Young Musa came from its apex; the Sadrs were one of the most celebrated clerical and scholarly families in that world. He brought with him into Lebanon the prestige of his lineage and his birthplace. Moreover, he claimed descent from Jabal Amil. This is the way Musa al Sadr represented himself:

I am from a family whose origins are to be found in Lebanon: I am a descendant of the Imam Musa Ibn Jafar [the seventh of the twelve Shia Imams, d. 799]. My ancestors left Lebanon when Turkish oppression had reached an all-time high, when our books were burned and our ulama were killed. My ancestors then left for Iraq and Iran. In the two countries they established a large family.

I was born in Iran where my father, Sadr al Din al Sadr, lived and established a religious university, in the city of Qom. I first studied in that university, then I obtained a law degree at the University of Teheran. I completed religious education in Najaf, in Iraq. I assumed my religious duties in the south of Lebanon after the death of my relative, Sayyid Abdul Hussein Sharaf al Din.[4]

He was a newcomer. But he was no upstart. The fastidious country to which he had come had its deeply held notions of men born to lead and men fated to follow. Men of the clerical establishment and the literati of Shia Lebanon who journeyed to Iran and Iraq knew of his *bayt*, his family. Sayyid Muhsin al Amin (1867–1952), one of the most prolific of the literati and ulama of southern Lebanon, recorded a journey he had made with a cousin of his to Iraq and Iran in 1934, when Sayyid Musa himself was six years old. In Iraq, he was hosted by the al Sadrs, and in Meshed, where the eighth Imam, Imam Ali al Rida, was buried, his host was Sayyid Musa's father, Sadr al Din al Sadr: "Our host there was *al alim*, the scholar Sayyid Sadr al Din al Sadr. He used to live in Qom and oversee the seminary, *al madrasa* of Shaykh Abdul Karim al Yazdi. He was its noted presence, its leader. Then he moved to Meshed, to the Shrine of Imam Rida, where he was in the forefront of its *ulama*. After we left his home for a house we rented for the length of our stay there, he came to visit every morning and evening; he accompanied us on our return visits to the homes of people who called on us."[5] Fame traveled. Men were their reputations; and they inherited the reputations of their elders and ancestors. A man carried his *nasab* (genealogy) and *hasab* (inherited merit, to which he could add) with him in Muslim society. Knowing a man's hasab and nasab was essential to "estimating his worth." A man's relation to others didn't start from scratch. His hasab and nasab enabled others to judge what a man was made of. There was a presumption that an heir to a distinguished heritage had to live up to the tradition of his ancestors. As one historian put it, "A man whose ancestors had great talent and high estate would fear the loss of the collective 'force' that his ancestors had bequeathed to him."[6]

In both his paternal and maternal lineage, Sayyid Musa al Sadr carried the burden and the gift of a distinguished ancestry. He was the son of Ayatollah Sadr al Din al Sadr (1882–1953); his maternal grandfather, Ayatollah Hussein al Qummi (d. 1945), was an activist cleric in

[4]*Al Irfan* (Sidon, Lebanon) 58 (May 1970), 129.
[5]Muhsin al Amin, *Rihlat al Sayyid Muhsin al Amin* (The Travels of Sayyid Muhsin al Amin) (Beirut: Dal al Ghadir, pp. 190–191.
[6]Roy Mottahedeh, *Loyalty and Leadership in an Early Islamic Society* (Princeton: Princeton University Press, 1980), p. 101.

the forefront of the opposition to the Iranian ruler Reza Shah Pahlavi, and to the latter's effort, launched in the late 1920s and early 1930s, to centralize the state and undermine the role of the Shia clergy.

An awed biographer of Sayyid Musa al Sadr, writing in the mid-1960s, a bare seven years after his subject had arrived in Lebanon, started with a hadith of the Prophet. The Prophet Muhammad is reported to have said: "I and my family are a tree in Paradise, with branches in this world. Whoever holds on to those branches finds a way to his God." Sayyid Musa, said this biographer, "is a branch of this tree, with the prophecy as its base and the Imamate as its branch."[7]

The biography traced Sayyid Musa's roots to Jabal Amil, to Marakah in the district of Tyre, one of Jabal Amil's three hundred villages. Sayyid Musa's ancestor, Sayyid Saleh Sharaf al Din was an "accomplished alim," a "God-fearing and pious man." Late in the eighteenth century, Saleh Sharaf al Din was subjected to the persecution of an Ottoman governor, Ahmad Pasha al Jazzar (ruled 1775–1804), a harsh man depicted in the annals of Shia historiography as the quintessential tormentor of the faithful. Two of Sayyid Saleh's sons were killed; he himself was sentenced to death and "his home and books and treasures were burned." He was imprisoned, the biographer says, but legend had it that his prison guards were moved by his piety and prayers and that they let him escape. After his escape, Saleh Sharaf al Din made his way to the Shia holy city of Najaf in Iraq, home to a large clerical and scholarly community. His two surviving children, Sadr al Din (Sayyid Musa's great-grandfather) and Muhammad Ali, were brought to him in Najaf. In Najaf Sadr al Din became one of the distinguished *ulama* (religious scholars). He later—at a time left unspecified—left Najaf and settled in Isfahan, in Persia. He fathered five sons, all of whom became ulama.

Sadr al Din's most outstanding son was Ismael al Sadr (Sayyid Musa's grandfather). Ismael, born in Isfahan, completed his religious studies in Najaf, Iraq, and returned to Isfahan. Ismael, we are told by the biographer, studied with the great *mujtahid* (religious scholar) Mirza Hassan Shirazi (d. 1894), who led a major revolt in Iran in 1891–1892 against the Shah's granting of a tobacco monopoly to a British concern. Sayyid Ismael fathered four sons: Sayyid Muhammad Mahdi who participated in an Iraqi revolt against the British in 1920; Sayyid Sadr al Din (Sayyid Musa's father), Sayyid Muhammad

[7]Najib Jamal al Din, *Al Shiah ala al Muftraq* (The Shia at the Crossroads) (Beirut: n. p., 1967), p. 155.

Jawad, and Sayyid Haidar, all men of piety and learning. Sayyid Ismael rose to the rank of *marja* (source of imitation); he spent his last years in Najaf, where he died in 1919. The *sira* (the life and conduct) of Ismael al Sadr depicts him as a man with a "clean hand" in matters of money.

> Great wealth came to the marja, Sayyid Ismael al Sadr; but he refused to handle it himself and he trusted financial matters to two men known for their honesty and piety. Once, the two treasurers noticed the shabby attire of the marja's four sons and tried to get his permission to spend four pounds on the attire of the young boys. They did not tell him the purpose for which they sought to spend the money for they knew in advance that he would refuse to authorize it. The marja insisted on knowing what the money had to be spent on. One of the two treasurers stormed out, saying the money is for four descendants of the Prophet whose fate it has been to know an oppressor such as yourself.[8]

Clerics made their choice: they could embrace this world, *al dunya*, or they could rise above it. They could hoard wealth, pass it on to sons and heirs, or they could use the wealth made available to them by rich contributors to aid orphans and widows and the students of religious science who came to study with them. The temptations of *al dunya* were there for Sayyid Ismael, says the biographer, but he rose above them.

Ayatollah Sadr al Din al Sadr, Sayyid Musa's father, the biographer continues, was a modest man "more given to solitude than to crowds." He studied with two of the most distinguished luminaries of Shia scholarship in Najaf. Then in the mid-1920s, he crossed the border to Iran, where he settled in Khurasan and finally made his home in Qom. Sayyid Sadr al Din al Sadr was one of the pillars of the *madrasas*, the religious seminaries of Qom. "It is known," writes the biographer, that the position of *Marja al Taqlid* (the highest source of imitation), occupied by Ayatollah Hussein Borujerdi (d. 1961), "would have been Ayatollah Sadr al Din al Sadr's had he sought it." Sadr al Din al Sadr died in Qom in 1953, a man of great distinction and modest financial means. The biographer was told by Sayyid Musa, "I was twenty five years of age then. I don't remember ever seeing a Persian carpet in my father's home."

It was in such a home of "marjas and mujtahids and rebels" that "in Qom, in the Hijra [Islamic calendar] year of 1347, or A.D. 1928 was born that Lebanese Arab, Musa the son of Sadr al Din al Sadr, the son

[8]Ibid., p. 26.

of Ismael, the son of Sadr al Din, the son of Saleh Sharaf al Din, the rebel against al Jazzar in the south of Lebanon." Hasab and nasab were more important than birthplace. The man who arrived in the coastal town of Tyre as its *mufti* (religious judge) could trace his ancestry back to an alim from the south of Lebanon, and further back still to the seventh Imam. The Shia world—in Iran and Iraq and Lebanon—gave Musa al Sadr his legitimacy. The Iranian birthplace, problematic to those Sunni Arabs who asserted the primacy of nationality over faith, did not trouble the men who followed Musa al Sadr. The biographer acclaiming the cleric paid homage to Qom: Qom, he said, was to *ahl al bayt* what the city of Medina in the Hijaz (Islam's second holy city) was to the Prophet Muhammad and what Mecca was to God: It was a "blessed place."[9]

It is doubtful whether Sayyid Sadr al Din al Sadr, Sayyid Musa's father, thought of his move from Iraq to Iran in the 1920s as the crossing of an international frontier. It was a time of great political changes. The Ottoman empire had collapsed in World War I. Patterns of rule elaborated in Iraq over the course of centuries which rested on a balance between the imperial authority and the power of local notables and customs were shattered. When it held sway in the geographic entity of Iraq, Ottoman authority had to reconcile itself to the diversity of the country—a land of Sunni and Shia Muslims, Arabs and Kurds, small communities of Christians and Jews. The power of the Ottoman officialdom, based in the large towns of Mosul, Baghdad and Basra, was never able to penetrate into the countryside and the mountainous areas. Though a Sunni multinational state, the Ottoman empire had not sought to pacify the Shia majority of the country. By Ottoman rules and practice the Shia were excluded from public office. But their religious cities were permitted a great deal of latitude and autonomy. In the Shia holy cities of Najaf and Kerbala, clerics taught and held court and preserved the Shia scholarly tradition. The two cities were, an English scholar noted, "independent enclaves in which the Ottomans tended not to intervene unless provoked." Ties of faith, commerce, and family bound Najaf and Kerbala to the Persian religious centers across the borders. Najaf and Kerbala "looked more towards Qom and Mashhad than towards Baghdad or Basra."[10]

As World War I drew to a close, Iraq came under British control. The British had made their way there early in the course of the war,

[9]Ibid., p. 48.
[10]Peter Sluglett, *Britain in Iraq* (London: Ithaca Press, 1976), p. 301.

arriving for defensive reasons, in October 1914, to protect British interests at the head of the Persian Gulf. There were British interests in the oil fields of southern Iran and there was the long-standing concern of the British authorities in the India Office with the security of the empire in India, and that of its trade and communication routes. But in the course of the war, and then in its immediate aftermath, what the British called "marching into Mesopotamia" was transformed into British hegemony over Iraq. The awarding of the Near Eastern Mandates at San Remo in 1920 had given that "defensive" British move into Iraq a legal sanction of sorts. With the mandate, and the power of the Royal Air Force, the British set out to mold a new Iraqi polity. This could be done, they believed, and British interests in Iraq could be secured if a "native administration" were to be given the trappings of authority while British advisers exercised effective power.

In a land that had a Shia majority and large Kurdish, Jewish, and Christian minorities, with stubborn and rebellious tribes in the hinterland, the British propped up and set out to work through a minority government recruited from the urban Sunni notables and ex-Ottoman officers and bureaucrats. Initially, when they had made their way to Iraq, the British were convinced that the alienation of the Shia from the Ottomans would reconcile the former to British power. But the Shia holy cities would not submit. In plebiscites administered by the British in 1918–1919, the Shia mujtahids in Najaf and Kerbala came out against British rule in Iraq and against the government being installed by the British. It was clear that Britain wanted a minority regime, a desire that precluded an alliance with the Shia. In one scholar's apt summation: "With the Sunnis in power, the British could control the country through them; with the Shia in power there could have been no mandate."[11] For the British design to work, the power of the "reactionary Shia divines" (the words recur in British dispatches from Iraq) had to be broken and the more rebellious among them forced across the border to Iran.

Gertrude Bell, the remarkable traveler and Arabist who served as Oriental Secretary to the High Commissioner in Iraq, kept a diary of this turbulent time. She wrote, repeatedly, of the difficulty of "getting into touch with the Shias," particularly with their clerical leaders, the mujtahids. In her entry for March 14, 1920 we run across the Sadr family: "there is a group of these worthies in Kadimain, the holy city, eight miles from Baghdad, bitterly Pan-Islamic, anti-British. . . . Chief

---

[11]Ibid., p. 314.

among them are a family called Sadr, possibly more distinguished for religious learning than any other family in the whole Shiah world."[12]

An "advanced Shiah," a "free thinker" of Baghdad took the Oriental Secretary to visit one of the grand mujtahids, Hassan al Sadr, and his son, Sayyid Muhammad, a cousin of Musa al Sadr's father and a politically activist mullah then in his early thirties, who was to play a leading role in Iraqi politics over the next quarter century. (Sayyid Hassan al Sadr, a cousin of Ismael al Sadr, was a descendant of the same Saleh Sharaf al Din, who had fled his home in Jabal Amil in the early 1780s; Saleh had two sons, and Sayyid Hassan was a descendant of the younger son, whereas Ismael al Sadr belonged to the elder's branch.) The visit of Gertrude Bell, it should be noted, was made by a foreign woman of independent spirit who refused to be veiled for the occasion:

> Saiyid Hassan's son, Saiyid Muhammad stood on the balcony to welcome us, black robed, black bearded, and on his head the huge dark blue turban of the mujtahid class. Saiyid Hassan sat inside, an imposing, even a formidable figure, with a white beard reaching half way down his chest, and a turban a size larger than Saiyid Muhammad's. I sat beside him on the carpet and after formal greetings he began to talk in the rolling periods of the learned man. . . . We talked of the Sadr family in all its branches, Persian, Syrian and Mesopotamian; and then of books and collections of books in Cairo, London, Paris and Rome. . . .
>
> I said I wanted to tell him about Syria and told him all I knew down to the latest telegram which was that Faisal was to be crowned. "Over the whole of Syria to the sea?" he asked, with sudden interest. "No," I answered, "the French stay in Beyrout." "Then it's no good," he replied, and we discoursed the matter in all its bearings. Then we talked of Bolshevism. He agreed that it was the child of poverty and hunger, "but," he added, "all the world's poor and hungry since this war." I said that as far as I made out the Bolshevist idea was to sweep away all that ever had been and build afresh. I feared they didn't know the art of building. He approved that.[13]

A few months after this meeting took place, a full-scale rebellion in which Sayyid Muhammad al Sadr was to play a leading role erupted against the British in Iraq. A Western historian described Sayyid Muhammad as "the most active of the Baghdad Shia nationalists."[14] Another mujtahid of the Sadr family, one Sayyid Muhammad Mahdi

[12]Lady Bell, ed., *The Letters of Gertrude Bell* (London: Ernest Benn, 1927), p. 484.
[13]Ibid., pp. 484–485.
[14]P. W. Ireland, *Iraq* (New York, Russell & Russell, 1970), p. 146.

al Sadr (a paternal uncle of Sayyid Musa) was also to be found among the ranks of rebellious Shia divines. The Grand Marja Muhammad Taqi Shirazi gave the revolt religious sanction when he issued a *fatwa* (binding opinion) that "none but Muslims have a right to rule over Muslims."[15]

The rebellion, which raged throughout the summer of 1920 was overwhelmed in the autumn of that year. Its harvest was deeper Shia alienation from the British. The shape of things to come was much clearer in its aftermath: Britain would increase its reliance on the urban Sunni notables and the ex-Ottoman political class; and the emerging Iraqi regime would go it alone and exclude the Shia. Gertrude Bell herself recognized the problem. In her diary for January 22, 1921, she wrote: "The present government which is predominantly Sunni isn't doing anything to conciliate the Shiahs. They are now considering a number of administrative appointments for the provinces; almost all the names they put up are Sunnis, even for the wholly Shiah province on the Euphrates."[16]

The British-backed regime in Iraq was soon to be supplied with a monarch from outside Iraq and with more ex-Ottoman officers and bureaucrats. The monarch, Prince Faisal, the son of Britain's ally in World War I, the Hashemite Sharif Hussayn of Mecca, had staked a claim to Syria and had established there a short-lived "Arab kingdom." But the French had other plans for Syria: Syria was theirs, they insisted. France's "honor" and France's interest required a presence in the Levant. And so in the summer of 1920, the French had expelled Faisal and his entourage of officers and bureaucrats. Faisal was now a prince in search of a domain of his own. His British admirers and friends, among whom could be counted T. E. Lawrence and Gertrude Bell, pushed his "candidature" (the euphemism was important; the fiction had to be preserved that Faisal was the free choice of the people of Iraq) for the Iraqi throne. The British wanted a king who would reign but not rule. Faisal, a Sharif, a descendant of the Prophet but an outsider to Iraq, was an ideal candidate. In late June 1921, one year after his expulsion from Damascus, Faisal arrived in Iraq, a stranger dependent upon the power and the goodwill of his British patrons. Aboard the ship that brought him from the port of Jeddah were several Iraqi notables, escorting him to the country whose throne he sought, and among them was Sayyid Muhammad al Sadr, son of the grand mujtahid, Hassan al Sadr. It was still possible for someone like

[15]Abdallah Fayyad, *Al Thawra al Iraqiyya al Kubra* (The Great Iraqi Revolt) (Baghdad: al Irshad Press, 1963), p. 168.
[16]*The Letters of Gertrude Bell*, p.585.

Muhammad al Sadr to hope that the new regime and its proposed monarch would reach out to the Shia.

"Somehow or other," wrote Gertrude Bell in her diary for June 30, 1921, "Faisal has to be proclaimed King." All was not "smooth yet," she conceded: "We get reports about the lower Euphrates tribes preparing monstrous petitions in favour of a republic and of Shia mujtahids being all against Faisal." She would "never engage in creating kings again; it is too great a strain," she wrote in her diary entry of July 8, 1921. The work of "creating kings" was done by late August of 1921.[17]

The mujtahids continued to press for Iraqi independence from the British, to summon their followers to rebellion, to urge noncooperation with the British. It was hard to tell where ulama opposition to British rule ended and opposition to Sunni dominion began. In October 1922, the influential marja Mahdi al Khalisi denounced the Hashemite monarch and said that the people of Iraq were released from the pledge of obedience they had made to King Faisal. In November, a fatwa was issued by several leading mujtahids against proposed elections that the British and the monarchy wanted in order to ratify an Anglo-Iraqi treaty and to bestow greater respectibility and acceptance on the British presence in Iraq's political life. In mid-May of the next year the ulama of Najaf sought the support and opinion of their colleagues in the religious town of Kadhimain; they wrote to the marja Mahdi al Khalisi, to Sayyid Hassan al Sadr and to Sayyid Muhammad Mahdi al Sadr, asking them for a fatwa of their own against the elections. After the three of them provided a particularly strong ruling against the elections, the British authorities and the Iraqi cabinet ordered the expulsion from the country of the marja Mahdi al Khalisi, who had emerged as the spiritual head of the resistance to the Iraqi regime and its British patrons. A number of other mujtahids crossed the border to Iran in a show of solidarity with Mahdi al Khalisi.

The world of the mujtahids was being increasingly undermined; the culture which gave them a good deal of control over religious and educational matters was being subordinated to a state with a completely different cultural and political temperament. Faisal himself, the anointed head of this state, was a worldly and tolerant man. As a Sharif (though a Sunni) he traced his descent through Imam Hassan, the second of the Twelve Imams, to the Prophet. He had no particular hostility to the Shia. But the political class around him was made of

[17]Ibid., pp. 607 and 610.

different material. Some in his entourage brought to the new polity a rigid, really a Germanic, view of nationalism that was almost racialist in its assumptions about who was "an Arab" and who was not. The mujtahid culture in the Shia holy cities, composed as it was of Persian and Arab, was a world that the new political class was determined to break. An educational system whose orthodoxy was imposed and defined by one Sati al Husri (1880–1968), the most influential Pan-Arabist ideologue of his time, saw the Shia society of Iraq and its religious class as obstacles in the way of a uniform, organic culture. From his position as director general of the Ministry of Education, Sati al Husri, who had been a zealous Ottomanist, enforced a system of education which rewrote much of Islamic history, giving pride of place to its Arab core, dismissing and distorting the contributions of the high medieval culture of Persian Islam. In the "pure" Arab historiography of Sati al Husri and his political class, the Shia and their mujtahids were men beyond the limits of the "Arab nation." Iraq, in the vision of Sati al Husri and like minded ideologues, was to be the nucleus of a larger Arab entity. Its differences were to be leveled; its heterogenous sects were to be subordinated. The British political historian Elie Kedourie summed up the outlook and mentality of this political class: "The attitude of the ruling classes to the population they ruled was one of disdain and distaste: they were townsmen ruling over a population of primitive countrymen; they were the government in its exalted majesty and boundless power, the others were the subjects who must be prostrate in obedience."[18] A popular Shia saying expressed the growing sense of political dispossession on the part of the Shia: "Taxes and death are for the Shia while posts are for the Sunni."

Those among the mujtahids who would not bend with the wind or play by the new rules chose to make new homes for themselves in the religious towns in Iran. A combination of forced deportations of mujtahids and voluntary exodus to Iran was to deplete much of the Shia clerical community in Iraq. Sayyid Musa's father, Sayyid Sadr al Din al Sadr, was part of that exodus. A traveler from Lebanon depicted its impact on the clerical community in Iraq. Some twelve thousand religious scholars had studied in the *madrasas*, the seminaries in Najaf, before the coming of the British; now, he noted, "the number is decreasing day by day; it is feared that religious learning might one day become extinct."[19]

[18]Elie Kedourie, "The Kingdom of Iraq: A Retrospect" in Kedourie's collection of essays, *The Chatham House Version and Other Middle Eastern Studies* (London: Weidenfeld and Nicolson, 1970), p. 261.
[19]Muhsin al Amin, *Rihlat al Sayyid Muhsin al Amin*, p. 106.

The Shia *madrasas* in Iran were given a great boost by the events in Iraq. Over the course of the preceding century, in the words of one American student of Iran, Qom's *madrasas* had fallen into "disuse and ruin and the town had suffered what a leading editor and pedagogue calls an intellectual famine."[20] The newcomers needed the sanctuary in Qom and they set out to rebuild it. One of the new arrivals was Shaykh Abdul Karim Yazdi (d. 1935), the main force behind this revival; another was Sayyid Musa's father, Shaykh Yazdi's colleague and principal associate.

On the face of it the passage across the border from Iraq to Iran made by Ayatollah Sadr al Din al Sadr was a passage to a state of the faithful, to a Shia state. But in Iran, too, it was a difficult time for Shia clerics. An ambitious soldier, Reza Khan, later Reza Shah, was to declare himself monarch in 1925 and launch his own "revolution from above." Reza Shah was a merciless man. Rival centers of power—the tribes, the mullahs—were to be broken. It was a time of frustration for the mullahs. Reza Shah was determined, wrote a Western historian, "to replace Islam as the cohesive force of society by loyalty to the territorial state. He regarded the religious classes as an obstacle to his policy."[21] In 1929, one year after the birth of Sayyid Musa, "modern dress" was decreed for all Iranian men. The hold of the ulama over the educational system was being challenged. In 1931, Muhammad Reza Pahlavi, Shah Reza's son, then a boy of twelve, was sent off to school in Switzerland. The religious schools in Iran languished: such schools were for the poor, and they were of the past in a place attempting to walk away from the past. Then in 1935–1936, another symbolic struggle was launched over the unveiling of women. The state picked this highly charged issue to highlight the struggle between its new ways and those sustained and defended by the clergy.

A modernizing autocracy placed the men of religion on the defensive. Help for the clerics came from the bazaar, the fortress of national tradition. But there was a price to be paid: such assistance rendered the custodians of the religious institution so dependent on public opinion and on the financial contributions of the bazaar that they were too timid to attempt any great innovations. Shaykh Yazdi, himself a man of relatively enlightened ways, once thought of dispatching some religious students to Europe to study foreign lan-

[20]Michael Fischer, *Iran: From Religious Dispute to Revolution* (Cambridge: Harvard University Press, 1980), p. 109.
[21]Ann Lambton, "A Reconsideration of the Position of the Marja' Taqlid and the Religious Institution," *Studia Islamica*, 20 (1964), 118. See also Nikki Keddie's authoritative *Roots of Revolution* (New Haven: Yale University Press, 1981), pp. 79–112.

guages and learn European ways. But the bazaaris vetoed the idea, theatening to cut off their contributions, and the project was abandoned. Enrollment in religious schools declined. Sayyid Muhsin al Amin, a scholar from the south of Lebanon who traveled to Iran in 1934 and met Sayyid Musa's father, writes of a religious educational system in the throes of a crisis. There were nine hundred students studying with Shaykh Yazdi, he says. They had their own physician provided by Shaykh Yazdi, and they were fed and housed from funds available to the shaykh. "We raise and educate the students," Shaykh Yazdi said to his visitor, "But when the education comes to fruition, the student takes off his turban and wears the attire of *ahl al hukm* (the men in power, the bureaucrats) and joins one of the government departments."[22]

Young Musa al Sadr himself was drawn to the secular educational system. Although son of an alim—and it was normal for religious scholars of the sayyid class to follow the path of their fathers—Sayyid Musa recalls that he began a secular educational course, though he was persuaded otherwise by his father. Islam and Islamic education were "in peril." His gifts were needed to shore up a clerical profession then on the defensive. The paternal command was adhered to—but not without some equivocation. The fact that Musa al Sadr enrolled at the law school at the University of Teheran when he was in his mid-twenties is indicative of a modern cast of mind, a certain dissatisfaction with what the world of the clerics and the education of the clerics had to offer. The world of the clerics was, on the whole, an isolated ghetto. And there was in this one sayyid a curiosity about the world beyond.

It was this alertness that brought Musa al Sadr to the attention of the relative who invited him to Lebanon. Sayyid Abdul Hussein Sharaf al Din (1873–1957), the mufti of Tyre, had seen young Musa during one of those trips that clerics from Lebanon made to Iraq and Iran. There were close family ties between Sayyid Abdul Hussein's household and Sayyid Musa's. Sayyid Abdul Hussein was a decade older than Sayyid Musa's father. Young Musa caught his eye on a journey to Iran he made in the mid-1930s. He kept track of the young student. In 1955 with Sayyid Abdul Hussein in his eighty-second year, an invitation was sent to Sayyid Musa to visit the Sharaf al Dins in Tyre. The purpose was to interest Sayyid Musa in Lebanon. A Shia observer from the Gulf who knew the Sharaf al Dins and the Sadrs said that Sayyid Abdul Hussein, a man of some distinction in the Shia

[22]Muhsin al Amin, *Rihlat al Sayyid Muhsin al Amin*, p. 170.

world, a man who had been born and educated in Iraq, was disappointed with the caliber of his own sons. The clerical mantle had to be passed; and Sayyid Abdul Hussein, despairing of his own sons, thought of Sayyid Musa as a worthy inheritor. Sayyid Abdul Hussein had spent much of his first three decades in the holy cities of Iraq, among the Sadrs. His maternal grandfather was one of the Sadr family, his maternal uncle was the grand mujtahid Hassan al Sadr (the cousin of Sayyid Musa's grandfather) whom we encountered earlier. Sayyid Abdul Hussein had been taken to Lebanon by his father when he was eight years old while his father completed his religious education; he returned a decade later for his own studies and stayed in Iraq until 1905, when he was in his early thirties.

In his time Sayyid Abdul Hussein was something of an activist and a reformer. He had returned to Lebanon during the waning years of the Ottoman empire. His biographer describes the time of his arrival as a "dark age" of ignorance and feudalism; it was a time when the masses, *al ama*, were terrified of their masters and landlords, of the Ottoman officialdom, a time when the flock, in the words of the biographer, took life as "slavery and obedience."[23] To this remote corner of Greater Syria Sayyid Abdul Hussein brought an energetic clerical style; he had an active interest in political matters. When the stirrings of protonationalism made themselves felt in this rural community after the collapse of the Ottoman empire, some literati and notables in Jabal Amil pushed for an independent Greater Syria under Sharif Husayn's son Prince Faisal. Sayyid Abdul Hussein was active in this movement. He headed a Shia delegation to Damascus in 1920 to make the case for Syrian unity. The effort failed. The French mandate in Syria and Lebanon put off the question of Syria's independence. And in that year, the Shia world in Jabal Amil, the Bekaa Valley, and the (Sunni) coastal cities of Sidon and Tripoli and Beirut were appended by the French mandatory power to the Maronite core of Mount Lebanon. Greater Lebanon was a gift made by the French to their Maronite dependents.

The French mandate was a time of some difficulty for Sayyid Abdul Hussein. His home in Tyre was looted by French soldiers, his books and manuscripts were confiscated, another home in a neighboring village was burned. He fled to Damascus but had to quit that city for

[23]Abd al Hussein Sharaf al Din, *Kitab al Muraja'at* (The Book of Disputations) (Beirut: Dar al Andalus, 1963), pp. 12–13. Further biographical information about Sayyid Abdul Hussein Sharaf al Din and his generation and elders among the Sadrs can be found in Abbas Ali, *Sharaf al Din: Hazmat Daw ala Tariq al Fikr al Imami* (Sharaf al Din: A Ray of Light on the Imami Road) (Najaf, 1968).

Egypt and then for a brief stay of several months in Palestine before he was allowed to return to his base in Tyre. With the limited resources available to him in that city and with some contributions made by its expatriates in West Africa—men driven out of the south of Lebanon by poverty—Sayyid Abdul Hussein managed to build a mosque and a secondary school which Tyre desperately needed; he even built a school for girls in 1942. This last deed was proof of the man's relatively tolerant ways.

The fiefdom in Tyre enabled Sayyid Abdul Hussein to write the books he continued to write on religious matters, to build for himself a respectable scholarly reputation in the faraway *madrasas* of Najaf and Qom. And there remained in him a healthy interest in political matters. In mid-May 1945, the French, trying one last throw of the dice to retain a foothold in Syria and Lebanon in the face of local and Allied opposition, dispatched Senegalese troops to Beirut to reinforce the French presence. Violent resistance broke out against the French in Damascus; petitions were sent to the British and to the Americans urging complete independence for Syria and Lebanon. A petition in the files of the American Legation in Beirut was sent by the mujtahid of Tyre, Sayyid Abdul Hussein Sharaf al Din: "We inhabitants of Jabal Amil protest strongly against landing of foreign troops in our country, which is free. This is a slighting of our liberty and a disdain of our honor. We are prepared to defend our independence. We would not hesitate to shed the last drop of our blood to that effect."[24]

It was this modest inheritance that Sayyid Abdul Hussein wanted to pass on to Musa al Sadr. The offer was extended by Sayyid Abdul Hussein's sons after the death of their father in December 1957. Musa al Sadr had by then completed four years of religious education in Najaf, Iraq, and had returned to Qom. In Najaf he was a protégé of the Grand Marja Ayatollah Muhsin al Hakim (d. 1970). Muhsin al Hakim wielded great religious influence over the Shia of Lebanon; the old cleric, presiding in Najaf, thought of Shia Lebanon as a domain of his. Some wealthy men there made their contributions to Sayyid Muhsin, took him to be their marja. Muhsin al Hakim's own father, Sayyid Mahdi, had lived and worked in Bint Jbail, a town in southern Lebanon; the death of Sayyid Abdul Hussein had left a gap in Lebanon that the marja thought should be filled by a cleric of promise. Sayyid Muhsin advised his young disciple to accept the invitation extended him from Tyre. Letters were dispatched to the Shia notables

[24]Sharaf al Din's petition in Monthly Political Review of American Consulate, Beirut, May 24, 1945.

of Lebanon by the marja, Sayyid Muhsin, telling of the gifts of Musa al Sadr.

The Iranian-born cleric took his time before he accepted Tyre's invitation. Consider Iran with its great cities and its 628,000 square miles and set it alongside Lebanon with its 4,105 square miles; the cleric's reluctance to go to the small place is easy to understand. Besides, Iran was Musa al Sadr's home, its language his first language. The myth in Lebanon about the "Arab" born in Qom notwithstanding, Musa al Sadr was a man of Iran, formed by its currents of thought. An intensely political man, he was in his teens when his maternal grandfather tried to rein in Reza Shah's drive against the clergy; he was in his mid-twenties in the early 1950s when Iran went through a nationalist eruption which culminated in the brief triumph of Mohammed Mossadeq, a Western-educated liberal nationalist, over the Shah and in the exile of the latter. (The back of the Mossadeq experiment was broken in 1953 by an American-led effort against him.) Sayyid Musa, the son of a leading ayatollah, and on his maternal side the grandson of an Iranian ayatollah of great distinction, was under no compulsion to leave his birthplace. His was not a case of a man being banished by his country, and needing to seek fame and fortune in another place. A shrewd man, he knew that he would have to charm and court a new country, learn its ways, seek its acceptance. Furthermore a political and clerical endeavor waged in the late 1950s, by a man of Iranian birth in an Arabic-speaking place, was no easy task. A strident kind of Arabism held sway in the Levant in the late 1950s and early 1960s. A young man of Iranian birth pondering his options must have worried about what awaited him in the land that he had visited only once in the summer of 1957.

But the invitation was accepted. On the face of it, the move from Iran to Lebanon was to a lesser place. But 1959 was not such a bad time for an Iranian-born cleric to try his luck in a distant Shia realm. The time of Musa al Sadr's departure from Iran was a "quietist" time for the ulama of Iran.[25] Even the firebrand Ruhollah Khomeini, who incurred the government's wrath by instigating a popular uprising in the summer of 1963—which led to his exile from the country in 1964—kept a low profile in the late 1950s.

The leading Iranian cleric of this time, the Marja al Taqlid, was Ayatollah Hussein Borujerdi (d. 1961). Borujerdi, a cleric of conservative temperament, was not unfriendly to the Shah. He believed in the

[25]See Keddie, *Roots of Revolution*, pp. 142–182; and Lambton, "A Reconsideration," pp. 118–120.

separation of religion and politics and frowned on political activism.[26] Royal dictatorship was in full stride in the late 1950s. The view of Borujerdi's entourage on the role men of the religious institutions should play was summarized by one cleric as follows: "Our duty is to advise, not to fight."[27] It was in this spirit that Borujerdi refused to come out against the overthrow of the popular prime minister Mohammed Mossadeq in 1953.

The clerics had their grievances against the Iranian monarch. But they lacked the self-confidence and the ideas to combat Muhammad Reza Shah's dictatorship. Aided by American funds and support and by oil wealth, the Shah had set out to remake Iran in a Western image. There were enough carrots and sticks in his arsenal to overwhelm the clerics. Besides, the latter were between a rock and a hard place. Opposed as they were to a monarch who viewed them with contempt, they were also worried about the appeal of the Communist party in Iran. This was not the clerics' time. The disillusionment with modernity which gave them their chance in the late 1970s had not yet come. Iran was groping its way in the 1950s: the yearning for change, for the things and the ways of the West, was strong enough to put the ulama on the defensive. No "Islamic" or clerical response had been formulated to cope with the dilemmas of a society increasingly urbanized and literate. Some efforts in this direction were to be made in the early and mid-1960s, a few years after Sayyid Musa left his birthplace. Some of the enlightened clerics and some Muslim liberals realized the need to adapt the message and the content of religious discourse to a changing society: they feared, and rightly so, that unless the attempt was made the religious institutions would become hopelessly obsolete. But 1959 was not exactly springtime for the clerical community of Iran. It made sense for a restless and ambitious cleric to give a new place a try.

The new place was not without its attractions: though Lebanon was far smaller than the country of Sayyid Musa's birthplace, it was also a more fluid environment. The Shia religious institution was nowhere near so elaborate, so hierarchical as that of Iran. For that reason, it was an easier structure to subvert and to challenge. In Iran Sayyid Musa al Sadr would have had to work his way up through the ranks and fight for his own place. We have no precise figures on the num-

[26]Keddie, *Roots of Revolution*, p. 200. See also Hamid Algar, "The Oppositional Role of the Ulama in Twentieth Century Iran," in Nikki Keddie, ed., *Scholars, Saints, and Sufis* (Berkeley: University of California Press, 1972), pp. 231–255.
[27]The statement is attributed to Ayatollah Arbab Isfahan in W. G. Millward, "Aspects of Modernism in Shia Islam," *Studia Islamica*, 37 (1973), 115.

ber of mullahs in Iran in 1959 when he left for Lebanon. There are figures, though, for the late 1970s, which put the mullah population of Iran somewhere between 120,000 and 180,000. Iran could have had a hundred thousand clerics when Sayyid Musa came to Lebanon. Even so gifted a man as he would have had a very crowded field in which to make his way.

Moving some distance from the place where his father and maternal grandfather excelled could have been another incentive for coming to Lebanon. In Iran Sayyid Musa would have remained the son of Ayatollah Sadr al Din al Sadr, the grandson of Ayatollah Qummi. (Such was the fate and choice of his older brother Rida, born in 1922, who stayed in Qom.) In Lebanon, he had a chance to begin anew, in an environment of his own. The prestige of the lineage carried into the new place. But the burden of the ancestors was lighter.

Creativity is often easier in a new place. Self-fashioning and the playing of roles, so essential to creativity, is harder to do in familiar surroundings. A new place releases a man's energies. Lebanon was to do this for Musa al Sadr. The newcomer's instincts about the possibilities afforded by a new country were to be borne out in record time.

Musa al Sadr's talents lay in the political realm—in his ability to lead men, in a remarkable capacity to relate to strangers. He was no great mujtahid. Not for him were the heavy treatises that clerics had to write if they were to "emerge" and stand out among their colleagues in Iran and Iraq. The professional standards, heavy, imposing, and stilted, that would have shackled him in Iran could be violated with relative impunity in Lebanon.

The skills and perspectives learned in Iran could be played out and experimented with in Lebanon. Musa al Sadr brought with him to Lebanon the talents of the great Iranian ulama and ayatollahs. It was not that he tried to reproduce Iran in Lebanon. He was too shrewd a man, too much a pragmatist, to think in such ways. He knew Iran; for him it was not a textbook or a land of the imagination as it was for some of the Shia in Lebanon. But he had come to Lebanon long after his formative years were over. Even as he learned a new environment, his birth place—its ideas, the great deeds of members of the clerical profession—continued to beckon and to inspire. For over four centuries, since the introduction of Shia Islam to Iran, Iranian ulama had supported and opposed kings, raised and paid for private armies, put together coalitions that spanned the entire political spectrum, all the way from rich merchants to urban mobs. That kind of knowledge and history the Iranian-born cleric brought with him to Lebanon.

[47]

"Out of the mud we can make a prince," said a Russian testifying as to why he and thousands of others followed Emelyan Pugachev, a pretender, in a furious uprising in 1773–1774, when a claim was put forth that the pretender was the deceased tsar Peter III. Peter III had been murdered in 1762; the pretender bore no physical resemblance to him. But he promised the mutineers threatened by an expanding state "eternal freedom, the rivers and the seas, and all sorts of benefits and subsidies, food, powder and lead, rank and honor, and liberty for centuries to come."[28] Men make their leaders when they want them, when they need them.

In no time, the man born in Qom was to stand out in Lebanon. No great effort, however, had to go into making of Musa al Sadr what he was not. In so many ways he was a casting director's dream of a cult figure. From his imposing height (six feet six inches) in a land of relatively short men, to the flamboyant way he wore his turban, and the cleanliness and elegance of his attire, he fitted the role. Lebanon has long been a country finicky about the looks, the aura, *al haiba* of a leader. The Shia in particular have been noted to be a people of some vanity. In the Shia tradition, the Imams were not only morally infallible men (an Imam was said to be *masum*, not subject to error), but also physically perfect beings. A blind man or a lame man would not have been accepted as an Imam. Musa al Sadr, a handsome man of striking looks, was true to his people's fantasy of what a man of piety and distinction and high birth slated for bigger things should look like. He was, in addition, a dazzling speaker in a culture that exalted the spoken word and those who could express in classical Arabic what was on the minds of others.

He was, as it was said of him many times, a "man unlike others." There was something special about him. It was a quality that even men beyond the Shia faith, outsiders, readily saw. An American diplomat who visited him on one occasion cabled home the following message:

Made one hour courtesy call on Imam Sadr.

Although we conversed through an interpreter, he is without debate one of the most, if not the most, impressive individual I have met in Lebanon. He is over six feet tall, has piercing, deep-set eyes. Although he spoke in a quiet, detached manner, I could well imagine him inciting a group of men to go to any extremes that he desires. His charisma is obvious and his apparent sincerity is awe-inspiring.

He dwelt at some length on his admiration for our country's attach-

[28]Paul Avrich, *Russian Rebels* (New York: Norton, 1976), pp. 192–193.

ment to the rights of man and the books he read on Washington, Lincoln and our other leaders. He then discussed the Communist menace. . . . He is optimistic that peace can return to this part of the world and that Muslims can devote their energies to repairing the inroads that the Communists had made in recent years. . . . He believed that GOL [Government of Lebanon] and other observers here have underestimated the effectiveness of Communist propaganda which has found fertile soil among young southerners who are able easily to compare Beirut extravagence with backwardness and poverty that exist only an hour or so away from the affluent capital. The "rulers" in Beirut are only slowly realizing the importance of this problem.[29]

A Lebanese publisher of Greek Orthodox background, one of Lebanon's most moderate men, who stood above the feuds of the country and knew Sayyid Musa al Sadr over a number of years, recorded his impression of the cleric:

Calm, "the tranquil force," his face marked with deep gentleness, the Imam Musa al Sadr seemed to come from nowhere. . . . By his charisma, he obliged his enemies and friends alike to venerate him, to respect his clairvoyance. His credibility was never questioned, in spite of the rumours concerning his origins. . . . [He was] tall, very tall: To the point of seeming to soar above the often frenzied crowds that his presence drew together: black turban tilted with a slight negligence. His enemies seemed charmed by his enigmatic and benevolent smile, whereas his friends found that his bearded face constantly reflected profound melancholy. . . . One often had the impression, watching him, that his immense head was constantly trying to rise even higher. And his hands gave the impression of gathering up his floating robe, the *abaya* in which he wrapped himself, as if he were preparing himself to step out of some antique miniature.

Even while he harangued the masses, his words were calm and sybilline, an oracle of love and hope, punctuated with mysterious accents of some mystic vision that appealed as much to reason as to the heart.

His personal contacts were a ritual of seduction. When he would humbly open the door and invite you to enter a modest office or an ordinary salon of some home which sheltered him, one would wonder why this man was there, by what mystery, and how such a mythic persona could seem so familiar. Then, as in a Persian miniature, one would sit at his feet, looking to reap the teachings of the master, only to leave with more questions than one had brought him.[30]

[29]Ambassador George Godley to State Department, U.S. Embassy telegram 5059, Beirut, April 1974.
[30]Ghassan Tueni, *Une guerre pour les autres* (Paris: Jean Claude Lattès, 1985), pp. 97–98.

The words and impressions of two outsiders to the Shia faith: these must be faint echoes of what men who took Musa al Sadr as a piece of their history, who understood his symbols and words, saw in him.

There are occasions, said one Shia observer with a literary bent and a good deal of education, when "history walks on two legs." And in the case of Sayyid Musa, he added, Shia history walked on two legs. There were Persian miniatures which portrayed the Imams of Shia history and the members of *ahl al bayt* as men with black turbans, flowing *abayas* (gowns), and imposing looks. Folk poetry and *marathi* (set pieces of lamentation for the sufferings of *ahl al bayt*) depicted the twelve Imams and the other members of the Prophet's family as men of courage and noble manners. With his black turban and height and his persianized Arabic, Musa al Sadr embodied that history, summoned its power. Tales were told by the impressionable Shia of Lebanon about the newcomer's eyes, about the power people saw in his eyes. It must have been that in a historically intimidated community, they were impressed by the fact that he had no apology and no fear in the way he looked at other men. They said of him, not so long after he arrived to Lebanon, that he knew seven languages. He really knew two, Arabic and Farsi. (He was familiar with English and French.) But the newcomer who rose like a meteor in Lebanon cultivated an aura of mystery and invited it. In a very small country which had little space for secrets and privacy, this was the stranger's advantage: men could imagine things about him, impute all sorts of power to him. He was beyond his followers' self-doubt and beyond the self-contempt men projected onto others like themselves. In a country where men and women had a long memory for feuds and the foibles of men, it was a newcomer's edge that he had an unfamiliar past.

> He appeared like a creature not only of another kind but of another essence. Had they not seen him come up in a canoe they might have thought he had descended upon them from the clouds. He did, however, come in a crazy dug-out, sitting (very still and with his knees together, for fear of overturning the thing)—sitting on a tin box—which I had lent him—nursing on his lap a revolver of the Navy pattern —presented by me on parting—which, through an interposition of Providence, or through some wrong-headed notion, that was just like him, or else from sheer instinctive sagacity, he had decided to carry unloaded. That's how he ascended the Patusan river. Nothing could have been more prosaic and more unsafe, more extravagantly casual, more lonely.[31]

[31]Joseph Conrad, *Lord Jim* (Harmondsworth: Penguin, 1949), pp. 174–175.

That is Conrad on the modest arrival of Lord Jim, the stranger who had come to redeem himself in a remote corner of Malaya, who was loved and obeyed in his new place. The tale of Musa al Sadr, too, had modest beginnings. Two decades before his disappearance in Libya, he arrived in the small coastal city of Tyre with letters of introduction from the marja Muhsin al Hakim in Najaf to a fairly small fiefdom; he arrived with a twenty-year-old Iranian wife—herself the daughter of a mullah—and two male children, a child of four and a six-month-old infant. He came to work amid a politically quiescent population in a republic where the Shia were a marginal community—and the bearers of a tradition of lament and submission.

[2]

The World the Cleric Adopted

There was a Shia way of telling history in Jabal Amil, a way mixing pride and lament. The pride was in the valor of men, in their learning, in the vast literary and religious tradition of which they were the presumed inheritors. The lament was for the results all around—the ruined landscape, the harsh villages, the poverty that drove men from this hinterland to the far ends of the earth.

And there was a figure in that history symbolic and evocative of the harshness and the ruin: that of the late eighteenth-century Ottoman governor Ahmad Pasha al Jazzar (al Jazzar literally meant "the butcher"). It was apt that the events that ended the al Sadr family's history in the south of Lebanon, the ruin and flight of their forefather Saleh Sharaf al Din, were laid at the doorstep of al Jazzar. The rule of al Jazzar and his military campaigns were like some great divide in the history and folk memory of the Shia of Jabal Amil. Earlier times were depicted as days of prosperity and independence, those that followed as eras of dispossession. A native chronicler of the Shia world gives the time before al Jazzar the nostalgic glow that agrarian populations give, in retrospect, to some imagined age of bliss and plenty.

> The people of Jabal Amil lived in dignity and prosperity even during times of war and catastrophes. No taxes overwhelmed them; no rulers oppressed them and plundered their wealth. . . . After storms blew over they devoted themselves to their agricultural work, to exploiting their land the way they wanted to without taxes, without fees, and without monopoly. Their own rulers were merciful toward them. If a Shia traveled to some other place beyond his land, he traveled proud of his heri-

tage, with none daring to challenge or belittle him. Peace reigned among the *zuama* (the leaders) and they were united. Each *zaim* (leader) was free in his own territory, governing it, protecting its borders, preserving it. No authority was higher than that of the *zaim*, and no guardian, except the authority of the ulama.[1]

There had been books, and massive libraries, the Shia chronicles and storytellers said, but they were taken by al Jazzar to the seat of his power in nearby Acre, where they were burned. So massive was the output of the Shia literati and ulama that the books kept the ovens of Acre going for six days. Men had been independent, but al Jazzar snuffed out their independent spirit.

Stripped of the romance and the lament, the history of al Jazzar's rule was part of the recurrent struggle which bedeviled the Ottoman empire between *multezims* (tax farmers, "strongmen," local shaykhs) and the *walis* (the governors) of Ottoman provinces. Jabal Amil, a remote corner of Greater Syria, a world of tucked-away villages and towns, had fallen under Ottoman control early in the sixteenth century when the Ottomans overran much of the Muslim world around them. All that this Shia hinterland of a (Sunni) Ottoman state could hope for was to be left alone to its age-old ways. And with the exception of occasional incursions from the center of the province in Damascus, the world of Jabal Amil (the Shia of this part of Syria were then known as Matawlah or Metoualis) was cut off from the culture and the ways and the reach of the Ottoman state. By the mid-seventeenth century, Ottoman power established a separate *wilaya* (province) in the nearby coastal city of Sidon. But the spirit of localism and the weakness of the Ottoman order kept the power of the state at bay. By the mid-eighteenth century, we are told by a careful work of the historian Amnon Cohen, the authority of the wali had shrunk to the town of Sidon itself.[2] In the years that preceded the arrival of al Jazzar, the Shia world had come within the orbit of a celebrated tribal leader from Galilee by the name of Dahir al Umar. Dahir al Umar had exploited the weakness of the Ottoman center; in the early 1770s he emerged as master of the whole of Palestine. The leading families and clans in the Shia world of Jabal Amil attached themselves to him and ignored the power of the Ottoman governor. It was in Dahir al Umar's dominion, in the city of Acre, where the cotton then grown in Jabal Amil was marketed. From Acre, French traders of Marseilles op-

[1]Muhammad Jabir, *Tarikh Jabal Amil* (Beirut: Dar al Nahar, 1981), p. 104.
[2]Amnon Cohen, *Palestine in the Eighteenth Century* (Jerusalem: Hebrew University Press, 1973), p. 83.

erated, made loans to the growers, and bought their crops. The place knew a period of relative prosperity. Dahir al Umar respected the workings of the system of clans and notables. He took his share of taxes but left the Shia world to itself. A network of marriages cemented the bonds between him and the local notables.[3]

There matters stood until al Jazzar sought to put an end to Dahir al Umar's dominion and to impose a central regime of his own. Ottoman walis were sent into the provinces and in effect asked to run self-sustaining principalities, and to send the state's share to the Ottoman capital. Al Jazzar was an ambitious and ruthless man. He was, in the words of Baron de Tott, a French diplomat and traveler of the times, a "lion let loose against humanity."[4] The thriving cotton trade and its profits were to be his; the regime of Dahir al Umar and that of the Shia clans allied with him had to be broken.

Religious zeal inspired the Ottoman soldiers, giving the fight between al Jazzar and the Shia clans added ferocity. In one Ottoman chronicle written after a campaign against the Shia hinterland, an Ottoman official said that the ruin inflicted on the Shia was "a revenge taken for the life of Abu Bakr and Umar,"[5]—who were, respectively, the first and second caliphs of Islam, figures from Islam's first century. Some eleven centuries had passed since the time of those two caliphs. The Ottoman official was dredging up an old Islamic account between the Sunnis and Shia. And, a fitting note of irony, he did not know his Islamic history: no revenge had to be taken for the life of Abu Bakr. Of the first four caliphs—the Guided Caliphs—to succeed the Prophet, only Abu Bakr had died a natural death; the three others had been murdered. That historical detail eluded the Ottoman official. But the Sunni-Shia chasm between a centrally administered empire and "heretics" of the hinterland was more than enough to justify the harsh measures.

Events beyond the small world of Jabal Amil added to its misery and its marginality within the Ottoman realm. On the level of imperial politics, the Ottoman state had long been engaged in protracted conflict with the (Shia) Safavid state in Persia. Shiism may have rescued the Persian state, marked it off from the expanding Ottoman empire. But men caught on the wrong side of the divide—Sunnis in Safavid realms, Shia in the Ottoman state—were destined to suffer.

[3]See Ali al Zayn, *Lil Bahth an Tarikhna fi Lubnan* (In Search of Our History in Lebanon) (Beirut: n. p., 1973), pp. 457–603.
[4]Baron de Tott, *The Memoirs of Baron de Tott* (London: G. G. J. and J. Robinson, 1785), p. 321.
[5]Cohen, *Palestine in the Eighteenth Century*, p. 102.

The Ottoman Turks had seized the banner of orthodox, Sunni Islam. They brought to their view of Islam the zeal of new converts, a literalist cast of mind. At its inception the Sunni-Shia split had erupted within the confines of Arab society, a battle of clans. The revered figures of Shia Islam—the first Imam Ali and his son Hussein, the third Imam—had come from the apex of Arab society. The Ottoman Turks, late-comers to this fight, had imbued the Arab dispute with an excessive tone of righteousness vs. deviation. The Ottoman empire's long struggle with the Safavids had further deepened Ottoman alienation from Shiism and its adherents. Al Jazzar, wreaking havoc on the Shia hinterland, bringing its revenues and its cash crop under his domain, must have also been convinced that he was doing God's work and upholding the true faith.

Comte de Volney, a Frenchman who took his inheritance and traveled during this period throughout Egypt and Syria, visited this Shia corner of Syria after one of al Jazzar's major campaigns. Volney recalled the existence of a "small nation," a "distinct society": the "Motoualis" of Syria. He noted their religious separation; he doubted that they would survive: "It is said that they have long existed as a nation in this country, though their name has never been mentioned by any European writer before the present century. . . . Like the Persians, they are of the sect of Ali, while all the Turks follow that of Omar. . . . Since the year 1777, Djezzar, master of Acre and Saide [Sidon] has incessantly laboured to destroy them. . . . It is probable they will be totally annihilated, and even their name become extinct."[6]

They were not to be annihilated. They and others who came in al Jazzar's way had to bide their time and, as Baron de Tott said, "wait for the destruction of the tyrant."[7]

Al Jazzar's system came to an end a quarter-century after it was imposed. But the memory lingered: For the Shia, the tale of al Jazzar taught the futility of political action. Power was the attribute of capricious men. Shia history had transmitted that kind of aversion to the world of power; al Jazzar was true to the expectation. What the Shia derived from the memory of al Jazzar was an attitude of political withdrawal and defeat. Half a century after al Jazzar's time, a British traveler heard fresh tales of his deeds. The traveler recorded the lament of a local Shia host: "He then said one hundred villages had been entirely ruined, that the country had never recovered from the ravages

[6]C. F. Volney, *Travels through Egypt and Syria* (New York: John Tiobout, 1798), p. 56.
[7]de Tott, *Memoirs*, p. 326.

of Jezzar Pasha, that they had no water and had heavy taxes. He hoped better days are coming."[8] This was a grievance of the mid-1800s. It was to stick. This was a world which when it meditated upon its condition grieved for itself.

The nineteenth-century British traveler, David Urquhart, captured the marginality of this beaten community:

> Whence it came, how it came, what its race, what its character, and whence its name have been matters . . . of much doubt and mystery. To all inquiries respecting them, even on their immediate border, the only answers to be obtained were fables revealing utter ignorance mixed with fear and hatred. This is certain, that they do not belong to the original people of the Lebanon, and that their introduction dates but from a recent period; certainly not before the fourteenth century, and more probably, or at all events principally, in the middle of the seventeenth century. In their character, which combines dignity of manners, and pride of descent with ferocity and lawlessness of disposition, may be traced a deviation from a noble stock, and a succession of many generations of struggle, misery, and persecution. In religion they are Shiites, in race Arabs. To this anomaly, which alone would render them unclassible, must be added another; that they have ceased to be nomads, without passing either into the condition of citizens or of mere cultivators, but hold the districts they inhabit as a feudally dominant class. . . . They have lost the tribe character of a people; they have been prevented by their religious schism from being included in the administrative order of the empire. Their position in the Lebanon was neither that of princes called on to govern nor . . . that of a tribe which has displaced the original population and occupied the soil.[9]

"Unclassible" men, in some intermediate zone between Arabs and Persians. They were, Urquhart said, "hated by the Persians as Arabs, and by the Turks and Arabs as Shiites."[10] The themes glimpsed by Urquhart—the hostility to the ruling Turks, the Persian connection—are repeated in the diary of another traveler, Lawrence Oliphant, which he entitled *The Land of Gilead* (1870): "The Metawalies feel a strong, secret dislike to the Turkish government; and not withstanding outward professions of loyalty which they make, all their secret sympathies are with the Persians, to whose country they look as the stronghold of their religion and the bulwark of their faith."[11]

[8]David Urquhart, *The Lebanon (Mount Souria): A History and a Diary* (London: Thomas Coutley Newby, 1860), p. 330.
[9]Ibid., pp. 94–95.
[10]Ibid., p. 96.
[11]Lawrence Oliphant, *The Land of Gilead* (London, 1870), p. 14.

The "secret dislike" was a tendency with foundations in Shia psyche and doctrine. *Taqiyya* (precautionary dissimulation, concealing one's faith) had been authorized by Shia Imams and jurists; it was a response of an embattled minority to a larger Sunni world and to a harsh balance of forces. Men on the run, dissidents living under adverse political circumstances, Shia travelers in Sunni realms, resorted to the practice of Taqiyya. Shia history turned inward. In the main it was a history of righteousness and quietism. Ottoman dominion was endured in this Shia realm. Shiism, and the habits and insularity of a hinterland, had prepared men for political withdrawal.

As the nineteenth century drew to a close, the Ottoman empire was clearly living on borrowed time. When it finally collapsed after World War I, no one grieved for its demise. The Shia hinterland did not bring it down, however; the Shia were a people who neither waged nor faked a great anticolonial struggle. The "Arab awakening" which exaggerated the distance between the ruling Turkish element and the Arab realms of the Ottoman empire, was alien to this impoverished and quiescent population. History here remained raw, unobscured by illusions. The "Arab awakening" had in effect rewritten history; it had read modern doctrines of nationalism into an earlier time when Ottomans and Arabs had accepted an Islamic definition of the community, and when the Ottomans were just another military dynasty that had governed in the name of Islam. Early Arab nationalism was an ideology of the cities of the Arab world; it was also manifested in the pamphleteering of Christian Arabs, who saw in the imminent demise of the Ottoman Muslim state an opportunity to put forth a modern concept of secular nationalism which would have a place in it for their political yearnings and ambitions. Some Shia voices claimed a piece of that invented nationalist historiography. A scribe from the Shia town of Nabatiyya, Muhammad Jabir (1875–1945), expressed the anxiety of the few Shia literati who wanted it noted that they too were there when Arab nationalism set out to challenge the Ottoman empire:

No Syrian congress was convened, no Arab nationalist meeting was held without the Shia representatives being there in the vanguard, protesting the conditions of their world, demanding being part of Syrian unity. Had it not been for difficult circumstances that were tormenting them, weakening their economy, sending their sons and the flower of their youth to faraway places, they wouldn't have endured a reality so contrary to their nature.[12]

[12]Muhammad Jabir, *Tarikh Jabal Amil*, p. 230.

A large multinational Muslim state had collapsed; a nationalist idea was poised to inherit its mantle. The pamphleteers and the publicists of the Arab cities had stout lungs; the few literate Shia wanted to belong. But the new nationalist movement too kept its distance from the hinterland.

Some honest Shia writers contemplating the fate of their people got it right: this place was on the margins of nationalist history. Ali al Zayn, an independent and daring critic for his time and place, provided a realistic interpretation of the politics of the Shia of Jabal Amil when he wrote: "The Shia notables and clerics did not know of nationalism and nationalist ideas. They were pessimists and sectarians—a tendency which made them stay away from any political movement or rebellion." They, the clerics and the notables, did not want to repeat the history of the eighteenth century which brought them "death, hunger, and exile."[13] Rebellion had been tried in times past. And it had led to ruin. Men were confirmed in their political caution, in their avoidance of political causes.

One set of strangers replaced another in 1920; Ottoman rule was replaced by the French mandate. The bid for an independent Arab kingdom in Syria made by Prince Faisal and his cohorts was denied. The Shia world in Jabal Amil and the smaller Shia community in the Bekaa Valley were appended by the French to Greater Lebanon with its Maronite core. The French had divided their newly acquired domain in Syria and Lebanon into four territorial entities: Greater Lebanon, Syria, Jabal al Druze (the Druze mountain in southeastern Syria), and the territory of the Alawites in another corner of Syria.

French rule in Syria and Lebanon was established after colonialism had had its heyday. It was popular only among the Maronites in Mount Lebanon. France had long been the protector and ally of the Maronites. But among the Muslims and the Druze, the French were particularly resented. The mandate offended the nationalists in Damascus who wanted to run their own affairs, who resented the heavy-handed way in which the French had ousted the Hashemite Sharif Faisal from Damascus. And soon after the French came, their rule ran afoul of the sensibility of the Druze in their mountainous and traditionally independent realm in Syria.

Fierce communalists, the Druze wanted to be left alone in their own territory. Under Ottoman rule, they had been given substantial au-

[13] Ali al Zayn, "Athr al Ananat Fi Tarikhna (The Influence of Confusion on Our History)," *Al Irfan*, 58 (May 1970), 36.

tonomy and exempted from taxation and military service. The structure of authority that anchored Druze society, the rule of a "princely" family and of the men of religion, was left intact. The leading family in Jabal al Druze, the Atrash family, had held sway in its own domain. Its authority had survived the upheaval that engulfed Ottoman territories when the Young Turks set out, after 1908, to challenge the traditional political concepts and practices of the preceding Ottoman centuries. And then Druze society had witnessed the coming of the Hashemite regime to Damascus and its expulsion; the Druze notables had looked upon that short-lived regime with a good deal of skepticism. France promised the Druze autonomy, and as such, the Druze adopted a wait-and-see attitude. But three or four years into the mandate, French colonial officials began to push Druze society harder than that society could tolerate, challenging, by word and deed, the authority of the Atrash family. By all indications French rule now seemed determined to level Druze society, to regiment it, to impose a system of taxation and forced labor, to deny the chieftains their prerogatives, to impose on the Druze an education system staffed by Christian teachers brought by the French from Maronite Mount Lebanon. Rebellion was not far behind. It broke out in mid-1925. In November of that year the Druze swept into the Mount Hermon region in southeastern Lebanon, and into Shia Lebanon. For a moment, it seemed that the rebellion might spread through the south of Lebanon, perhaps to Beirut itself.[14]

The great Druze rebellion of 1925 found the Shia their quiescent selves. "The Shia Sheiks of Jabal Amil," noted one dispatch, "have sent letters to the High Commissioner affirming their loyalty."[15] In a work of oral history, recorded nearly half a century after the rebellion, the rebel chieftain, Sultan Pasha al Atrash, was forgiving and benevolent toward the Shia. They were, he said, asked by the French to form units to resist the Druze but they refrained from doing so.[16] The Shia dodged the fight. The Druze heritage was one of rebellion, that of the Shia one of submission.

The Druze rebellion was crushed. It was, as one observer put it, a rebellion of the "sixteenth century against the twentieth."[17] But the

[14]See *Mudhakarat Sultan al Atrash* (The Memoirs of Sultan al Atrash) (Jerusalem: Matbat al Sharq, 1969). Sultan al Atrash was the celebrated leader of the 1925 revolt by the Druze. There are other accounts of the revolt: "In the Djebel Druz," by Wolfgang von Weisl, in *The Atlantic Monthly* (December 1925); A. Ryan, "The Syrian Rebellion," *Contemporary Review* (January–June 1926).

[15]*The Times* (London), December 9, 1925.

[16]Sultan al Atrash, Memoirs, p. 219.

[17]Von Weisl, "In the Djebel Druz," p. 854.

Druze had given evidence that they would fight for their separate communal identity and their autonomy. No similar upheaval erupted in the Shia hinterland.

A memoir of roughly the same period written by a Shia scribe provides a glimpse into the ways and political attitudes of the Shia. It describes a visit by French High Commissioner Maxime Weygand (April 1923–November 1924) to the coastal town of Tyre. A sumptious, elaborate meal was prepared for the French visitor. The surrounding villages arrived in delegations to pay homage to the High Commissioner. The author of the memoir, then a schoolboy, screwed up his courage to petition the High Commissioner, to tell him of the needs of the district of Tyre and of the villages in the south. "You can't go beyond Tyre," he told the commissioner; "the villages beyond lack roads and schools and clinics." The commissioner patted the boy on the back and asked him what he would prefer to have first for his village: the road, the school, or the doctor? The boy said that he preferred to see a road. The road, he trusted, would then bring the doctor and the school. The road was promised.[18]

A photographer who accompanied the High Commissioner then stepped forth and snapped a photograph of the courageous youngster. Some months later, the photo was mailed to him. (The photo is proudly displayed in the memoir.)

The road, though, was another matter. It was begun but the execution of it . . . well, it didn't happen. Many things were begun in this region, never to be completed.

The scene with the High Commissioner would be reenacted many times in the years to come, both before and after independence was granted by the French in 1943. One thing changed with independence: the visitors were *beys*, feudal lords of this community or ministers in successive cabinets. Native-born, the new visitors did not have to pat young boys on the back or mail photographs. If a visitor happened to be a member of Parliament, he would promise that he intended to take up the matter of schools and clinics with the prime minister if need be. There was no need to worry, the villagers were told: the waters of the Litani River would, in time, bring electricity and irrigate the harsh earth; the paved roads would come; the tobacco acreage that had to be licensed by a tobacco monopoly would be increased. There would be fairer prices for the tobacco crop paid out by

[18]Hassan al Amin, *Al Dhkrayat* (Recollections) (Beirut: Dar al Ghadir, 1973), pp. 78–80.

the tobacco monopoly. And just in case the visiting member was pressed, he could always complain of the ingratitude of the villagers.

A note drafted in 1943, the year of the country's independence, gave this description of the three hundred predominantly Shia villages of the district of southern Lebanon: "Not a single hospital in all the district, but a health office exists in Sidon, Tyre and Nabatiyya . . . . It is also deprived of irrigation schemes and the bulk of the people drink stagnant water."[19]

There was very little that the Lebanese state could or would do for the Shia hinterland. Two dominant ideas had been brought together in the Lebanese polity: a Maronite concept that stressed Lebanon's Christian identity and a Sunni Arab conviction, upheld by the merchants of Beirut, Tripoli, and Sidon, that the country was a piece of a larger Arab world. Both conceptions were alien to the Shia: the Shia were Lebanon's hewers of wood and drawers of water. On the eve of independence, Lebanese statistics (for whatever they are worth) put the Shia at some 200,000 inhabitants out of a population of a million Lebanese, Numerically, the Shia were behind the Maronites and the Sunnis. But the disadvantage was not merely, not even mainly, numerical. Both the Maronites and the Sunnis brought into the new polity large ideas of themselves and their place in a Lebanese republic. For the Maronites, their Lebanon was a Christian nation set apart from the Muslims of the cities and the plains, a nation with roots in an independent mountain, with its own monasteries and monks and traditions. As for the Sunnis of the coastal cities, they were the inheritors of the culture of the Ottoman empire of the preceding four centuries. In this latter conception, Lebanon looked to its east and partook of the culture and the ways of the larger Arab and Muslim world.

The Maronite sense of separatism had given the Maronites the self-confidence and the self-consciousness to assert their independence vis-à-vis the Arab world around them. Maronite history was built around the theme and the ethos of separatism: a Christian sect had migrated, in the seventh century, from the plains of Syria to the purity of its own mountain. What it left behind was tyranny; what it built was a realm of purity. "That land [Syria] was the land of persecution and a place that threatened to eradicate one's identity; this land [Lebanon] is the land of freedom and integrity," wrote a Maronite, summing up the psychological outlook of his people; what was

[19]The text of the note was submitted by the president of the "Muslim bloc," one Mohamed Jamil Beyhum to the president of the Republic. Beyhum's memorandum was reported in a U.S. Consular Dispatch, Beirut Legation, January 26, 1943.

within the new piece of land was a "separate identity"; what was beyond it was "a stranger or an enemy."[20] Maronite history, articulated by scholars and priests, led to a militant kind of Lebanonism with the Maronites as its proud bearers. Conversely, the Sunni membership in a larger Arab world had given that community a settled sense of self and purpose. For the Sunnis, Lebanon or, more accurately, the coastal cities they inhabited were a fragment of a larger world.

The Shia were in an intolerable position. Like the Maronites, they were men of Lebanon. But unlike them, they had not spelled out a doctrine of independence and autonomy. Like the Sunnis, they were Muslim; but they were schismatics. What Shia books there were were at times shrill and anxious to assert that the Shia were "Arabs," that they had come to Lebanon during "the dawn of Islam" from the Arabian Peninsula. Shia scribes and genealogists did the normal thing in a society that exalted genealogy: they traced their roots to an Arabian tribe. The inhabitants of Jabal Amil, said one chronicler, were descendants of "Amila the son of Siba of the Yemenite tribe of Qahtan." But there was no genuine sense of identity with the wider Arab world. Shia history stood in the way; so did rural insularity.

Over the distant horizon loomed the large Shia realm of Iran. Iran was known to a few Shia travelers and clerics and literati. There were small consolations to be derived from the imagined exploits of a large Shia state. But when all was said and done, Persia, the realm of the *Ajam*, was far away. It had its own language and habits. Its reach was limited. Besides, to the extent that the Persian connection was imputed to the Shia of Lebanon, it was to suggest that they were strangers to Lebanon, newcomers, that Lebanon was not for them a "final homeland," a *watan nihai*. Iran had adopted Shiism; in doing so, Iran had changed Shiism. Shiism, one recent historian points out, "became finally and inalienably associated with Iran as its homeland and stronghold."[21] The adoption of Shiism in Iran had in effect "Persianized" the Shia in Arab realms. It was a case of a recent event reinterpreting and recasting a distant past. It did not matter that Shiism had been an Arab fight, that the battle of Kerbala was fought some eight centuries before the Safavid imposition of Shiism in Iran. This was a world both fastidious and final in its phobias and in the lines it drew between those who belonged and those who didn't.

[20]Hamid Mawrani, *Al Wijdan al Tarikhi al Maruni bayn al Qadim wa al Jadid* (Maronite Historical Consciousness between the Old and the New) (Beirut: n. p., 1981), pp. 66–67.
[21]Hamid Algar, *Religion and State in Iran, 1785–1906* (Berkeley: University of California Press, 1969), p. 5.

Lebanon's "special identity" had represented a compromise between the Maronite idea of the mountain and the Sunni heritage of the city.[22] The Shia had to make their way between these two conceptions.

Denizens of an inarticulate hinterland, the Shia population was represented in the Lebanese polity by a handful of feudal families; the beys, the big men, *al zuama* were the descendants of landed families. The leadership of the big man, *al zama*, was the organizing principle of social and political life. Rather like the principle of kingship, al zama had its aura and mystique and expectations. As a general rule al zama was inherited. An ideal zaim (big man) was the son of a zaim. There was a limited measure of mobility in the system. A man, if he was lucky enough or gifted or rich enough, could fashion his own zama. Great wealth and, by the 1950s, advanced university degrees were helpful in launching a new bid. But the success of such bids was never assured. A "real" zaim was *Ibn bayt* (literally, the son of a household), meaning the son of a noted family. A man making a new bid had to be exceedingly generous with money; he had to have "an aura," and render services to those coming to him for help; he had to live down the skepticism of those who knew him or who knew his family "back when." And, more frustrating still, such a bid had to begin under the tutelage of one of the old zuama who had a gift for spotting anxious new talent—and an equally remarkable gift for cutting the aspirant to size right when the bid for a new place was beginning to show some promise.

The country's Parliament, a body with a fixed quota for each of Lebanon's religious sects, was the gathering place of the zuama. A man with some wealth and new ambitions aspiring for a place had to come as a supplicant before one noted zaim or another. He had to bear the humiliation and play second fiddle to the big man. He had to sweat out the length of a four-year term in the Parliament, never assured that the next Parliament put together by the big man would still have room for a vulnerable newcomer. And there wasn't much that men from a backward community could accomplish when elected to the Parliament. Every now and then one of them would stand up and make the "perennial demand" of their community for justice. As always, the government promised benevolence. The daring member, who had to fight down his panic in order to stand up in Parliament to make the demand, returned home to say that he put before the Parlia-

<hr>

[22]See Albert Hourani's insightful essay on the tension between the (Maronite) mountain and the (Sunni) city, "Ideologies of the Mountain and the City," in Roger Owen, ed., *Essays on the Crisis in Lebanon* (London: Ithaca Press, 1976), pp. 33–41.

[63]

ment of the nation the demands of his sect, the demands of his *taifa*, the deprived taifa.

The few words said in panic in the faraway Parliament were embellished by the local politician and his clan and his friends. In the Parliament that brought together men of power and means, the honorable member from the south spoke with reluctance. In the villages he represented (a generous and inappropriate term) a few words spoken in Parliament were turned into a grand epic: the words absolved him of further responsibility. He had screwed up his courage and said a "word of truth," *Kalimat Haq*, in the presence of men who did not want to hear it. Stories then went around about how the eloquent member, faithful son of the south, had silenced the enemies of the south, how he had outdone the arrogant Sunni leaders of West Beirut or the Maronite members from Mount Lebanon. The word of truth said and disposed of, the members of Parliament from the south were an obedient lot. From a foreign dispatch in 1951: "The deputies from South Lebanon always gave reliable but unspectacular support to the government debate. On several occasions they stressed the serious problem of the lack of drinking water in many villages of the South, and the government has promised to make every effort to alleviate this situation."[23] In another dispatch a Shia member of Parliament is described listing his community's demands. The prime minister of course agreed with him, "cleverly agreed with him," the dispatch says, "in his usual facile manner, but promised nothing."[24]

The quintessential zaim of the 1940s and 1950s was Ahmad Bey al Assad. (In the 1960s the mantle was passed to his son Kamel, who was, as late as 1984, the speaker of Parliament, the highest Shia post in the country.)

In his heyday in the 1940s and 1950s, when he held such posts as minister of public works and got himself elected speaker of Parliament, no one really challenged the way Ahmad Bey saw and took the world. That was a time when southern Lebanon was one large electoral district, sending fourteen members to a national Parliament of seventy-seven members. Ahmad Bey prided himself that, if he wished, he could get his cane elected to Parliament. Thirteen members of Parliament could ride his coattails. Electoral "reform" came in 1953, subdividing the south into smaller districts. Ahmad Bey lost some of his power. In the ruinous election of that year his bloc of fourteen members dwindled to himself and his son Kamel. The old

[23]U.S. Consular Reports, Legation Dispatch 117, August 30, 1951.
[24]U.S. Consular Reports, Monthly Political Review, May 1944.

bey had hit rock-bottom. To add insult to injury the Parliament, when it convened, elected his archrival Adel Bey Osseiran as speaker. Osseiran, a more enlightened bey, came from a Shia district close to Sidon, by the coast. He had always presented himself as the more en- lightened voice of the south; but though a graduate of the American University of Beirut, he was no match to Ahmad Bey in the more remote villages and towns of southern Lebanon. He did not have Ahmad Bey's electoral machine and Ahmad Bey's thugs. Still, he could mount some challenge. In 1953 luck came Osseiran's way, and he ended up with the coveted Shia post, speaker of Parliament. Not particularly used to such blows to his prestige, Ahmad Bey left the country in a fit of rage. He stayed away in Damascus for seven months. Rumors circulated that he was plotting the dismemberment of Lebanon with Syrian dictator Adib Shishakli. But it was a tall story. Ahmad Bey returned to resume his old seat. His faithful followers were told to accompany the Bey to the Parliament in style, to compen- sate him for the humiliation of the election. On March 9, 1954, he showed up for his first session at Parliament accompanied by a mass of demonstrators and armed followers. Ahmad Bey returned to par- liamentary life in a fitting way. He wanted the prime minister to apol- ogize for having accused the Assads, father and son, during a previ- ous session, of "ruining the country." The offending words were stricken from the record. All assumed that the matter was resolved. But Ahmad Bey's honor required more. An American diplomat de- scribed the sequel:

The aftermath of the session proved more exciting by far. After telling his supporters who had been awaiting him outside the Parliament building, that he had been vindicated, Ahmad Bey was borne in triumph to his car where he was surrounded by his followers who decided to escort him to his Beirut residence. Unfortunately their route took them through the quarter controlled by Mr. Yafi [the Prime Minister] and, at an opportune moment, Yafi supporters attacked the procession. In the resulting melee, one person was killed and eight wounded by gunfire.[25]

With or without electoral reform Ahmad Bey had remained him- self. His followers—humbled, frightened, treasuring a word or a ges- ture from him—confirmed his view of things. A young man relates an all-too-typical tale of the time: the young man's father, a peasant of modest means, used to take a lamb of his own and slaughter it in the bey's town and offer it to the bey. The bey did the old man the honor

[25]U.S. Embassy Dispatch, 566, Beirut, March 11, 1953.

of accepting his lambs. Then in a fit of generosity, the bey once gave a small cut of lamb to the old man. The old man returned with the cut of meat to his village, to show off what the bey had given him. He had been to the bey of Tayyaba's "palace." Our bey, the old man said was a generous bey and the old man had a special line to him.[26] There was no reason for Ahmad Bey to learn new lessons or to change his mind.

To the eye of an outside observer Ahmad Bey seemed like a "bandit chieftain," a "smuggler in a big way," an "outstandingly incompetent member" of the Lebanese cabinet: the words occur in a foreign diplomatic dispatch.[27] To his followers, Ahmad Bey's presence almost stalked the landscape of southern Lebanon. He was the focus of their conversations, of their love, of their hatreds. They organized their politics around him and around his whims. In a land of frightened people, a "bandit" lived out the fantasies of ordinary men. The laws were decisions made by aliens and outsiders and broken by them whenever they wished. Ahmad Bey, their own bey, in breaking the dreaded laws, was doing what they could not do.

Ahmad Bey hated ambitious peasantry. Stories are told of how he once berated a sensitive young man for suggesting that the young man wanted to study law. The young man, good at school, had finished his secondary education. He was brought into the presence of the bey by his father; a peasant's son had passed the official examination and was showing some promise. The father wanted the bey to bless the effort. In time, perhaps, the father must have thought, the bey would have to intervene on behalf of the young man if the young man was to secure a coveted government appointment. This had been an old Shia dream: peasants getting on the government payroll, receiving the praise and obedience of less fortunate men. But Ahmad Bey, who sincerely believed that the land and the men who worked the land belonged to him, was not so charitable that day. "No," he said, "my son Kamel Bey is studying law." The young man was commanded to choose another field of study.[28]

The thought that a modern system of education would give the son of the peasant and the son of the bey the same opportunity struck Ahmad Bey as some dark, sinister development playing havoc with the world. Of his people Ahmad Bey said on one occasion: "There are

[26]This exquisite tale was told to me by a young raconteur of southern Lebanon, Hussein Hijazi.

[27]U.S. Consulate General, Dispatch 545, Beirut, November 14, 1942.

[28]This vignette comes from Ambassador Mahmud Hamud, who, violating the orders of the bey, went on to study law, and to a distinguished career in the diplomatic service.

no great feelings among them because news and incitements do not reach them. They are poor and ill-educated and have almost no news-papers." Peasants were peasants, Ahmad Bey thought. Schools, roads, clinics had to be denied them if the world and its familiar land-marks were to remain the same. To a delegation of villagers who came to plead for the establishment of a school, Ahmad Bey gave one of his vintage answers. There was, he said, no need for a school for he was educating his son Kamel Bey for all of them. There was no need of many other things: peasants, the beys believed, bit the hand that fed them. It was more important to keep the peasantry down than to serve them and change things.

For his followers, Ahmad Bey offered a different kind of satisfac-tion: to be his men, by his side, on occasions that his (and presumably their) honor warranted. They escorted him to greet his son whenever the young man returned from Paris, where he was studying. On one such occasion, five hundred of them were by his side, with their pis-tols, a foreign dispatch of 1951 noted: they "paraded the streets of Beirut and around the airport, shooting in joy."[29] But the gendarmes were not far behind. They arrested a few of them and dispersed the others.

"Shooting in joy": the men who came from villages and towns with stagnant water, places without schools, without medical care, cele-brating the triumphant return of their chieftain's son. The education acquired in Paris stood for something old: communal pride, men with pistols showing off before other clans. No one asked what the young bey would do with the education. It was not a functional thing, the acquiring of a degree, the preparation for something new. Pride had required the new education: it had to be obtained in a faraway place, then celebrated and displayed. Ahmad Bey's only son acquired a de-gree to buttress Ahmad Bey's honor. The celebration worked: it infu-riated one of Ahmad Bey's rivals. Yusuf Bey al Zayn, a contemporary of Ahmad Bey, a lesser bey but nevertheless someone to be reckoned with in the district of Nabatiyya, someone whose sons also were in time to inherit his domain, was beside himself about the celebrations of the Assads. It was Yusuf Bey who apparently brought matters to a head and interrupted the celebration around the airport. He tele-phoned the director of the Ministry of the Interior, complained about the license given his rival and about the use of arms, and threatened "to do the same at his first opportunity."[30]

[29]U.S. Embassy Dispatch, 396, Beirut, February 28, 1951.
[30]Ibid.

[67]

The honor of Ahmad Bey was a very serious thing. It was not to be trifled with. And the old bey had a flair for displaying his might. He had a "private army," to use the words of a gullible outsider, which "keeps watch among the rocks throughout the wide area of the surrounding countryside." A foreign visitor invited to lunch noted the presence of "some 30 to 50 armed men." But the old bey, it was whispered, could field a thousand men. Alas, the flair could not carry off the act: "The arms in evidence consisted mainly of rifles about World War I vintage and a sprinkling of concealed pistols. Knives of course were also common. I saw nothing of any heavier firepower, though there was talk of tommy guns."[31]

There was always talk of something beyond the shabbiness. The "palace" at Tayyaba was more modest than the word implied. It was a large house of stone, a villa; the presence of the bey there was what gave it dignity. During the civil war that broke out in 1958, which pitted the Maronite president against the Sunnis of West Beirut and the Druze of the Shuff Mountains, Ahmad Bey said that he could send into battle thousands of men. He never did. That war remained an affair of West Beirut and of the Druze mountains. The war that signaled the breakdown of the so-called "national pact" between Sunni Pan-Arabists and the Maronite-based state went on beyond the universe of Ahmad al Assad and his followers.

Ahmad Bey al Assad wore a fez and had a mustache of the old-fashioned kind that twirled and pointed upward at the sides of his mouth. He was a boss of the old school. His son would have nothing to do with a fez. He was a "modern" man, a product of the city. He had studied law at the Sorbonne; he listed tennis as one of his hobbies. But in mentality the young bey was more inflexible about power and the prerogatives of power than his father. Ahmad Bey died unlamented. But his son who succeeded to his power in the early 1960s would make the men of the south miss the old man and his fez and his old-fashioned tyranny. The old man's cruelty and slights could be brushed off as the ways of a patriarch, a father. He was rough, but he was of his people. He spoke their language. He had land and he had power, but he had their ways. He spoke and ate like the rest of them. And he blew his nose in the village square and the markets like the rest of them. When the promises he made did not materialize, the old bey could complain about *al hukuma*, the government, like any helpless peasant. He could make himself, whenever he chose to, a sharer of their defeat and marginality.

[31]U.S. Consular Reports, Memorandum of May 22, 1947.

On his deathbed, the storytellers say, Ahmad Bey told his son that he was going to do very well for he was bequeathing him a "million mules." Such was Ahmad Bey's view of his Shia followers. The numbers, like all Lebanese numbers, were inflated for it was a more modest realm. But the sentiment of the old bey was shared by his son. The old man was just more natural about it.

The younger bey, Kamel, hated the south and its ways. He openly mocked his men and his region. He had studied French, and with his father's money had made the trips to Paris which were required of the men of power and the men of culture in Lebanon. He knew, it was said, the red light district of Beirut, the Zaituna, like the palm of his hand. And the promiscuity and sexual conquests were admired badges of distinction.

When power came to Kamel Bey after the death of his father, the world was beginning to change in very threatening ways. Peasants were leaving the land in droves. New Shia money made in Africa was appearing. Enough boys had been hounded and beaten into getting university degrees. Kamel Bey was uncomfortable with those winds of change. They only made him more rigid. His power came with insecurity. No Shia, it was reported, was allowed into the younger bey's presence with a necktie. Accomplished men with education and money ushered in to see him had to remove their neckties. Only the bey himself could wear modern attire. The rest had to avoid his wrath; they had to be peasants, to identify with his power, with his sexual exploits, with the way he humbled this or that man by having his way with the man's wife. They had to live off his triumphs, a man of their own faith, walking for them into alien worlds.

Kamel Bey was good at mimicking the Shia manner of speech and those Shia words that mothers said to their sons, the words of peasants—the words of piety and defeat. When a Shia man from the south stepped out of line, he was in for a dressing down. Kamel Bey loved to humiliate men in the presence of others. The more accomplished, the more "uppity" the man, the more Kamel Bey enjoyed humiliating him in public, mocking his achievements and his education.

Kamel Bey played on the other side of the cultural divide. Not for him were the hearty peasant women of Shia Lebanon with their bright dresses, with the smell of onions, with their peasant accents. Kamel Bey saw them all, men and women, as peasants. No modern attire would fool him. Underneath the modern act, the young bey knew his Shia. He saw them the only way he had known them, when he was taken every now and then—against his will, no doubt, and

[69]

overshadowed by his awesome father—to their home in Tayyaba close to the Israeli border. The young bey had to be taken there to be socialized and to learn the ways of leadership. He was his father's only son. The father had "doubts" whether the son would make it. All the fathers in this place had such doubts. The doubts were the sword the fathers held. With the doubts, sons were manipulated and kept in line.

The son inherited his father's domain and prerogatives—those of the lord of the Shia of the south. Kamel Bey yearned to outdo his father. Since there were no public projects to excel in, the young bey's battle with his father's shadow and legacy was conducted in the only way men saw and practiced politics here. The son decided he should be more cruel than his father, more awesome and terrifying in the way he stared at men, more snide in the way he put Shia men of southern Lebanon in their place, and more relentless in his attempt to get money out of the lucky ones who returned to Lebanon from far away places with new money, with a new measure of their self-worth.

The men who returned from West Africa and other places where the Shia had gone ached for respectability. So many of them wanted to be members of Parliament, to run on the bey's parliamentary slate. Men with new money believed that they could buy their way onto the bey's list of candidates. The bey taunted them about their lack of education. He talked of the new men with university degrees and titles, the *dakatra* (men with Ph.D.'s), the *mohandissin* (engineers), and the lawyers who coveted the same seats. The bey had room for both the new money and the new degrees. He disdained them both with equal *hauteur* and hardness. The men with money had to buy their way onto the bey's list. They had to have enough for the cars and buses that took the Shia squatters of Greater Beirut back to their villages to vote. The Shia never believed in registering to vote in the city and the ghettoes that had become their home. A vote in Beirut was a wasted vote, they believed. They kept their registration in the places they had left behind. And every four years, during those festivals and competitions of clans that passed for elections, the cars and buses took them back to their villages and towns in the south and the Bekaa to cast their votes for this or that bey, for Kamel Bey or against him, for Yusuf Bey al Zayn or against him. Then the cars and buses returned: those who had backed the losers quietly slipped back to the city, but the cars of the winners' supporters returned in triumph, horns blowing, women ululating. Their man had won and their rivals had been vanquished. It was a simple matter. It was about vanquishing the other man. Men savored the most vicarious of triumphs. They had so little else to celebrate and to savor.

In the district of Bint Jbail, the Bezzis, one clan whose leader was willing to do anything to get himself elected to Parliament, either defeated their rivals, the Beydouns, or were defeated by them. In the district of Marjayun the Abdallahs of Khiam believed that a parliamentary seat for one of their kinsmen was a birthright. The clan as a whole partook of the honor. There were very few services that rival candidates could render. What mattered was the intangible honor, the feeling, as the Bezzis of Bint Jbail put it, that they themselves went to bed satiated while their rivals went to sleep on an empty stomach. "Ideology," wrote a foreign observer, was a "stranger to Lebanese elections."[32]

The candidates had to have money for the cigarettes and the coffee, for the thugs who protected the bey and his candidates, accompanying them to towns where threats had been made against the bey and where complaints were heard about his style and his arrogance and his lack of concern for the unpaved roads and the pricing policy of the tobacco monopoly. Above all, there had to be money for the bey himself, master of the realm, the man who was raising them to new heights of power, who was promising them one of the special license plates that members of Parliament were assigned. Of course there were not license plates enough for all, and rather than bidding for a seat in Parliament, some of the men with new money just wanted to hang around the bey, to be part of his entourage, to turn up in photographs of him and his dinners and his gatherings. They wanted to have the word spread in the town or village they had come from that they had been consulted by the bey, that they advised him on political matters, that they were privy to his judgments on Shia men and issues. The bey knew how badly the men with new money wanted to have the distinction of an association with him. And he knew how to make them pay for this kind of honor. It cost money to have dinner with the bey, to be photographed with him, to ride in his car, to be in his presence.

The money paid Kamel Bey would be put to good use. Some of it he stuffed away. Some went to maintaining the men who protected him, who rode with him to towns and villages where he was not wanted. A good deal of the money was spent in the seedy bars and nightclubs of Beirut, on the virgins that the bey was said to be so fond of deflow-

---

[32]This accurate summation comes from a U.S. Embassy report of July 28, 1971, entitled "Youth in Lebanon 1971" (File designation A228).

ering. This was power over other men. Other men were served the bey's dishes cold, after he had sampled them and walked away. This was how the bey thought of the world. And this was one kind of politics that the Iranian-born cleric had to do battle with.

The old politics of clans, with all its theater and consolations and futilities, was the dominant politics among the Shia. But by the time the 1950s drew to a close, some fifteen years after Lebanese independence, a rival political current was attracting some of the young: the "ideological" parties of the left and the right that promised to change the old ways of the country. Parties like the Communists, the Baath, the Syrian Socialist Nationalist Party, the Arab Nationalist Movement, found ready adherents among the first generation of Shia young men breaking with the insularity of their elders. More and more Shia were making their way to Beirut and its suburbs and shantytowns. By 1959–1960 the per capita income in Beirut was some five times larger than it was in the country.[33] The importance of the land was being annulled; the politics that derived its power from the land and the ways of the land was being eroded. In effect the old beys promised nothing but the humiliations of the past—the past disconnected from its webs of meaning, from the little shelter and the little security they once gave. The new ideological parties gave an illusion of something new, a new language. A new political style, a new sensibility, made its appearance in once-remote towns and villages.

It was easy to see that the new parties labored in a hostile environment, that the country of sects and clans eluded the borrowed vocabularies and constructs. But the young flocked to them. More than anything else, the new ideological parties supplied frightened men with some self-respect. The young displaced peasant speaking of Marx and Lenin and Stalin, the primary school teacher pushed off the land yet without a new world to anchor him, with a family still on the land making claims on his salary and sensibility, found in the ideological parties a world that could be made their own. The books and the pamphlets provided a larger view of the world than the politics of clans and notables. The harsh, impoverished land, the stern elders, and the isolated villages closed up the world; the new pamphlets and political ideas opened it. A sociologist who hails from the town of Bint Jbail made an insightful study of the ideological change that swept that town in the 1950s. The Baath party, a Pan-Arab party founded by

[33]See Roger Owen's helpful discussion of the Lebanese economy: "The Political Economy of Grand Liban, 1920–1970," in Owen, ed., *Essays on the Crisis in Lebanon*, pp. 23–32.

two intellectuals from Damascus, spread with amazing ease in Bint Jbail in the early and mid-1950s. Membership in the Baath provided schoolteachers and small artisans with an opportunity for political self-expression. Across the border from Bint Jbail, a great fight over Palestine had been fought and settled in a drastic way in 1948 with the establishment of the state of Israel. A familiar world had been re-made. Public secular schooling had come to Bint Jbail about the same time. Of some seven thousand inhabitants in 1952, nearly six hun-dred were students enrolled in school. The balance of Bint Jbail was broken. New ideas were needed to explain the world. Hundreds from the town had found their way to West Africa and to the automotive factories of Detroit. Their remittances made possible schooling for a younger generation. This was the first generation to know anything beyond grinding poverty and the toil of the land. Baathist ideology, which preached the unity of the Arab world, may have held out no hope of changing the conditions of Bint Jbail. But nor did the old ways of the country.[34]

Lebanon, the country of rival sects, had its way of dealing with the new movements and the new language. It persecuted them when it could, when it needed to. The state, such as it was, may have been unable to pave roads or to pay for education. But it could crack down on those who wanted to rock the boat. The state did another thing: something more effective, something it was good at: it turned the new conflicts, the new categories of class, the new grievances into the old tribal feuds which the country knew so well and felt that it could handle.

A member of Parliament summing up the politics of the Shia at the time of Musa al Sadr's arrival put it this way: "It was a politics of polarities, feudalism, *al Iqta*, on one side, extremism, *al tatruf*, on the other. A new way had to be found."[35]

If men in this Shia society thought of political salvation in the late 1950s and early 1960s, they didn't look in the direction of the Shia mujtahids. Shia Lebanon sustained a clerical community that was on the whole economically depressed and politically quiescent. The cler-ics accepted the preeminence of the beys. The latter were the ones with the money, with the men with guns, and the land. The ulama

---

[34]Waddah Chrara, *Transformation d'une manifestation religieuse dans un village du Liban-Sud* (Beirut: Publications du Centre de Recherches, Université Libanaise, 1968).
[35]I owe this perceptive remark to a discussion with Sayyid Hussein Husseini, who made it as a summary of what he took to be the situation of the Shia that Musa al Sadr confronted.

were respectfully treated when they came into the presence of the beys. They were at hand when the beys made their grand tours of their domains. But whatever deference and whatever material help were offered the men of religion the beys saw as signs of their own fidelity, their own generosity. Piety was fine in its place; but it was the world of power, the world of affairs, that mattered. Muhammad Taqi Sadiq, the preeminent cleric of this period, was an ally of the Assad family. From his base in Nabatiyya, Shaykh Sadiq preached a conservative discourse. He was a man without political ambitions, without glamour. No special mystique surrounded the men of religion. Economically vulnerable, they took the world as it came. Better leave stones unturned, the clerics thought, so long as the men in power paid some homage to the religious institution and its custodians. The "limits" of the religious institutions were observed. Beyond these limits, things might snap; the man of power might declare a particular cleric a fool or a hypocrite. Some religious tale might then be found, perhaps related by one of the beys himself, maintaining that the men of religion were furthest away from God and his teachings. In a world of scarcity, there was always the suspicion that the cleric was a parasite, that he lived off the toil and the land of other men.

Men with peasant cunning mocked the religious professionals. It was said that the religious garb was often a cover for men who wanted to hide physical deformities and escape being taunted about them. And the learning of the religious professionals was always the subject of snide comments and of gossip. It was not unusual for sharp-tongued laymen to question the learning of this or that mullah, to doubt whether the clerics really knew their trade. In good measure, this stemmed from resentment over the monopoly on knowledge —basic reading and writing skills—that the religious professionals had had until modern schooling came into this Shia hinterland in the 1940s and 1950s. The monopoly broken, the sense of resentment was replaced with a newfound arrogance toward what the men of religion knew and the knowledge they peddled.

The Shia clerics were obscurantists. They told fantastic tales about the twelve Imams, about their valor and their eloquence—tales that the mind, even the believing mind, had trouble taking in. They were timid and conservative. The outside world frightened and bewildered them. A Shia layman who became one of Musa al Sadr's admirers expressed his despair and the despair of others like him with the clerics: "The man of religion in our midst covered himself with his abaya, put his head on his hand, and went to sleep. He woke up only to tell others to sleep. He lives a stagnant life; don't be fooled by any motion he

[74]

makes for it is usually backward. The man of religion does two kinds of harm: once when he falls behind, and once when he pulls others with him. . . . He, the man of religion, has stuffed his mind with the most impossible fantasies and miracles and myths."[36]

We have a testimony to the popular skepticism regarding the religious institution and its custodians from a noted Shia scholar and jurist, Muhammad Jawad Maghniyya. Maghniyya had toured some of the villages of the south of Lebanon in 1959, the year of Sayyid Musa's arrival. What he found on his tour was a disheartening spectacle: "Some youngsters and some of the elders as well are always complaining that the men of religion, *rajal al din*, do not fulfill their duties, do not visit and guide the faithful. But when a man of religion comes their way they escape from him as a healthy man avoids a man with a contagious disease. I told one young man in one of these villages that the purpose of my visit is religious instruction, that I was interested to hear from the young as to their concerns, for religion allows every skeptic to have his say. . . . The young man heard me out, promised to return in the evening with a list of questions and reservations, but he left never to return."[37]

The clerics were bearers of a stilted religious and educational tradition. It weighed them down; it rendered them unable to keep up with the changes—the real changes as well as the aspirations and pretensions—of their flock. The tradition they transmitted had no bearing on the reality that men knew and lived. They saw every new idea as *bida* (innovation, heresy), as a torch setting fire to sacred realms. They were on hand to attack the heresies of science, to say that the Quran anticipated the tape-recorder, to warn the young, the dissidents, of the follies of disobedience, to remind a rebellious soul of the Quranic injunction: "Oh believers, obey God and obey the messenger and those in authority among you" (Quran, 4:59).

It was not so much the shortcomings of this or that cleric, but the traditional system of education, the making of a cleric, that doomed the custodians of the religious institution. The gifted British scholar Edward G. Browne has given a vivid account of the making of a Shia cleric. Browne's material comes from Iran, but he was describing an entire tradition of Shia education, a world which "closely resembles that of the medieval European student."

---

[36]Najib Jamal al Din, *Al Shia ala al Muftraq* (The Shia at the Crossroads) (Beirut: n. p., 1967), pp. 100–101.

[37]Muhammad Jawad Maghniyya, "Ila Ulama al Shra fi Jabal Amil" (To the Ulama in Jabal Amil), *Al Irfan*, 47 (September 1959), 77–78.

We see the child prematurely torn from the games and amusements suitable to his age to undergo a long, strenuous, and arid course of instruction in Arabic grammar and philology, reading one grammar after another in an ascending scale of difficulty with commentaries, supercommentaries, glosses and notes on each; we see him as a boy, now fired with ambition, pursuing his studies in theology and law, half-starved, suffering alternately from the cold of winter and the heat of summer, ruining his eyesight by perusing crabbed texts by the fitful light of the moon, and his digestion by irregular and unwholesome meals, varied by intervals of starvation. Cut off from home life and family ties; submerged in an ocean of formalism and fanaticism; himself in time adding to the piles of glosses and notes which serve rather to submerge and obscure than to elucidate the texts whereon they are based; and at last, if fortunate, attracting the favorable notice of some great divine, and becoming himself a *mudarris* (lecturer), a *mutawalli* (custodian of a shrine), or even a *mujtahid*.[38]

Muhsin al Amin (1867–1952), one of the noted mujtahids of the Lebanese Shia community—often cited as its most distinguished figure of the time—left a rare glimpse of the world of its clerics. His autobiography, a most unusual undertaking for a cleric of a traditional mold, confirms Browne's portrait; it shows what a cleric like Musa al Sadr, a man with daring and flamboyance, had to work against.

Sayyid Muhsin was born in one of the more enlightened towns of southern Lebanon to a marriage of sayyids. It was typical of sayyids and religious scholars to intermarry. On both his father's and his mother's side, he documents a lineage of religious learning and piety. Of his father, Sayyid Abdul Karim al Amin, he writes: "Sayyid Abdul Karim was a pious, pure, and God-fearing man who made the pilgrimage to Mecca and to the shrines in Iraq; he wanted to visit Meshed, the burial place of Imam Rida, may God grant him peace; but it was suggested to him by his cousin Sayyid Kazem that he should spend what he intended to spend on that journey on the religious education of his nephews; he accepted his advice. . . . He died in Iraq and was buried there." Sayyid Muhsin's maternal grandfather was Shaykh Muhammad Hussein al Amili al Musawi, "a pious alim, God-fearing, a poet who went to Najaf in Iraq in pursuit of knowledge; he lived there for a while, then he passed away."[39]

Sayyid Muhsin recalls his years of schooling. At age seven, he was

[36]Edward G. Browne, *A Literary History of Persia,* vol. 4 (Cambridge: Cambridge University Press, 1978 edition), p. 367.

[39]Sayyid Muhsin al Amin, *Al Sayyid Muhsin al Amin,* edited by his son Hassan al Amin (Sidon: Al Irfan, 1957), pp. 6–9, and p. 8.

taken to the village teacher to learn the Quran. It was a regime of terror and rote learning: the teacher had in front of him two rods, a short one to reach the boys seated near him, a longer one for the ones further away. Games, the play of children, were not open to the seekers of religious knowledge. This harsh regime, he says, came from time past: it was used "even with the children of Caliphs and Kings and Princes."[40] After he mastered the Quran, it was time to turn to Arabic grammar, to concentrate on improving his handwriting: grammar and the rules of grammar occupied Sayyid Muhsin's evenings.

In 1879, when Sayyid Muhsin was twelve, a religious scholar returned from Iraq to a neighboring village. He had acquired a modest reputation, and Sayyid Muhsin was sent to study under him. It was hard going, says Muhsin: "As I was a boy, I could not understand what I was reading; my mind wandered; my thoughts were scattered. Meanwhile my peers were busy with their games. I reminded myself that I had come here to learn. I vowed to study in a serious way. . . . I put behind me the company of anyone from whom I could not learn."[41]

Four years later, a more learned cleric, Shaykh Musa Sharara, returned from Iraq to Bint Jbail, one of the larger towns of southern Lebanon. Sayyid Muhsin wanted to study under Shaykh Sharara. He could not make up his mind; he sought guidance in the Quran. The inspiration came, and with it the decision to go to Bint Jbail. It turned out to be a wise decision: Sayyid Muhsin's new teacher offered a thorough program of instruction in grammar and jurisprudence; the teacher had a compelling way of explaining the content and the meaning of the Quran. Sayyid Muhsin's attention was claimed by his studies. It was a time and a place of great scarcity. There was a dearth of water in Bint Jbail; in the summer the supply nearly dried up. Water had to be brought from a nearby village which had "a generous spring." The students did not want to fetch the water: carrying a jar was women's work—and called for some skill. When no woman came forth to help, one of the students took the jar to the neighboring village, filled it, and tried to lift it to his shoulder by one of its two handles. The jar broke; it had to be lifted with both handles. It took the intervention of Shaykh Musa to coerce one of the women in Bint Jbail into fetching water for the aspiring scribes.

After three years of studying with Shaykh Musa, Sayyid Muhsin was left on his own. The teacher died of TB; the school was aban-

[40]Ibid., p. 9.
[41]Ibid., p. 13.

doned. "Such was the practice here; a school's life came to an end when its master died, if not before."[42] Sayyid Muhsin now worked and studied by himself. He wanted to go to Iraq for religious studies, but his father was opposed. The family lacked financial means. Sayyid Muhsin spent five years (1885–1890) waiting for his chance to go to Iraq.

During this period military conscription reared its head. The Ottoman army had to be staffed. From Sayyid Muhsin's memoir we learn of the gulf between the Ottoman administrators and their Shia subjects—in part the "normal" distance between ruler and ruled, in part a doctrinal chasm between Sunni and Shia. Sayyid Muhsin reported to the authorities at the government's seat in the coastal city of Sidon. He went with others, who, like him, wanted exemption from military service on grounds of being ulama. There a Turkish officer, "quite violent in his prejudice against seekers of religious knowledge," sent Sayyid Muhsin and a few of his companions to Beirut with a note that they were not religious students, but farmers, "men who plough and reap." The religious scholars were dispatched to Beirut in the charge of a gendarme. The matter was effectively being decided: Sayyid Muhsin and his companions were on their way to becoming conscripts.

But there were cracks in the system. In Beirut, an Ottoman official of gentle disposition who spoke Arabic with a Damascene accent accepted that Sayyid Muhsin and his friends were students. The official inquired how Sayyid Muhsin secured his livelihood: "I said that God was generous to all his creatures, that we had families that helped us out. He told me that I was dressed like a merchant; I had on an Iraqi *abaya*; I was wearing it against the winter's cold. I told him that the examinations were upon us, and that knowledge did not depend on what a man wore."[43]

The young scribes sat for an examination. All of them passed. The military exemption was granted.

Sayyid Muhsin relates a revealing incident that illuminates the hard economic facts of the religious institution and the relations between *al ayan* (the notables) and the clerics. Sometime after the death of Sayyid Muhsin's teacher, a wealthy notable of Bint Jbail by the name of Hajj Suleiman Bezzi assembled other men of means in the area to plan for the invitation of another cleric from Iraq. A telegram was sent to Muhammad Hussein Kazimi, the highest marja in Najaf, asking for

[42]Ibid., pp. 30–31.
[43]Ibid., pp. 35–36.

one of two clerics: Ismael al Sadr (Musa al Sadr's grandfather) or Mahdi al Hakim (father of Muhsin al Hakim, who became the Grand Marja in Najaf and Musa al Sadr's patron). Mahdi al Hakim accepted the invitation. He insisted on a certain cash payment and it was made. He came from Iraq to the remote town of Bint Jbail. "I yearned to see him," says Sayyid Muhsin, "as a thirsty man yearns for fresh water."

Not long after his arrival Sayyid Mahdi al Hakim put the question of his livelihood before the notables. He wanted them to buy him a house and a small farm: "I came to these parts to 'enjoin the good and forbid the evil,' *Al Amr bi al Maruf wa al Nahy an al Munkar*, and this can't be done the way it should be done unless I am economically independent." This, reflects Sayyid Muhsin, would have been a reasonable request in Iran or Iraq. But here, where "the people are poor no religious scholar had ever made such a request." The notables put forth a compromise proposal: the farm could be bought, but it could not be Sayyid Mahdi's outright; it would be set aside for whoever occupied the position of alim in the area. The issue was not resolved; there was little wealth to give Sayyid Mahdi what he wanted. Of his request one of the notables attending the meeting had this to say: "We are poor; our men of religion live as we do. It is our custom for one of us to offer the alim a horse, for another to offer him some money, and so forth. If we have to buy a farm for each alim, it won't be long before the whole area here becomes a property of religious men. Where then would we go?"[44] The limitations of a poor country and the layman's suspicious view of clerics merge in his words.

Deliverance for Sayyid Muhsin came in 1890, when he was twenty-three years of age. He fulfilled his dream of being able to go to Iraq. His father's objections subsided. There was little money to spare for the venture to Iraq. But the father had relented, a good omen for the journey.

Of the Shia holy city of Najaf, of its schools and its ways, Sayyid Muhsin writes as a man writes of a promised land to which he finally attained: with awe and with some disappointment. The awe was for the history, for what the land evoked and was burdened with; the disappointment was for the curriculum. From Sayyid Muhsin we learn of the schools' defects: the mediocrity of the students, the chaos of a *laissez-faire* educational system, the formalism. He even found fault in the command of Arabic possessed by many of the *Ajam*, the Persians, in the religious schools. We also learn of the poverty and

[44]Ibid., p. 40.

material hardships of the students, of the difficulty of making ends meet. Sayyid Muhsin had apparently gone for religious studies with a wife and children. No marriage has been mentioned in his narrative to this point, but in relating the experience of ten years in Najaf, he does speak of a wife and several children. It was hard studying the obscure texts and feeding a family. Sayyid Muhsin tells of three difficult years—they are left unspecified—when prices skyrocketed in Iraq. It also happened that these were years of drought in his ancestral village. Very little money was sent to him during this period. Some books had to be sold to keep things intact. "The family nearly collapsed," he noted, "while I went on with my studying and reading." A generous soul whom Sayyid Muhsin had never met, a man of Shia Lebanon, made a financial contribution to seeing him and his family through hard times.[45]

In 1901, the "Shia of Damascus invited us to come and settle amidst them," writes Sayyid Muhsin. He did so, and it was between Damascus and his ancestral home in Shia Lebanon that he spent the rest of his working life. He avoided as best he could the upheavals of politics. He was in Jabal Amil, he tells us, when World War I broke out, and returned to Damascus, thinking that it was safer. But he left Damascus again when he realized that he was "further away from danger" in his ancestral home.

Sayyid Muhsin was a "bookish" man. Damascus, a wealthier place than his rural homeland, enabled him to write the "commentaries and supercommentaries" that clerics were known for. One of his works, *Ayan al Shia*, runs into fifty-six volumes. It is a grabbag. Here and there light intrudes; the bulk of the work, however, fits Browne's description of the output of clerics. Weighed down by a heavy scholarly tradition, harassed by poverty, and hemmed in by a view of the world that saw the realm of politics and power as one of compromise, the Shia clerics were hardly the men to whom others looked for change and for leadership. *Al Amr bi al Maruf wa al Nahy an al Munkar*, enjoining the good and forbidding evil: that was what Sayyid Musa's predecessors in Shia Lebanon took to be their proper realm.

In the early 1960s when Musa al Sadr was still searching for a role, a mullah in Shia Lebanon by the name of Shaykh Hussein Maatuq expressed the dominant clerical view of political involvement. He cited the authority of the highest cleric of the Shia world, the Marja al Taqlid, Ayatollah Muhsin al Hakim in Iraq. Ayatollah al Hakim, he said, refrained from having any dealings with the king of Iraq during

[45]Ibid., pp. 63–64.

the time of the monarchy or with the Baathists and Communists who overthrew the monarchy. Other clerics, lesser clerics were bound by Muhsin al Hakim's caution and distance from the world of politics.[46] Every now and then a village mullah—rather like some village priests in tsarist Russia who gave religious cover and sanction to intermittent rural rebellions—would dabble in radical politics. But the dominant clerical response to the world of power was a mix of historic caution, opportunism, and strict fidelity to the sacred text.

The tradition released the clerics who accepted and transmitted it from responsibility. One could come to a *modus vivendi* with the established political order; one could render it obedience without being implicated in its ways. To reform a social order one would have to accept a more committed kind of membership, but the quietist clerical interpretation ruled out such membership. It gave those who subscribed to it absolution from political and social responsibility. It placed a premium on scholarly and religious ritual. The inherited traditions, the weighty treatises, the written and oral history of the twelve Imams were massive and demanding enough to absorb the energies and vindicate the work and role of a cleric. Alongside such a trust, the "pollution" of daily life, the abuses of the state and the landlords, were matters that could be ignored or at least "put in proper perspective." The clerics had a flock to look after. Evil, unreason, and sedition stalked the lives of men. The men of religion had better concentrate on keeping things intact. This is a cast of mind illuminated by Joseph Conrad in words attributed to a character in *Under Western Eyes*: "Obscurantism is better than the light of incendiary torches. The seed germinates in the night. Out of the dark soil springs the perfect plant. But a volcanic eruption is sterile, the ruin of the fertile ground."[47]

Because the Shia faith had such a high emotional content, many clerics felt it part of their mission to be excessively sober and erect, to disdain popular passions, to keep away from ordinary men. The standing and dignity, *al maqama*, of the man of religion had to be preserved. This attitude served as a great barrier between clerics and laymen. Normal life—spirited discussions, tales of sexual exploits, banter between men and women, critical statements on religious matters—was not to go on in the presence of clerics. The world was defiled and polluted—and real. The men of the religious institution upheld that which was pure and correct—and contrived.

A cleric with political ambitions and social concerns walking into

[46]Shaykh Hussein Maatuq, "Waqfa ma al Zuama wa al Shaab" (An Encounter with the Leaders and the People), *Al Irfan*, 51 (December 1963), 548–552.
[47]Joseph Conrad, *Under Western Eyes* (London: Penguin, 1979), p. 36.

this society had his work cut out for him. But the newcomer who arrived in 1959 had some things on his side. Timing helped. Musa al Sadr arrived as people were feeling the possibility of some improvement in their lives, as new Shia money, some of it brought back by Shia expatriates in West Africa, was elbowing its way through the society. Most important, he came as urbanization was narrowing the gap between the city and the countryside. The work of a cleric and the charisma of a cleric needed an urban population. "We are *fellaheen* (peasants), what do we want of religion," said an exasperated peasant of the region to a curious missionary who kept insisting that every man including "the poor savage in the centre of Africa" had a religion.[48] Peasants inhabited a raw and limited world. Neither their imagination nor their subsistence living provided appropriate soil for an ambitious cleric. Had he arrived a decade earlier, Musa al Sadr would have found a burdened and cynical peasant population. Instead, he was lucky; he arrived after men had been released from the certainties and the uncertainties of the land, from the haven of tradition that it offered and from the grinding work and poverty that it made inevitable.

He was lucky as well in that he came in 1959 to a new political regime that emerged after the civil war of the preceding year. What happened in 1958 need not detain us long. The "national pact" of 1943 with its basic understanding between Maronite Lebanonists and Sunni Arab nationalists broke down in 1957–1958. The Maronite president, Camille Chamoun, violated the workings of this fine-tuned arrangement. During a period of intense Arab nationalism generated by the charismatic appeal of the Egyptian president, Gamal Abdul Nasser, Chamoun sought to push Lebanon into the orbit of the United States. Chamoun broke with the subtle assumptions of the Lebanese polity that the president (by agreement a Maronite) was first among equals in a system of chieftains and oligarchs speaking for the disparate communities that made up Lebanon. He rigged a parliamentary election in 1957—beyond the "normal" limits of the country's generous and languid sensibility. It was clear that he wanted to get himself elected to another six-year presidential term (yet another violation of Lebanon's unwritten rules). A civil war that brought the U.S. Marines to Lebanon, on the side of Chamoun, broke out in 1958. It ended in compromise; what issued forth was a relatively enlightened regime headed by the commander of the army, an officer with a no-nonsense mentality, by the name of Fuad Shihab. The old regime

[48]W. M. Thomson, *The Land and the Book* (London: Nelson, 1872), p. 227.

of Camille Chamoun had its Shia "notables" and props; the new regime, committed to some reform, to a decent measure of *étatisme*, was on the lookout for new men it could cultivate and work with in order to check the power of the feudal chieftains.

Furthermore, it was fitting that Musa al Sadr, a man who knew the power of imagery, came to Lebanon at the same time as the new television station. Some six thousand sets were to be found in Lebanon in the year of his arrival; a decade later, the country had more than one hundred and fifty thousand sets. The culture of the automobile was to spread in the decade that followed his arrival. Ten years earlier the isolation of the Shia villages and towns had been suffocating. By the early 1960s, when Musa al Sadr began crisscrossing this small country, automotive culture had narrowed the gap between the city and the countryside.

Luck and circumstances were on his side. He arrived in a country beginning to see the inequalities of men and classes in a new way. In the early 1960s, newly available statistics put before the Lebanese the inequalities of their country. In an economy which was heavily skewed in favor of the service sectors—banking, trade, and tourism —the top 4 percent of the country's population claimed 32 percent of the national income, while the bottom 50 percent took in only 18 percent of the income.[49] The figures were the results of a study commissioned by the regime of President Fuad Shihab and carried out by a French team. Men, being awakened to inequalities, now recited the figures, saw age-old imbalances as something that men had brought about and men could change. Wealth and poverty had lived side by side here as they did in every traditional social order: wealth was *nima*, a blessing and the possession of a few; poverty and scarcity were the lot of most. Now the state and some enlightened men saw inequalities as something that could be tinkered with and changed. "It is almost never when a state of things is the most detestable that it is smashed," noted Tocqueville, writing of the old regime in France, "but when, beginning to improve, it permits men to breathe, to reflect, to communicate their thoughts with each other, and to gauge by what they already have the extent of their grievances. The weight, although less heavy, seems all the more unbearable."[50]

Even distant African nationalism aided the Iranian-born cleric. Not

[49]These and other statistics on social change come from Tawfiq Beydoun, *Ithr al Nizam al Iqtisadi ala Tasruf al Musthalik fi Lubnan* (The Impact of the Economic System on the Consumer in Lebanon) (Beirut: Lebanese University, 1970).

[50]Alexis de Tocqueville, *Selected Letters on Politics and Society* (Berkeley: University of California Press, 1985), p. 296.

[83]

long after Musa al Sadr arrived in Lebanon, many of the Shia expatriates began to make their way back to Lebanon. Banished by poverty
in the preceding quarter-century, to Ghana, Sierra Leone, Liberia,
and other African countries, they had made enough money to return
to the old country. African nationalism, to which they were entirely
hostile and unsympathetic, added an incentive for putting their African years behind them. The men with money made in faraway lands
could not find a comfortable home in the old politics of beys and
clans. And the politics of the ideological parties were not for them.
They and the newly arrived cleric from Qom made ideal partners.
Like him, they were searching for a place in the country, some middle
course between feudalism, al iqta, and extremism, al tatruf.

[3]

The Path the Cleric Took: Sayyid Musa and His Companions

"There are those who cannot deal with dedication and commitment. They have linked my initiatives to political movements—local, Arab, and foreign—without shame, without any evidence. There is no reason for suspicion. The only reason is that I took the man of religion, *rajul al din*, into the social realm, that I removed from him the dust of the ages."[1]

The words were Musa al Sadr's. They were words of self-definition and self-defense. The turf in Tyre which was enough for his predecessor was for him only a beginning. As he set out to make his presence felt in Tyre and beyond, he faced the suspicions of this small land. He was a man with an agenda and in a hurry. Tyre could not contain him.

Histories of Phoenician times have made much of Tyre: the ruins on the coast were monuments to better days. The textbooks of the Ministry of Education which exalted Phoenician greatness spoke of Tyre and its trade and its splendor. But it was a ruined and impoverished realm. Official government reports put the population of the city and its surroundings at some seventy thousand inhabitants. Shortly after Musa al Sadr's appearance there, a newly elected member of Parliament, Jafar Sharaf al Din (a relative of Musa al Sadr; a son of Sayyid Abdul Hussein), stood up in Parliament to make a plea for Tyre and to describe the conditions of the coastal city and its surrounding towns and villages:

[1]As reported in *Al Irfan*, 54 (September 1966), 408.

The district of Tyre has sixty villages, to which God Almighty gave all kinds of beauty. But the rulers have deprived Tyre and the surroundings of their rights. Of these sixty villages only a dozen or so have anything that could be called a school or a paved road. Forty villages are without a school. These sixty villages go thirsty in this age of science and the machine, while a river [the Litani] passes them by on its way to the sea. All sixty villages lack electricity. Electricity is the fortune of more privileged districts. . . . These sixty villages are deserted, inhabited by old men and women; the young ones have departed to toil in the heat of Africa. Thousands more have come to Beirut, to toil among others of their kind. Tyre itself, the heart of the district, has suffered what no city can suffer. It has become a deformed, ruined place. Everything in it falls short of what a civilized place should be. The government should restore to Tyre its splendor.[2]

Yet despite the lamentation of its deputy, Tyre had its advantages for a young aspiring cleric. It was the only Shia coastal city: the other Shia towns were more insular and more unfortunate still. The majority in Tyre were Shia, but there were Christian communities, and a substantial population of Palestinians had lived there since their dispossession in 1948. Tyre was only a few miles from the Israeli border, and all sorts of political currents were to be found in it. The town was a microcosm of the country. The Palestinian community that had settled in Tyre was instrumental in introducing new political concerns, in importing Pan-Arabist ideas and doctrines. At the other end of the political and social spectrum was one of southern Lebanon's "feudal" families, the Khalils, with their age-old ways. The Khalils were known for being particularly rough and hard. The lord of the clan, Kazem, a "tough," had been defeated in the parliamentary election of 1960. He had been the darling of the previous regime, that of President Camille Chamoun, which had been pushed aside in the civil war of 1958.

Musa al Sadr courted and worked with the new regime of General Fuad Shihab. The charge made in later years that he was a "vassal of the regime" was both clumsy—and true. During his first decade in the country he worked through establishment politics. Sayyid Musa al Sadr was a reformer; he wanted vocational schools and clinics; he wanted civil service appointments for the Shia; he wanted a bigger share of the national budget for the neglected towns and villages of the south. He was a newcomer, and a stranger. He had to demonstrate his fidelity to the institutions and the welfare of the state. He

[2]Mahadir Majlis al Nawab (Proceedings of Parliament), Beirut, 1960 session, pp. 66–67.

[86]

had to pay homage to Lebanon, to its "special genius," to its "historic mission"; he had to say all those things that the country said about itself. Had he flung himself against the Lebanese state in the 1960s, it would have been a quixotic undertaking. Few brave souls in the Shia community would have followed him, and the effort would have fizzled out. He had to court, and learn the ways of, a new and bizarre place. He worked amid a supremely "realistic" community. The Shia then had so little margin for error; a man leading them had to deliver concrete benefits and services. Something said of old Russian peasantry applied to this population: they tended to believe in whatever worked for them.[3] A man wanting to lead had to show tangible evidence of his gifts and his concern.

Musa al Sadr's outlook and ambitions converged with the general thrust of the Shihab regime. In brief, Shihab's six-year rule (1958–1964) was Lebanon's first—and last—fling with *etatisme*. Shihab brought to the presidency the spirit and outlook of an apolitical army commander. He wanted for the country something more than the old politics of warlords and nepotism. He was the first president of Lebanon who realized that the "merchant republic" of ruling oligarchs and feudal chieftains had to come to terms with the dispossessed, that its chaotic life had to be organized in a new way. Lebanon's wild capitalism, Shihab understood, had to incorporate ideas of social responsibility, had to accept taxation. He wanted to increase the power of the state vis-à-vis the warlords. The organs of the Shihab regime were on the lookout for new men and forces who could be aided and propped up against the old order. Shihab sought a better deal for the Shia and for their neglected parts of the country. He knew that the political balance in Lebanon had to be changed, that his community, the Maronites, had to yield some of its power to the Muslims. But he, too, worked with the existing material—and with the verdict of the civil war of 1958. The rebellion of 1958 was launched by (Sunni) Muslim West Beirut and by the Druze. And these two communities emerged as the beneficiaries of the Shihabist reforms. As Lebanese historian Kamal Salibi sums it up, the reforms in the civil service and the changes intended to aid the Muslims went to the Sunnis and the Druze. The Shihabist reforms ended up with the Shia "losing a large part of their share to Sunnites and Druze"; they remained "the community most poorly represented in the public service, as they had indeed been before."[4]

[3]This is borrowed from Paul Avrich, *Russian Rebels* (New York: Norton, 1976).
[4]Kamal Salibi, "Lebanon under Fuad Chehab, 1958–1964," *Middle Eastern Studies,* 2 (April 1966), 219.

[87]

Still, Shihab made an effort: and this gave the agile cleric in Tyre some space. It was Faud Shihab himself who granted Musa al Sadr Lebanese citizenship. The deed was done, we are told by a well-informed Lebanese politician, with "some hesitation." The custodian of the Lebanese state, a man of Lebanon with an ordered army career behind him, thought of Musa al Sadr as "a man unlike others, a dangerous man."[5] This was not because of any tangible information that the general had. It was because of that mystery that trailed the cleric, that clung to him. The Shihab family was deeply Lebanese. Shihabs had ruled Mount Lebanon as its preeminent princely family from 1697 until the early 1840s. Fuad Shihab was through and through a product of a very small space. Musa al Sadr was different: his identity and background could not be so neatly categorized. But the doubts notwithstanding, the citizenship was granted, and some state funds were made available to Musa al Sadr's work in Tyre—principally for a vocational training center that was his pet project during his early years in the country.

It took only six or seven years before Musa al Sadr's reformist themes and his fame—his spark, said one observer—caught on. He emerged on the national scene as a reformer, an enlightened man of religion. He was a spellbinding speaker, a born persuader of men. In a country where some southern men lived and died without ever venturing to the northern coastal city of Tripoli, he was a tireless traveler. Much was made of the fact that he could wake up in Tyre, have lunch in Mount Lebanon, then spend the night in the eastern Bekaa Valley. It was a small country, but its lines were drawn and men, particularly Shia men of religion, rarely ventured beyond their small fragment of it. A man who grew up in Iran must have felt claustrophobia in Lebanon.

Musa al Sadr entered the political arena, elbowed his way into it. But we must recall that he did so as a man of religion. And it is with this aspect of his career and self-representation that we must begin. We have no way of assessing his, or anyone else's, piety. (In general, Islamic society has wisely dodged this question. The imputation of disbelief, *Takfir*, to someone is such a thorny and dangerous endeavor that men are taken at their profession of faith, that they are Muslims.) Some conservative clerics in Lebanon thought him an agnostic, doubted his religiosity. When he appeared at a church to deliver a sermon, his rivals in the clerical establishment circulated a photo-

[5]Karim Pakradouni, *Al Salam al Mafqud* (The Missing Peace) (Beirut: Ibr al Sharq, 1984), p. 118.

graph of him under a cross. No mujtahid, they said, could do such a thing and stay within the faith. When he traveled to Europe in 1963, they were sure that the trip itself defiled him. He must have slept in the infidels' world and eaten the infidels' food, they protested. There were those who believed that the turban of this thoroughly political man was a cover, that religion was purely an instrument, that a man of so much charm and drive and worldly ambition could have done what he did without the sanction and cover of the religious institution.

But the worldliness aside, this was a cleric, a sayyid, and the son of a cleric. His trademark and themes were religious ones; his language was suffused with religious symbols and metaphors. It was as a sayyid, and a descendant of the seventh Imam at that, that he represented himself. The men who were to follow him—the patricians and upwardly mobile professionals in his first decade, the Shia masses in the second—read into his life themes of Shia history, and projected onto him long dormant attitudes about legitimate authority and who was entitled to it. The career of an "Imam"—a religious and a political leader—had to be anchored in a religious base. The history working for him, aiding him against landed families with long-standing claims to power, against secular political parties with a sense of entitlement to power given them by the modern world of politics, was a thoroughly religious one. In Islam itself, the political community grew out of the religious. The exemplary leader had been the Prophet Muhammad himself; the Imams who in the Shia doctrine inherited his religious and worldly power worked out of the same progression— from the religious toward the political. And in Musa al Sadr's case, it was an inheritor of tradition who was insinuating—really bringing back—into the world of politics an old notion of the primacy of the religious over what was worldly and political.

He was not a great systematic thinker, or a writer of major treatises on religion. Lebanon did not need this kind of talent; there was no space for it. Besides, that kind of work would have required solitude, and Musa al Sadr was a man of hectic motion. He was a quick study, and he was obviously well read. His was the advantage of an intellectual and a political activist—one suited to, in his words, removing from religion and the man of religion the "dust of the ages." Musa al Sadr was interested in power and change. He had a "soft" and modernist reading of the Shia faith. His early discourses in the country, the ideas that attracted attention, that brought him fame and influential followers, were reiterations of the old themes of "Muslim modernism." We are familiar with the themes as they evolved over the course of the nineteenth century: they were elaborated by political activists and philosophers who sought an Islamic answer to the power of the West, and to the demands of a secular, scientific culture. The modernist defense of Islam—prodding it along, reading into scripture new needs and changes, "smuggling" change into an old tradition that had fallen behind the Occident—had had its exemplary publicist in Jamal al din al Afghani (1838-1897), an Iranian-born sayyid with an obscure and controversial background of political conspiracy and activism. In the course of a life which included concealing his own Iranian (Shia) birth and claiming an Afghan (Sunni) descent and which spanned India, Iran, Egypt, and Turkey, Afghani had set out the modernist themes for others to pick up: the compatibility of faith and reason, the openness of Islam to innovations, the need to reform Islam for purposes of "self-strengthening."[6]

These modernist ideas were the themes of Musa al Sadr's early years. Islam, he said in a discourse that echoed the concerns of the modernists, has been turned into "ritual." The "deviant" men of religion have gone along with this tendency. "Islam was once movement, vitality, and work; it now stands for lethargy and abdication. Why have the Muslims fallen behind the caravan of civilization? The woman is half of society. During the early days of Islam, women worked even though the opportunity for work was limited. Today half of society is paralyzed."[7]

Genuine faith, he said in a lecture before a gathering of secular intellectuals, "sustains scientific inquiry and supports it. . . . The believer who fights science, and reason, who fears reason, should realize that he is not fully committed to his religion; fear of truth means that one suspects that one's religion is at odds with truth." There are some believers, he added, who view man's incursions into outer space as violations of God's realm and his teachings; there are others who are quick to say that the Quran foretold all scientific advance. Both positions, he said, were wrong: the first because it is too timid; the second because it takes the Quran and submits it to a test of details which it is destined to fail.[8]

[6]The career and views of Jamal al din al Afghani are set out in Nikki Keddie's masterly biography, *Sayyid Jamal ad-Din al-Afghani: A Political Biography* (Berkeley: University of California Press, 1972). See also Keddie's edited work, *An Islamic Response to Imperialism: Political and Religious writings of Sayyid Jamal ad-Din al-Afghani* (Berkeley: University of California Press, 1983).

[7]"Why Did the Muslims Fall Behind in the March of Scientific and Material Progress" delivered in May 1967 in Beirut, reprinted in *Al Islam: Aqida Rasikha wa Manhaj Hayat* (Islam: A Firm Ideology and a Way of Life) (Beirut, 1979), p.108. This book is a selection of Musa al Sadr's early sermons and lectures.

[8]"Al Islam wa Thaqafat al Qarn al Ishrin" (Islam and the Education of the Twentieth Century), delivered in May 1965 in Beirut, reprinted in *Al Islam*, pp. 68–69.

These themes were put forward in a talk before Lebanon's "best and brightest," before al Nadwa al Lubnaniya (the Lebanese Forum). No Shia cleric had ventured there before. This was an organization for the learned, for the chic, for those who took pride in their capacity to handle ideas and lively discussions. The force behind the Lebanese Forum was Michel al Asmar, a Maronite intellectual of open horizons and generous temperament. Michel al Asmar, who was to become one of Sayyid Musa's close friends, had a deep interest in the Shia heritage; a Maronite, he believed that the Shia and the Maronites were the two principal communities of Lebanon, that bridges ought to be built between them as a way of offering an ideological alternative to the Sunni–Pan-Arab conception of Lebanon.

Sayyid Musa's lecture before this audience was delivered in classical and formal Arabic. The text shows something of the anxiety of a man displaying the range of his learning, the number of books he has read, his ability to harmonize the heritage, *al turath*, with the needs of modern men. In Islamic strictures, he said, were to be found so many of the modern dimensions of men's lives, "the social, the philosophic, even the psychological." Anxiety, *al qalaq*, sexual yearnings, envy were all dealt with in the Quran, in the *sira*, in the conduct and example, of the Prophet. "Our (Islamic) education connects heaven and earth, connects man, as an individual, as a social being, to his creator." He quoted and rebutted the Orientalist Sir Hamilton Gibb on the compatibility between Islam and modern ideas; he ranged over Islamic history to note contributions to science and philosophy. It was a tour de force that came straight out of the literature of Islamic modernism. He pointed to the work of the Muslim philosopher Sadr al din al Shirazi, known as Mulla Sadra (d. 1640). Mulla Sadra, he said, was a "son of the seventeenth century," yet his philosophical ideas and outlook were superior to what has been arrived at in twentieth-century European philosophy. In Mulla Sadra's work and in that of his disciples were the questions raised by the German philosopher Karl Jaspers, by the existentialism of Sartre: "From this forum I want to claim that in the realm of philosophy and mysticism, the East still illuminates the world of this century. My proof is a testimony of the French scholar, Henri Corbin, who says that Eastern philosophy can still rescue Europe from decline, from confusion, and that Europe is in desperate need of that timeless wisdom that issued from the East."[9]

The insistence that reason and revelation can be harmonized had long roots in Islamic philosophy, particularly in its Persian tradition.

[9] Ibid., pp. 67–68.

[91]

This was the tradition that Musa al Sadr had been exposed to. Religion and science "were born twins," he said in another discourse. "Together the two of these determine man's fate and his perfection. Science was a natural way that the work of the creator can be seen and can be known. . . . Science and the search for knowledge are an expression of man's designated role in the universe." The "common birth" of science and religion left the two of them with the same ailment during their years of infancy and growth. Both became domains of superstition and myth; as a result "man wandered through realms of ignorance and confusion." Humanity suffered; history was a string of tragedies. Then God sent his messengers to rescue men, to "set free both his science and religion." The idols were smashed; men were freed to know their creator and to search for truth. This is what accounts for the fact that the same geographic areas of the world—the lands of the Greeks and the Egyptians, and the Irano-Semitic lands—were the sites of scientific flowering. Then there came a time when the balance between science and religion was broken. Religion used its power "to oppress its twin, to shackle it, to confine knowledge to that which was discovered by the ancestors. The oppressors now claimed that all the truths of the world were known by the ancestors and that anything new was heresy and deviation. Thus it was declared that anyone who maintained that the earth was round, and that it revolved around the sun, was in a state of unbelief and atheism, *Kufr wa ilhad.*" Oppressing science as it did, the religious institution shackled itself: it denied itself the fruits of knowledge. Then the situation was reversed as the Middle Ages came to an end. It was now science's moment and its opportunity for revenge. Henceforth the role of religion was belittled and mocked. "Science became intoxicated with its triumph; religion was considered the enemy of all social revolutions in man's history; the religious institution was accused of protecting the oppressor, of sanctioning an illegitimate Prophet, of soothing the oppressed." The coming of the twentieth century has brought to this struggle between religion and science a new maturity: "Science has sobered up, has come in touch with reality, has realized that it alone cannot bring about human happiness. Science has felt alienated and estranged; it sees with greater clarity man's happiness, the ravages of war and oppression. . . . Science and all its branches are instruments of creation. . . . Man who created the machine, who created science, cannot kneel before his own creations, and worship these creations to the exclusion of God. Science begins with man and relies on man."[10]

[10]"Hikayat Al Ilm wa al Din" (The Story of Science and Religion), delivered in 1967, is reprinted in *Al Islam*, pp. 81–103.

Musa al Sadr had figured out the new country to which he had come. The Shia were its dregs. Erudition displayed before modern audiences was part of the seduction of an impressionable community. With some of the sensitive points of Shia doctrine he trod carefully. In an introduction to the work of the French Orientalist Henri Corbin on Iranian Shiism, he put forth his own interpretation of the doctrine of the Hidden Imam: "At the base of this idea is man's instinctive drive toward perfection in all realms of life and his belief that though he may suffer a setback he is sure to recover from adversity even if it lasted tens of years." The belief in the Hidden Imam redeeming the world enhanced "the mental readiness of men receiving calls to justice."[11] The doctrine was given an instrumental function. Musa al Sadr refrained from defending an idea that flew in the face of reason. But he walked a fine line: there was no need to hack away at the idea. The appearance of the twelfth Imam was not some literal phenomenon that men were destined to witness, some great miracle. It was a belief that emerged out of political denial and oppression. The cleric with the modern temperament and outlook knew that men doubted the faith, that it was no longer enough for the custodians of the religious institutions to declare some points of the faith sacred and beyond questioning. The twelve Imams, he said, were guides and sources of inspiration. But history did not stop with them. People have to go on living and making their own history.

Musa al Sadr knew the depth of anticlerical sentiment among the lawyers and civil servants and financiers he set out to engage in a political effort under his own leadership. He preempted that sentiment, gave expression to it himself. He repeatedly condemned the men of religion who groveled before power and powerful men. The son of an ayatollah, he had something to say about the clerical profession which appealed to several of his leading associates: We must, he said, break the triple alliance that brings together the oppressive ruler who calls himself Zul-u-Allah (the shadow of God), the exploitative man of religion who calls himself Amin-u-Allah (the treasurer of God), and the corrupt man of religion who calls himself Ayat-u-Allah (the sign of God). Man, he said, has been suffocated by this triple alliance; he has become a prisoner of the ruler's sword, of the loaf of bread, of religious obscurantism.

Was this just a clever act, a cleric placing himself on the right side of skepticism, pandering to the inclinations of the few associates who were privy to such thoughts? We have no way of knowing for sure.

[11]See Musa al Sadr, "With Professor Corbin" (in Arabic), *Al Irfan*, 54, Part I (July and August 1966), and Part II (September 1966). The passage on the Imamate is in the September issue, p. 201.

What is clear is that the radical reading of the faith and the assault on the traditional men of religion worked. In discussions with intimate followers, Musa al Sadr hinted that "under certain conditions" abortion was permissible, that a Muslim woman should be able to marry a Christian man and still stay within the faith; he doubted, he said, whether polygamy was really permissible by the lights of Islamic law. To a close friend of his he confided that his own father, Ayatollah Sadr al Din al Sadr, had had similar doubts about polygamy.

Daring views were put forth in the form of queries and tentative ideas. A cleric was making himself a partner to the religious doubts and probings of a small circle of laymen. Islamic philosphy had long perfected this technique: the faith and the scripture and the revelation were the realms of the masses, al amma, reason and inquiry were the affairs of the elite, al khassa. Islamic philosophers exposed to Hellenistic traditions, but living, as they did, in a culture that rested on faith and revelation, had perfected the double standard that men resort to in social and political orders that require conformity. The philosophical mind was allowed to roam freely, to inquire. But it paid homage to the orthodoxy, went underground when it had to. The philosophical elite, it was believed, could bear doubt, live with it, but still retain an ethical orientation; the masses needed faith, needed to be kept in line, for otherwise they would be overwhelmed and would be lost.[12]

Something of this tradition—its pessimism about the masses, its trust in the critical faculties of the few—was present in the behavior of Musa al Sadr. The beliefs that the pious masses held were not to be offended, but those who doubted were assured in subtle ways that the modern cleric shared their doubts. He was summoning men to a political endeavor. Ideas were weapons. What was important was to establish that there was nothing inherently regressive or doomed about the religious tradition—or its custodians.

Sayyid Musa winked at traditions with a daring uncommon to men of his clerical calling and background. He was a hit with women, who admired his looks and his elegance and were pleased that they did not have to scurry out of living rooms and meetings when he arrived, as they did with ulama of more conservative outlook. As befitting a man of the religious mantle, he refrained from shaking hands with women, and his aides and companions forewarned Christian women who were to meet him that they should not try to shake hands. But even this prohibition was violated now and them. A woman who ad-

---

[12]For an elaboration of this theme see Keddie, *An Islamic Response to Imperialism*. Roy Mottahedeh has explored the tolerance of skeptics and skepticism in his book *The Mantle of the Prophet: Learning and Power in Modern Iran* (New York: Simon & Schuster, 1985).

mitted being drawn to him, being nearly hypnotized by him, once held out a hand to him, and he took it between his two hands, saying that he was not supposed to do so, and that he was doing what he shouldn't be doing, that he would not do it again.

The Shia tradition, frequently petty and nearly neurotic about the permissible and impermissible, found in Musa al Sadr an attractive embodiment. A politician speaking about his early encounter with Musa al Sadr, some years after the event, was joined by his wife: the sayyid, she said, the Iman, respected women and had a place for them in his idea of what social reform meant.

The tradition—alive and fresh, renewed by men keen on changing and improving themselves but still doing it within the faith—had answers of its own to modern needs: this was Musa al Sadr's message. It was in this vein that he took on the Marxist ideas of the Lebanese left. Some of his early followers were men of means, committed to keeping what they had accumulated. The older clerics in the country had hurled the charge of atheism against leftists and leftist ideas and believed that that alone was sufficient. Musa al Sadr had a keener mind and a more sophisticated political sense; he knew that the country was changing, that one had to offer more "modern" answers. "Economic determinism," he said in a relevant discourse "offered a false and partial view of human history." Man, it was true, was the product of his own environment. But an environment was more than just the sum of economic forces. There were "cultural and religious factors" as well. That is why men born to the same socioeconomic class, he said, at times develop antagonistic ideological outlooks:

> Robert Owen, who was considered one of the main figures of Marxism in the world, was a property-owning capitalist. It was Owen who came up with the idea of limiting the number of working hours, of declaring child labor illegal. Owen did this without being a son of the proletariat. . . . We cannot ignore the role of hereditary, of religious, spiritual movements in the making of history. Try as we might, we cannot give a materialist interpretation for the Prophet Muhammad and his movement without playing havoc with history . . . for the movement of the Prophet was not a mere economic movement, but a moral one with implications for the economy, for civic society.[13]

It is doubtful that more than a handful of his followers (if that) knew of Robert Owen. What mattered, what stood out, were two things:

[13]"Ideology: A Lecture by Musa al Sadr," in *Nukba Min al Muhadarat* (A Selection of Lectures), made available by Amal (published in Beirut, no date), pp. 19–20.

the modern outlook of the cleric speaking for them; and the sense of the men with new wealth that they had an answer of their own, enunciated by a man of holy descent and calling, to the leftist parties, to the young Communists in the Shia community brazenly asserting that property was theft. The modern world with its ideas and threats was here; men could respond to it, learn its vocabulary and its ways, and still remain themselves. This was the message delivered by the shrewd cleric speaking of the "dialectic," of the thesis and antithesis working out a new synthesis. These had been subversive terms that frightened a timid community barely beginning to shed its agrarian insularity, its fear of defilement, its sense that anything new was profoundly threatening and polluting.

The trip to Europe that Musa al Sadr took in 1963, which agitated the "purists" in the clerical profession, he justified in the old style of the modernists' apologetics. "Europe," he said, "with all its good and evil, is the future of this part of the world. It is only in light of our knowledge of Europe that we can come up with a correct program and that we can learn to deal with the destruction that this European invasion brings in its train."[14] The answer could have come straight out of the polemics of Jamal al din al Afghani a century earlier; change was needed lest Islam be swamped by the outside world; one partook of that glamorous civilization out there, learned its ways, in order to prepare the realm of Islam for the assault of the West.

Musa al Sadr's political agenda emerged out of the way he interpreted the faith. Faith was not about ritual, but about social concerns, about the needs of men. Religion was not something that had to be quarantined and kept pure by stern guardians; it could be made to address modern needs. Thus the man of religion, *rajul al din*, need not hide and solely concern himself with old books and rituals. Political ambition—something that the traditional men of religion frowned upon, a defiled realm of greed and naked desire—Sayyid Musa neither openly asserted nor foreswore. Had he asserted it, he would have forfeited the measure of self-denial that he needed as a man of religion; had he forsworn it altogether, he would have had to reconcile himself to the age-old quiescence and piety of the Shia clerics of the country. The old-style politicians, who resented his aura of "saintliness," who wanted to blow him out into the open and make of him just another contender for power, just another beneficiary of the Deuxième Bureau (the Lebanese state's intelligence services), could never quite corner him. Nor could the older clerics of the community,

[14]Musa al Sadr, quoted in Najib Jamal al Din, *Al Shia ala al Muftraq* (The Shia at the Crossroads (Beirut, 1967), p. 75.

who wanted him to live by the limits and restraints of his profession. His was a more radical outlook. He was the harbinger of a religio-political movement that blurred the line between worldliness, *al dunya*, and religion, *al din*. He was a "saint," but his saintliness was of a particular kind. It was of this world; it was supremely ambitious while outwardly denying ambition. By the standards of his time and place, his saintliness was revisionist; it sought to bring back religion into the social and political realm. But there was in the background a far older, and potentially more legitimate Islamic and Shia conception, which subordinated the world of politics to that of the religious order. The beys eyeing the young cleric, watching his intrusions into the realm of politics, seeing in him a man raiding the political order, had a calculus of their own; but the ambitious cleric was not bound by it. He did not seek an open confrontation with the custodians of power in the Shia community. That was to happen in the second decade of his career. What he did in the first decade was to fight for a place of his own in the country, to establish his preeminence, to let his fame and his dedication speak for themselves, and to gather around him a nucleus of Shia men of standing and wealth.

Musa al Sadr tapped into deep wells of human energy and ambitions—and resentments. Little more than two decades after the country's independence, a new Shia intelligentsia—lawyers, civil servants, physicians—and some men with new money were breaking with age-old insularity. They were not particularly devout. Their Shiism was a matter of identity and culture; the society they lived in, organized as it was in sects and clans, allowed no ambiguity about such matters. No one seeking to organize these men had to remind them of their sectarian identity. They were and could only be Shia. The cleric appealed to the mix of hurt and ambition that the Lebanese social and political order engendered in these men in their thirties and early forties, mostly contemporaries of his. Success had taken some of them beyond the limitations of their elders, beyond the demarcated lines which had contained the lives of their fathers. Venturing as they did beyond their elders' world, they had discovered what anxious *assimilés* everywhere discover: that their primordial identity is difficult to shed, that doors are slammed shut in their faces, that others are not quite so anxious to take them on their merit.

Both the men with new money and the newly educated Shia who rallied around Musa al Sadr were men of their society. They were not revolutionaries. They were formed by the social order they were trying to elbow their way through. They, too, partook of the country's obsession with rank, privilege, and prerogative. The civil servants who worked with Musa al Sadr, who were drawn to him, wanted a fairer share of the spoils of the state for their sect—and themselves, of course. The men who had made money in the face of difficult odds wanted their wealth recognized and rewarded.

No great, sudden discontinuity in the social order was implied or demanded by Musa al Sadr's early efforts. The cleric was an organizer. He worked with exciting material. He put to better use Shia energies unleashed by new wealth and education, but still groping for ways of making themselves felt. A few years before he arrived in Lebanon, some Shia professionals in Beirut—physicians, members of the judiciary and the civil service, men with some money and a sense of loyalty to their poor kinsmen—had put together a committee known as the Committee for Social Struggle, Haiat al Nidal al Ijtimai, to express Shia grievances and demands. That committee had not gone very far. It was too early for such an effort to work; the group remained small and ineffective. But as in other similar situations, some seeds were planted and some experience gained. Several of the leading figures in this small committee were to be among the men who lent their support to Musa al Sadr, who in the late 1960s made possible the creation of the Higher Shia Council—Musa al Sadr's first platform in Lebanon.[15]

There was "room under the Sayyid's tent" for a diverse group of men, said one of Musa al Sadr's early companions. It was a broad coalition that the cleric sought—too broad and diverse for the political purists. Reminiscent of some of the coalitions that Iranian clerics participated in or put together in the late nineteenth century and in this one, Musa al Sadr's effort drew on a wide range of men and interests. Even *ancien régime* elements in the Shia community were welcomed if they were relatively "enlightened," if they were willing to help, if they were shrewd enough to realize that their own interests were better served by a movement that secured for the Shia of Lebanon a better deal from the state. Men with wealth were made room for.

The newly monied Shia were frenzied and pushy individuals. There was a frantic quality to their lives. They were ambitious for themselves and their children—and their sect. Many of the men who contributed to Musa al Sadr's work had made their fortunes in Africa; a smaller number had prospered in the Arabian Peninsula. So little in their lives had given them a positive idea of human association. They dwelled on how they made it "up country" in Sierra Leone or Liberia, of the adversity they had overcome. Theirs was a Darwinistic, harsh

[15]See the report by *Al Shira* magazine (Beirut) January 16, 1984, pp. 20–24.

view of social life. The voluntary associations and charities formed by bourgeois and tame (Sunni) West Beirut had no equivalents in the Shia community. Missing, too, from the Shia world were the clannishness and communal solidarity of the Druze. The Shia *nouveaux riches* had taken with them to distant lands the harsh saying of home: "You have a piaster, you are worth a piaster." In their eyes, human encounters were battles. A cleric interested in building institutions, in getting these men to part with some of their wealth, had a job ahead of him.

Musa al Sadr grasped the dilemma of the monied Shia, particularly of the majority of them who had prospered out of the country and returned. Shia wealth was inarticulate: it had no channels for political participation or expression. And with a keen scent for their predicament, he was to emerge as their spokesman. He sought them out and traveled to the lands where they worked—to Nigeria, Ghana, the Ivory Coast and Liberia, and Sierra Leone. He asked for their financial help. But he had something to offer in return. He gave voice to their own vague resentments and claims. The "flower of Shia youth," he said, had been pushed off the land to remote places. They toiled and prospered, and did so without the protection of the state. All they wanted from the country, he said, was a fair deal. They had proved themselves in faraway lands; surely, they should have some solid ground in their own country.

An astute lawyer who knows the temperament of this group of Musa al Sadr's supporters has pointed out another dimension of their receptivity to the cleric. These men thought of themselves as preservers of some sacred and durable traditions, traditions they tended to idealize. After ten to twenty years spent outside Lebanon, they returned with a conscious (really an anxious) sense of the Shia heritage, of the ways of the land and the clan. They were particularly susceptible to a leader who embodied Shia history, who deployed its symbols, who appealed to them in the name of old verities. The verities were all the more seductive because the country was changing, because these people and their offspring were losing their hold on the past and the "old ways." Sayyid Musa offered no diatribes about the illegitimacy of wealth. Their contributions were needed. Wealth was *nima*, a blessing, they were assured. But wealth had to be caring and responsible; it had to be ethically and socially concerned. For wealth to play its part, it had to be converted into political and social power. Musa al Sadr appealed to the vanity of wealthy Shia, and to their embittered sense that money had not brought social and political power for the Shia in its train.

[99]

Some of Musa al Sadr's early supporters were drawn to him by precisely these reasons. The suspicion of fellow clergymen that Musa al Sadr may have been an agnostic could hardly trouble them. So many of these men had doubts about the faith, about the conventional and literal ways in which it was interpreted. So long as the faith was a matter of instruction and was a monopoly of the traditional clergy, the new men had to bide their time; they had to keep their doubts to themselves. Musa al Sadr offered a compelling new alternative: the faith dusted off, made less shackling and more in touch with the world. Around him, men could change themselves, improve their own lot and that of their sect, without being written off as unbelievers. There was an alternative within the faith to the vanquished world that the traditional clergyman sanctioned and expressed. "Glamour" was also important to this group: the young cleric's style and daring and education were indispensable in Musa al Sadr's dealings with self-educated men who had made it in the civil service, with the newly monied men, and the patricians of the Shia.

Three important followers of Musa al Sadr—two in politics, one a financier—have described what they saw in the cleric when he entered their lives, and why they followed him.

My first informant, a politician, was a close companion of Musa al Sadr from the early 1960s until the cleric's disappearance in 1978. The politician was under thirty years of age when he and the cleric met. He was born to a family of standing and power in the Bekaa Valley. My informant's family were sayyids, they took pride in their lineage, in their Shia roots. But they were also a distinguished clan that believed that politics and power belonged to the right men. They were one of the country's preeminent families. The politician's paternal uncle had served as a minister in the government in three cabinets formed in the late 1940s and early 1950s, and as a member of Parliament from the district of Byblos, a mixed Maronite-Shia part of Lebanon. His father was a man of great influence and social standing in the Bekaa, a trained lawyer with a degree from Damascus University, the kind of man that clans prided themselves on having in their midst. He was a power-broker, a man of reputation and integrity, a pillar of his community, the kind of man that feuding men went to in order to bring feuds to an end, that dying friends entrusted with their wealth to look after their children. The father had been the guardian of a Greek Catholic politician and member of Parliament from the Bekaa Valley. The politician's father had died when his son was a boy; the father had preferred to have his son looked after by a man of his class, holding the same values of honor, *hasab* (inherited merit), and *nasab* (lineage), rather than by a member of his faith. The young politician was raised in a tradition of commitment and self-confidence. He was in every way a member of the establishment—a man of grace and style, open to other communities in the country, free of the Shia shrillness and self-doubt.

He remembers that he made up his mind about Musa al Sadr in a very simple and telling way. The first thing he noticed about the cleric when they met was the cleanliness of his turban and collar, the elegance of his appearance, the cleanness of his shoes: "This was the first cleric with a clean pair of shoes I had met." Though the politician came from a family of sayyids with religious claims and distinctions, he disdained the old ulama; he scorned the way they hustled for money, the way they groveled before men with power, the obscure sermons they gave, but above all, the shabbiness of their attire—the dirty, worn-out collars, the old shoes. Once every year on Id-al-fitr (the days of celebration after a month of fasting), the politician's father had forced him to call on an older relative who was a high religious functionary in Shia Lebanon. The politician had done what was asked of him. The visits to his relative exposed him to other ulama of his sect. And from those visits he always returned with contempt for the ulama's discourse and with real despair over their personal qualities—and their bearing and attire.

A devout anti-Communist and an upholder of the social order who worried about the radicalization of the Shia, my informant despaired of the ulama's ability to deal with modern ideas, with the challenge of the left. Early in his political career, before his election to Parliament, he had been mayor of his town in the Bekaa. He recalls hopeless encounters with the ulama; he remembers in particular clerics standing up on religious and political occasions to rail against Marxist doctrines, against the appeal of communism. On so many of these occasions, the young politician was forced to ask the clerics to cut the sermons short. The politician knew that better religious ammunition was needed to cope with the radical challenge. The old religious style was akin to "medieval weaponry" being pitted against the "modern artillery of the new politics," he said. Each time a cleric spoke against communism in so obtuse a way, my informant thought, he did that ideology a favor; he proved that the tradition, *al turath*, possessed no power or answers of its own.

The politician of high birth was not looking for a clerical guide when he and Musa al Sadr met. But when they came to know each other, they embarked on a political quest that became the cornerstone of my informant's political career. Beyond politics, the cleric had

[101]

touched something very vital in this poised and moderate patrician. The cleric's example and commitment had given this man of politics proof that Shia history did not have to be "rejected or thrown overboard" for the Shia of Lebanon to integrate themselves into the political order of the country.

Speaking of the cleric—of "Imam of Sadr" as he refers to him—the politician obviously believes that he was graced by something special, that a great figure entered his life and changed it in profound ways. "Imam al Sadr," he says, "was clean in another important way: he had a clean hand, he was clean with money. He was not greedy; his material needs were modest. Even some of the financial contributions given to him for his personal needs were passed on to the institutions and charities that he had set up." The politician knew his country, he knew that power in Lebanon sought to accumulate wealth, to hoard. The cleric's moderation in matters financial had earned him the admiration of the young politician. Wealth, he says, was not what "the Imam" was after: this was a public man with a public agenda that went beyond personal and worldly ambitions.

What most impressed the politican about the cleric, the occasions that most readily came to mind, were the performances of Musa al Sadr before the "modern" groups, the religiously mixed political and social gatherings, in the city of Beirut. The politician wanted to bring the Shia into the mainstream in Lebanon. He wanted them to be as "advanced" as other communities were. Though he never quite said it, he believed that Shia institutions and habits were themselves defective, that their lot in the country was not just the result of Maronite or Sunni schemes. It was that yearning for change in the Shia psyche and situation that brought the politician and the cleric together. Theirs was a natural alliance: a political man of high birth, and a cleric of distinguished lineage and calling. It takes no great imagination to see that this politician would not have rallied behind an ordinary man of religion. His aristocratic temperament would have prevented such a choice. Dwelling as he does on the history of the Sadr family, it is clear that the politician saw in the cleric a reflection of his own preferences and sensibility.

The second example of the kinds of men who were drawn to Musa al Sadr is a lawyer born in the late 1930s, a man of the same generation as the companion of Musa al Sadr just described. But the lawyer was the bearer of a different tradition. Whereas the first companion of Musa al Sadr was born at the apex of Lebanese society, the second was born in Sierra Leone, son of a small trader—one of a predominantly Shia Lebanese "colony" that limited means and small plots of land had banished from Lebanon.

The traffic to Sierra Leone that took the lawyer's family and others from southern Lebanon had started early in the century. The story of the migration was a bizarre one: the early "pioneers" made it to West Africa by accident. They were on their way to the New World, or so they thought. But in Marseilles they discovered that they lacked the necessary funds and health certificates. West Africa was presented to them as an option by unscrupulous agents in Marseilles. It was the best they could do; they could not return to the harsh land they had left behind, to the judging relatives. In Sierra Leone, they worked as smalltime hawkers of coral beads, then as middlemen between the European colony and the African farmers. Other Lebanese—relatives, friends—followed. Diamonds, discovered in the early 1930s in Sierra Leone, brought more Lebanese eager to join in the windfall.

The Sierra Leone of the lawyer's birth in 1938 was a small colonial outpost. Graham Greene depicted it—including the life and the anxieties and intrigues of the Lebanese colony—in a travel book, *Journey without Maps*, and in his masterpiece of fiction *The Heart of the Matter*. Its capital, Freetown, where my informant's family lived and worked, was an "old trading post, left to rot on the beach," a "spectacle of decay." The Lebanese who lived there lived with a dream of redemption and return. The old country had expelled them. But they wanted to reenter it, to return to it, on better terms.

This companion of Musa al Sadr had been brought to Lebanon soon after his birth. As a boy, he was schooled in the town of Bint Jbail, the small regional "capital" of his part of southern Lebanon, before he settled in Beirut. Bint Jbail, as I mentioned, was a haven for the political ideology of Arab nationalism represented by the Baath party, and the Baath was the lawyer's first political romance. He joined the party as a young man, a typical choice of an *assimilé* Shia. It was a time before self-conscious sectarian politics.

In the early 1960s, the young Baathist was enrolled in the state-run Lebanese University, studying law. Most likely he was the first of his clan to go to a university. He was active in student politics, a driven young man. (Even two decades later, when he was undoubtedly a successful man, there still appeared in his constant reiteration of old hurts and accounts the frenzy of the newcomer, the Shia sense of disinheritance and persecution.) His political activism at the university brought him to the attention of the cleric. As the lawyer recalls, it was on the initiative of Musa al Sadr that the two men met. As was Sayyid Musa's habit when he spotted talent in the Shia community, he sought out the young political activist, after he saw him making a statement on a television program. My informant approached the cleric with reserve and some hostility. The lawyer/activist said that he had always been hostile to Shia ulama; he doubted if he and Sayyid Musa had anything in common. When they did meet, something more than the lawyer's anticlericalism stood between them; there was also his Pan-Arabism, garnered from the pamphlets and books of the Baath party. Recollecting their initial encounter, the lawyer remembers questioning Sayyid Musa as to why he had come to Lebanon from Iran. Iran was then anathema to young men like this one; it was associated with the Shah, with the Shah's intelligence, SAVAK, with the Shah's pro-American policies. The cleric gave the question the answer that he must have supplied hundreds of times, in his new land and then in the Arab realms he was to visit in the late 1960s after he had acquired greater fame and stature: he said that his ancestors were men of southern Lebanon, that he had "returned" to his ancestral land to serve his community. The lawyer wanted to know what the cleric thought of Gamal Abdul Nasser: For the lawyer, this was the litmus test of one's political orientation. The cleric said that the Egyptian president was a "great personage," that he was looking forward to an audience with him on a planned visit to Cairo.

There was no doubt in the lawyer's mind that this was a man of special gifts. But he did not drop his "reservations" about the man's Iranian birth or his innate hostility to ulama. This was an ambitious young man. It was still a farfetched idea to think of a sectarian movement, a Shia movement led by a cleric, having any chance in Lebanese politics. The Baath party may have been doomed in Lebanon. But it was a party of the wider Arab world, and it was a party that young Shia wanting to go beyond their elders could devote themselves to.

Under what circumstances, then, did the lawyer cast his political lot with the cleric? The lawyer remembers an incident which clinched the matter for him, which persuaded him that there was something there for him in the political project launched by Musa al Sadr. The cleric gave a sermon at a church in Beirut, a deed of daring and innovation. The lawyer was impressed. So sharp a break did that particular deed represent with the isolation and timidity of the Shia clerical establishment, that it was then possible for a politically ambitious young man to see that there might after all be a future for this cleric in Lebanon's politics. When several years later, in 1969, Sayyid Musa and his entourage secured from the Parliament and the country's president approval for establishing the Higher Shia Council, the young lawyer made a bid for one of the twelve seats on its executive committee open to laymen. He did not prevail in that election. But he was to remain within the political movement of Musa al Sadr. It was that movement that was to bring him a piece of the country's power.

The Baath Party had been a way out of the confines of old ways, an initiation into the world of politics, an attempt to give history a meaning beyond the passions and feuds of families and clans. But the politics of the Baath in Lebanon were doomed to frustration. A religio-political movement of kinsmen, of men of the faith, was to be a better vehicle for an ambitious lawyer of modest background. Family, ambition, some money made in a faraway place, and personal drive had brought this lawyer an awareness of possibilities—and a sense of violation. He recalls a time after finishing law school when he was genuinely convinced that he had been passed over for a government scholarship to study in France in favor of a Christian graduate. He appealed the decision, fought it, and won. The Shia of Lebanon, he was convinced, were like the blacks of America. That comparison stuck with him from the early 1960s after he made a brief trip to America to participate in one of Martin Luther King's rallies. The "civil rights" of the Shia had been trampled on in Lebanon, he believed. Musa al Sadr's moral authority, the promise of mobilizing apathetic Shia masses that he held out, were the things that swayed this one follower. The lawyer was hardly a man of piety and religious learning. He was part of the Shia culture and history without being particularly religious. He was young and representative of many others of his generation, who bore the burden of Shia history even without being deeply familiar with it. That history could not be buried under the Baathist label, nor could it be exorcised by a course at the law school of a state-run university. Education had opened up new possibilities, but the country's gates, the gates that mattered, were almost entirely closed to him. Even small openings were carefully monitored. The men who went throught the gates went in as Sunni Muslims, as Greek Orthodox, as Maronites, as Shia, and so on. The country kept track of such things, was precise about such categories. It rid men of the illusion of university; it taught them the futility of trying to get away from the claims of rival sects.

My third example of the kinds of men who accepted Musa al Sadr's leadership and gave it impetus is a financier who grew up on the docks, in the rough-and-tumble world of the port of Beirut. His family—hailing from the southern hinterland—was one of the first Shia families to prosper in Beirut. Back in the 1920s when the family had already established itself in the city, and gained some wealth in land and land speculations, there were no more than a thousand Shia in the entire city, this man estimates. (He was close, for the available statistics put the Shia population of Beirut in the 1920s at something like 1,500 of more than 120,000 inhabitants.[16])

The financier is just a bit older than my other two informants. By the time of his birth, his father had secured a turf for himself in the port of Beirut—no small undertaking, but an endeavor requiring "manliness" and toughness and all those stereotypical qualities called forth by a relatively free-wheeling port in a city of transients and trade. Wealth on the docks came to men who secured virtual protectorates of their own, who had the men to see to it that cargo was unloaded and guarded, who had the political backing and muscle in government circles that counted. This was the world that the financier had known, and it obviously shaped his character: he gives such terms as loyalty, "manhood," and courage the seriousness and directness they must have possessed in the world he knew as a boy.

The financier remembers the Beirut of his young manhood, the late 1930s and early 1940s, as a city of difficulties and humiliations for the Shia. He recalls times when mosques were closed to them, when they were despised outsiders in the city. "We had," he says in his own vivid language, "to pay a tax of blood to make it in the city, to endure the humiliations." "There was a time," he says, "and it was not so long ago when Muslim Sunnis who encountered a man who was obviously a Shia, whom they knew to be one, would command him to step out of the way; *shamil* (turn leftward), they would say."

Militancy came to this man in a natural way. It came out of the rough environment in which he and his father worked; it came out of the discrepancy between the wealth they possessed and the social slights they endured. There was an obvious Shia dialect that men of the southern hinterland spoke, a particular intonation that gave the Shia away. The young man who grew up in the city insisted on many occasions on speaking the dialect of his Shia kinsmen rather than the dialect common in his city surroundings. It was his way of defying the city, of saying that he didn't have to squirm about being a Shia, he did not have to hide it from others.

Poverty in the Shia hinterland, pushing men off the land, brought timid Shia migrants to the stronghold of the financier's family, to their home in the city. They came seeking help from a man of faith.

[16]See Leila Tarazi Fawaz, *Merchants and Migrants in Nineteenth-Century Beirut* (Cambridge: Harvard University Press, 1983), p. 50.

"They were terrified people," recalls the financier, of the migrants who came to Beirut in the late 1930s and early 1940s. He describes his father's attitude toward them as "protective" and "paternalistic."

Such was the environment that shaped this man's world—and his father's. They were Shia, but they were city men. They had no apology to make about their origins, but they were painfully conscious of the city's patterns of exclusion and discrimination. They possessed wealth and commanded men and disposed of resources, but there was a discrepancy between how far they had gone and the place of their own sect and faith in the city. The financier's father, a man of means, gave of his wealth to charities and to the poor—something one did because of one's religious obligation and one's social standing, because of a man's image of himself and his place. *Sahm-al-Imam* (the Imam's share, a contribution made to the religious institution) was part of that generosity and obligation.

An old bond existed between the father and the marja al Taqlid in Najaf, the grand cleric Sayyid Muhsin al Hakim. It was a bond cemented by letters and visits, and by contributions to the marja. A letter from the Muhsin al Hakim—something that the financier's father would take with great respect and seriousness—introduced young Sayyid Musa al Sadr to this family's home and attention. My informant's family had a soft spot for mujtahids and ulama. One family member had gone to Najaf for religious studies, but his work had been cut short by premature death. Young religious scribes and clerics were henceforth welcomed by the family, for they reminded them of the young scribe they had lost. Musa al Sadr, coming as he did with an introduction from Najaf was especially welcome. The letter that came from Najaf described the young cleric's lineage and history. It asked the financier's father to lend the newcomer a helping hand, to "open doors for him," and look after him. It assured the man who had carved out a place for himself and his son in a highly competitive world that this young cleric was destined for good works and distinctions, that he would not let down those who stood by him.

My informant, a man of readily obvious vanity about himself and his own looks, had received the kind of impression that others who knew the cleric also volunteered about him: the handsome face, the elegance, the commanding height. From his description—so attentive to physical features, to the cleric's penetrating eyes, to his aura (*haiba*), to his "perfect" posture and physical qualities—it was easy to see that an ordinary man, shorter of stature, less sure of himself and his impact on others, would have had a hard time swaying this unsentimental judge of people.

The Vanished Imam

The financier described himself as a man impatient with words, a man who believed in deeds. He saw his own "seriousness" and drive in the cleric. He was impressed that Sayyid Musa had no time for much leisure or long sessions of gossip. Probing his mind for what appealed to him about Musa al Sadr, he said "For the sayyid, business was business." "Personal attachments," he went on, "were not paramount in Sayyid Musa's world. He used the talents of those in the community whom he needed, but he avoided personal entanglements." The unsentimental observer saw in the cleric some of his own sense that tasks at hand were more important than loyalties, that in this small country feuds and entanglements had a way of sweeping aside larger objectives.

The financier, *par excellence* a man of Lebanon with its obsession with "elegance" and "style," its rampant and unabashed materialism, singled out a particular action of the cleric's that appealed to him: when the time came to house the Higher Shia Council, Musa al Sadr chose an elegant and imposing building in a suburb overlooking the city of Beirut. The sayyid chose well; it was a building, said the financier, worthy of the "community," the Shia community, and its aspirations. The financier contributed generously to this project. Shabbiness and simplicity were not for him. He knew, and so did the cleric who chose the building, that power should have trappings, that the lowliest Shia peasant or shantytown dweller wanted an imposing place to house the sect's leading institution. The downtrodden community had the values of Lebanon clearly implanted in it.

The cleric knew how to get things done; that also appealed to this practical man of affairs. Charisma may have moved more susceptible and impressionable souls in the Shia community. But charisma and the power of the Imamate were not for this man. He was more sober and harder. Charisma had to deliver tangible proof of its power.

It was easy to tell that this informant was not star-struck and did not stand in awe of a great legacy. He had his "reservations" about the cleric. He would not dwell on them. There were hints—hints that stardom spoiled Musa al Sadr when it came his way, that he tended to forget the people who were by his side during the "lean first years." Furthermore, Sayyid Musa, the financier said, was "mysterious" at times, one did not know what "his larger game" was, perhaps Iran was more important to him than Lebanon. But all these reservations were "water under the bridge," said the financier, and "didn't matter anyway." What mattered, he said, was the "Shia cause." And toward that end, the sayyid had made a "historic contribution."

[108]

It was fear that the financier believed to be the root cause of the Shia dilemma in Lebanon. Sayyid Musa, he said, helped men break with that fear. He credits the cleric with "turning the Shia history in Lebanon upside down." Before Sayyid Musa, he said, the young Shia were either too frightened to stand up to anyone or were the "tails," the followers, of the leftist parties. "The parties led them astray; those parties, too, had their own pashas and beys, their masters and owners." The parties peddled useless words, he said, words that did not feed or shelter anyone. "We had to get our young people back; no doubt the sayyid did this for us."

The country, said the financier describing Lebanon, had its "pampered sons," and "we were the country's rejected step-children." "We had some spineless men who tried to make it on their own, who married Beiruti women, who would not deign to acknowledge their roots. We could not continue on that path. We had to organize a movement and Sayyid Musa, a man of religion, was the ideal man to do this."

The city of Beirut had formed the financier. It had given him means, and it withheld from him its full acceptance. For this man, Musa al Sadr and the movement he led were vehicles for the settling of a historic score.

Three different men with different political sensibilities. The first, a man of conventional politics, wanted something outwardly simple and conservative; he wanted his people to be as others were. The second, a more populist figure, wanted a political movement in which men of modest background and relentless ambitions, men such as himself, would have a chance. The third man had in him an unresolved grudge against a city that had been home but whose power was in the hands of other men. The genius of the cleric—that chameleonlike quality in him that made his critics doubt his sincerity—was his ability to lead a movement that took in the aspirations of these men and others like them. Musa al Sadr stood on the shoulders of men of differing temperaments, and purposes.

By the mid-1960s Musa al Sadr had become a name and a force to reckon with. A program he launched to rid the city of Tyre of vagrants had succeeded. The school for vocational training was beginning to take off. But beyond these concrete achievements, there was the man's promise, his increasing ability to express the yearnings and ambitions of the Shia. Increasingly, opinion leaders embraced him.

A peasant culture, even one recently alienated from the land, is a "chatty" culture. Fame spreads; small accomplishments are turned into legends; a performance of some distinction by a man of the faith before a gathering of Christians and "Beirutis" is recounted as something of an epic in which a man of the faith proved once and for all the excellence of the Shia heritage, *al turath al Shi'i*. Tales of this kind and their embellishment had once been reserved for the big men of the land, for the beys. Musa al Sadr was now the stuff of such tales.

Sometime in early 1965 fame brought to his door in Tyre a curious visitor: Kamel Bey al Assad, the feudal overlord of southern Lebanon. Kamel Bey was in his prime then, strident and self-assured. He and Musa al Sadr were contemporaries: The bey, born in 1929, was just a year younger than the cleric. Kamel Bey's father, Ahmad, the old bey, had died a couple of years earlier; the young man was now on his own, an election in 1964 had given him and his slate nearly a clean sweep of the south; the young chieftain had secured the election of eleven members to a national Parliament of ninety-nine men. And in 1964 he had been elected to the country's highest Shia post, that of speaker of Parliament.

The meeting between the cleric and the feudal zaim was attended by one of Kamel al Assad's deputies, a young, newly elected member of Parliament from one of southern Lebanon's districts. The meeting ended in a stand-off: the two men "circled one another," said the member of the Parliament. The bey had come to see if the rising cleric could be co-opted; he had come to see for himself "the phenomenon of Musa al Sadr." The young bey, so self-consciously a man of the city and the world, had never had to bother with clerics before; he could be patronizing and condescending in dealing with them, assuming his own preeminence and their subordination. It was not long into this meeting before the bey realized that he was dealing with "someone different." The bey, the witness to the meeting reported, "withdrew into a shell." The ground was laid for an enmity between the two men that raged until Musa al Sadr's disappearance in Libya.[17]

This one bey and several lesser ones were to see behind the rise of the cleric foreign schemes and conspiracies: "More than one question mark," said Kamel Bey, hovered over Sayyid Musa, question marks about people behind him "here and abroad." The hints of foreign connections were standard practice in a country that was a cockpit for all kinds of foreign and Arab schemes and intrigues. Everyone suspected everyone else of some foreign connection or another. But Musa al Sadr in particular, again and again, invited such speculations. The Iranian birth, the Persianized Arabic, the obvious ambi-

---

[17]This episode was described to me by the witness, Mamduh Abdallah, former member of the Lebanese Parliament, in a taped interview, October 1984.

tion, the striking looks—all these suggested some hidden design or purpose.

The old beys responded to the cleric with methods of which they were masters. In 1966, a smear campaign was stage-managed by one of southern Lebanon's old politicians, Kazem Bey al Khalil. He procured the services of a woman in Tyre, who was willing to tape a statement telling of an affair with Sayyid Musa. The sexuality of clerics had always been a matter of suspicion and insinuation. Rumors of promiscuity were one way in which upright clerics putting forth a holier-than-thou image could be ridiculed and shown to be the scoundrels everyone presumed them to be. Underneath the facade of rectitude, underneath the clerical garb and the turban, laymen were ever anxious to see lust and sexual license. This was the case here. And to some, Sayyid Musa's striking looks and magnetism made the tale more plausible. Surely a man of such physical appeal, his rivals thought, was prey to sexual temptations.

The scheme backfired. Located, the woman repented and retracted her story. A married man who had presented a scrupulous image of himself was as good as his claim. The cleric had been subjected to an ordeal and had emerged intact.

Now that he was more sure of himself and his new environment, Musa al Sadr's sermons of the faith began to give way to more obviously social and political themes. His trail could be picked up in the diplomatic cables of these two years. An American "reporting officer" called on him in October 1966. The discussion had the reporting officer "complimenting" Sadr on his efforts to build a vocational training center in Tyre. The visitor found the building itself "largely completed . . . an impressive edifice." Funds, said the cleric, came from the government, from "Shiite businessmen." The visitor inquired whether light industry was feasible in the South. The cleric didn't think so; more pressing, he said, was the "mechanization of agriculture." Families were being separated and broken because of the condition of the countryside; "young people are forced to go to the urban areas and to Africa." The "social problems" that resulted were immense. There were "health problems among the population which could be prevented by timely medical attention." But the villages and towns of the south were without medical facilities. Then came one of Musa al Sadr's recurrent themes:

Sadr then stressed that as far as he was concerned the most dangerous element in the situation was the psychological outlook of the Shiite community itself. He said that after so many years of neglect by the government, the South had become a depressed area not only materially but also psychologically. As a religious leader of his community, Sadr said he felt obligated to restore the spiritual values of his people and to give them a sense of self-respect. Sadr said that this psychological element was probably the most depressing result of the poor economic and social conditions which prevail in the South.[18]

A dispatch of a year later accords the cleric greater recognition: "Sadr," it said, "is gradually becoming the leading and accepted leader of the Shiites of Lebanon. He is a very intelligent man who is actively working on social and educational projects for the Shiite community. He engenders much respect, and, among the poorer classes, he is almost a charismatic figure."[19] In this and in other American diplomatic reports of this period, the cleric is represented as a potential rival of Nasser, a bulwark against Nasserite influence in the Shiite community in Lebanon. The emphasis on his distance from the Nasserite current shows, in part, the preoccupation of those dispatching the cables. Nasserism was America's Middle Eastern obsession in the mid-1960s. A political officer making his way through Lebanon's tangled politics kept in mind Nasserite and anti-Nasserite elements. But there was more to this than the conditioned reflexes of American diplomats. Sayyid Musa al Sadr and his Shia program were not part of Cairo's weight and presence in Lebanon. Cairo had its beneficiaries, clients, and adherents in the country, but Musa al Sadr was not one of them. "We had serious questions about him," said Mohamed Heikal, Nasser's confidant, remembering Cairo's view of the cleric. "There were rumors about Musa al Sadr's connections to the Shah of Iran and the like. Lebanese politicians came to Cairo: they reported on one another. Because of what was said about Musa al Sadr, we had a cool and suspicious attitude toward him." The cleric eventually went to Cairo, not wanting, in Heikal's words, to be "left out of the bazaar." But the reservations and the suspicions remained.[20]

From the very beginning of his political quest, Musa al Sadr had a political project of his own, one that could not have been easily harmonized with what passed for Nasserism in Lebanon. To be sure, the sayyid appreciated the fervor that Nasserism generated in the country. He knew that many of the young Shia *assimilés* groping for a way out of insularity and out of the politics of feuds and factions were drawn to Nasser's Pan-Arab conception; he no doubt saw Cairo as a

[18]U.S. Embassy Dispatch, Beirut, October 23, 1966. State Department File A–430.
[19]U.S. Embassy Dispatch, Beirut, November 3, 1967.
[20]Interview with Mohamed Heikal, January 1984.

great city of the Muslim world. But his mental geography was different from the Pan-Arab map of those years which had Cairo at its center. It was in the direction of Iran and Iraq, via Syria, that he looked.
He was born and raised to a tradition that exalted the importance of
Persia and Iraq. It would have been self-defeating for Musa al Sadr to
try to outbid the fervent Pan-Arabists and Nasserites of (Sunni) West
Beirut and those among the Palestinians. He was too proud and too
shrewd a man to attempt such a thing. He knew that Pan-Arabism in
Lebanon and the Fertile Crescent was a wrapping for Sunni political
culture and sensibilities. He must have known by heart the history of
Sunni-Shia antagonism in Iraq that drove his father across the border
to Iran a few years before his birth.

A Shia cleric venturing into politics, Musa al Sadr had a corporatist
view of what a primary political grouping should consist of, what
kind of sentiments and loyalties it should rest upon. He had a cleric's
innate hostility toward political parties; this made him a natural rival
of secular and leftist movements. It was a community of the faithful
that he sought to organize and lead; this made him a rival of Cairo's
influence in the 1960s and a beneficiary of its relative eclipse in the aftermath of the Six Day War of 1967. The large ideological conceptions
of Nasserism or any other ideology would not have attracted his early
supporters and financial backers or carried them along. The two
kinds of men who flocked to him—the civil servants and professionals, the men with money made in West Africa—were hostile to
ideological abstractions and partisan politics. It was a concrete sectarian project in Lebanon that they wanted. The civil servants were obsessed with their disadvantage vis-à-vis the Maronites and the Sunnis. The *nouveaux riches* of the Shia community were searching for
respectability and a role in Lebanese society. A project that engaged
these men had to be a Lebanese project, something solid and familiar, of a piece with their ambitions and resentments. The idea of the
Higher Shia Council, a corporate body representing the Shia before
the state, had been kicked around before Musa al Sadr picked it up.
The majority of Shia clerics had not been excited about the prospect.
It smacked of entanglement with power and with the state. And there
was competition within the ranks of the ulama: if one mujtahid were
to rise above others through the channels of such an official body, it
would have surely been to the detriment of all the rest. No single
mujtahid before Musa al Sadr had had the daring and energy to push
his way beyond the limits of his colleagues' abilities and acceptance.
The one cleric who was accorded greater recognition than others,
Shaykh Muhammad Taqi Sadiq in Nabatiyya, remained a strict con-

servative, frowning on all political activism. Indeed it was only after his death that the idea of the council managed to make its way through the Parliament in 1967, to be endorsed by the Lebanese president, and to come to life in 1969 with Musa al Sadr as its chairman.

The council's structure and conception, hierarchical and neatly bureaucratic, were true to the sensibility of the men who pushed for it. It was to have forty-three seats on its executive committee—nineteen reserved for the nineteen Shia members of Parliament, twelve alloted for mujtahids and religious functionaries, and twelve for laymen. The spirit moving this bureaucratic body was a bid for political and doctrinal independence on the part of the Shia of Lebanon.

When the council was established, it was the sixteenth such corporate institution in the country. All the other sects—the Druze, the Maronites, the Greek Orthodox, and so on—had religious institutions of their own. The Shia had lacked an institutional body. The Sunni in Beirut claimed the Muslim mantle. The Grand Mufti (the highest religious judge and authority) of the Lebanese republic, a man of the Sunni faith and of the Sunni establishment, was the presumed representative of all Muslims. The Shia were in a cleft stick. So desperately anxious to stay within the fold of Islam, so disadvantaged when compared to the Sunni world of Beirut with its continuity and courts and schools and philanthropic associations, they had been unable to establish a measure of doctrinal and political independence vis-à-vis the Sunnis. The Grand Mufti, with his entourage of urban merchants, notables, and scholars, was hardly the man to represent the heterodox Shia peasants and their urban descendants. But that had been the pattern of the uneasy Sunni-Shia relationship in Lebanon.

A doctrinal and cultural schism separated the Sunni coastal cities from the Shia hinterland. Indeed no other relationship in Lebanon was as tangled and difficult as that between the two principal sects of Islam. Sunni Islam could take a benevolent view of men beyond the faith. The Sunnis shared the ways and the professions and the trading outlook of the coast with the Greek Orthodox community. These two groups had lived side by side in Beirut: they had learned to coexist. The Maronites of Mount Lebanon were the Sunnis' political rivals, but the Maronites had their own political world, their own truth and piece of the country. The Sunnis accepted and made peace with the fact that political power had to be shared with the Maronites, that the Maronites had the preeminent political role in Lebanon. For the Sunnis, the Shia were a wholly different problem. The Shia were Muslim schismatics; they were a break-away sect, but they remained just outside the bounds of orthodoxy, claiming that they represented the true spirit of Islam, speaking in the name of the Prophet's family, *ahl al bayt*, and their disinheritance. From the Sunni viewpoint, the Shia were too close for comfort. The Shia were not "strangers"—not quite; they were not and could not be another minority. Between the two communities, there were no easy ways that lines could be drawn and respected.

The urban-rural divide further deepened Sunni-Shia antagonism. The Sunnis were men and women of the city; they had their settled ways and their institutions. The city and its mosques and schools and cafés were theirs. The Shia peasants making their way into the city, with their shabby attire and their distinct dialect, could never quite belong. The city judged, and it judged harshly. Both the Shia squatters and the newly urbanized class of relatively prosperous Shia were either too contrived in their manner when they tried to be accepted or too coarse and distinct. Hard as they tried to fit in, they were bound to miss the mark. Now and then, some high civil servant of Shia faith or some physician could make his way in the city, putting his past behind him or trying to. There had been groups of such men in the Beirut of the 1940s and 1950s. They were loathed and (secretly) envied by other Shia. But this solution could not work for the swelling numbers of men knocking at the gates in the 1960s; nor was it an option for the majority of the Shia, who were not willing to do such violence to their identity. A few men could slip through the doors undetected; several thousand couldn't, even had they wanted to.

The Shia had to build institutions of their own. They needed to break free and place themselves a little further away from Sunni control and judgment. The formation of an independent sectarian body was the clearest way of doing it, and the most Lebanese way at that. The country of sects acknowledged the coming of age of another sect. A community set apart from the Sunnis by doctrine and by a legacy of insularity and backwardness had to go its own way. The Higher Shia Council, noted a foreign diplomatic dispatch, resulted from the "general feeling" in the Shia community that it had been "unable to compete with the wealthier, better educated and organized Sunni community."[21]

The organizing charter of the council reads like an assertion of doctrinal independence: "The Islamic Shia sect (*taifa*) is independent in its religious affairs and endowments and institutions. It has its sons who speak in its name according to the rules of the *Sharia* (Islamic

[21] U. S. Embassy Dispatch, Beirut, May 27, 1969, State Department File A–213.

law) and to Shia jurisprudence as set by the opinions of the Grand
Marja of the Shia in the world."[22] A new theme is struck and emphasized as well in the reference to the Grand Marja. Men were saying that they did not stand alone, that there was a large Shia world
beyond Lebanon of which they were a part. The reference to the
marja of this outside world was to be one of Musa al Sadr's recurrent
themes, a way of lending courage and spine to the Shia in Lebanon. It
was also vintage Lebanon: the tendency to borrow the prestige of the
foreigner, to refer to a community beyond this small country. Maronite discourse was laced with references to the "free world," to the
West, to Catholicism. The Sunni self-view was anchored in the prestige and resources of the Arab nations to Lebanon's east. The Shia of
Lebanon had lacked outside patrons and a sense of belonging to a
larger world. The statement of the Shia council implied a jury and a
community beyond Lebanon.

Some leading Christian politicians extended what support they
could to the Shia endeavor. "Several Christian leaders," noted an
American diplomatic dispatch, "have told us that they are pleased by
the formation of the Shia Council. . . . They say that they are helping
it in any way possible; this situation may explain the good publicity
Sadr gets in the rightist and Christian press."[23] The Christian politicians who backed the Shia project—and who were among Musa al
Sadr's early sponsors—had a mixture of motivations. It included the
old and understandable game of divide and rule. Promoting the independence of the Shia was a way of undermining the claims of Sunni
Islam. Then, too, there were some enlightened men who believed
that the Shia had to be brought into the country's political system. No
crystal ball could have foreseen what the Shia were to make of themselves down the road. In the late 1960s, the challenge that the Christian population feared came from Pan-Arabist doctrines, from the Palestinians. There were clouds on Lebanon's horizons. The country
was beginning to feel the tremors of the Arab defeat in the Six Day
War of 1967, of the radicalization of the Palestinians. Foreign capital
was being scared away. The country still had its clichés, its sense that
it could walk back from the brink. But sober men with a view of the
future were beginning to worry about Lebanon's ability to withstand
the chaos. From the Christian elite's viewpoint, it made sense, then,
to court the Shia, to give them a stake in the country's stability. Musa
al Sadr and his conservative companions seemed like a safe bet to the
custodians of Lebanese power.

[22]As quoted Najib Jamal al Din, *Al Shia*, p. 117.
[23]U.S. Embassy Dispatch, Beirut, October 10, 1969, State Department File A–414.

Musa al Sadr now had his platform. He had been eager for such an official institution, in part because of his ambition, in part because of his search for legitimacy in a country which was not quite home for him. His election to the presidency of the council had the elements of the coronation of a man who had secured a kingdom and wanted the trappings and the pageantry of kingship as a way of confirming his success. He had got both platform and presidency in the face of strong clerical opposition. He had risen outside of the organizational structure of the Shiite religious order. The politically quiescent clerics who had never raised a finger in the face of outside authority issued their predictable objections to the whole idea; in its pristine form, they said, Islam had never known such an institution. More than half of the country's principal clerics stayed away from the election which convened the council. There were rumors that it was rigged. The clerics who did participate had put up a conservative from their ranks, one Shaykh Suleiman al Yahfufi from the Bekaa Valley. Yahfufi's supporters charged that laymen were dressed as clerics by the supporters of Musa al Sadr and brought to the meeting to vote for the man who carried the day. But this, too, was a tale of Lebanon: rigged elections, both rumored and real, were of a piece with the country's ways.

But something unprecedented did happen on that day—a small gesture foretelling changes to come. On the day Musa al Sadr was elected to the council, the speaker of Parliament, Sabri Bey Hamade from the Bekaa Valley stood up and insisted on kissing his hand in public. Not only was the speaker the highest Shia official in the land; this one was a bey of the old school. In times past clerics had appeared before Sabri Bey seeking favors, pledging loyalty to him. Now Sabri Bey was acknowledging a shift in the balance between secular and religious authority. Most likely no great things were read into his gesture. Men probably took the deed as evidence of Sabri Bey's fiber and fidelity to religious truth; turning points are always established with the benefit of hindsight. But this was one of those episodes that men looking back on this small fragment of history could identify as a straw in the wind foreshadowing greater change to come.

Sayyid Musa of Tyre was now head of the Shia community in Lebanon. The triumph of the man himself was like a coming of age for the Shia. The newly elected head of the Shia Council was giving the men and women of his faith concrete expressions of their identity which they had lacked—a preeminent clerical religious guide and a seat of power. In a multisectarian society, he was giving them what other major sects in the country possessed.

The Maronites had their spiritual leader: at his headquarters in

Bkerke, deep in the Maronite territory of Mount Lebanon, the Maronite patriarch presided over a fiercely independent church with an elaborate hierarchy, kept watch on the politics of the country, pronounced on political matters as much as on those of theology, and at times competed with, plotted against the (Maronite) president of the republic. Local politicians and foreign ambassadors made frequent pilgrimages to Bkerke to discuss matters of state and elections and even the diplomatic alignments of the country. The seat of Maronite power and the man who presided over the church were vivid expressions of Maronite characteristics: the pride in separate history, the suspicion with which the Maronites viewed the Muslim world around them, the zeal and vigilance with which things and ideas Maronite were elaborated. Likewise, the Druze, in their stronghold, in the Shuff Mountains, had their one religious leader, *Shaykh al Aql* (literally the shaykh of knowledge, the possessor of knowledge). The canons of the Druze faith—an eleventh-century faith, esoteric, hermetically sealed against the outside world, known only to the initiated (*al Uqqal*) among the Druze themselves—gave the religious men and tribal chiefs nearly absolute control over their sect of fierce and independent mountaineers. The Shaykh al Aql, with his long white beard, the traditional fez of his people, and the baggy trousers of times past, embodied the Druze truth: the "impenetrable secrecy" of a sect that keeps to itself, the brooding silence and watchfulness. Just as the Druze banned all preaching, refused any converts, and held the "door of salvation" to be finally closed, their Shaykh al Aql never bothered to explain himself to the outside world. Holding aloof from the squabbles of the country, he communicated the determination of his sect—which had governed the heartland of the country in Mount Lebanon until the Maronites overtook them in the nineteenth century—to view contemporary reality with profound indifference.

The Sunni Muslims of the coastal communities of West Beirut, Sidon, and Tripoli had their religious center, *Dar al Fatwa* (literally, the home of rendering opinions) in Beirut and their grand mufti, its leading cleric. The Sunni mufti—whoever he happened to be at a particular time—inherited the deep-seated Sunni sense of belonging to the larger Muslim-Arab world around Lebanon. By custom and precedent the mufti was a man of property and standing. Historically, the class of Sunni ulama, who presided over courts and religious endowments, had emerged out of a process that emphasized order and consensus and social hierarchy. Merchant culture in Muslim Beirut—and to an even greater extent in a city of Sunni Islam such as Damascus—produced the class of Sunni ulama, stamped

them with its caution, its spirit of compromise, its aversion to anything smacking of charisma and social upheaval, its fear of minorities
and of the hinterland beyond the city. Shaykh Hassan Khalid, mufti
of the Lebanese republic during Musa al Sadr's emergence, was true
to the role: he was a pillar of the city of Beirut, a man of the social hierarchy and the status quo, a man to whom the fundamental concerns
of Islam were the administering of men and social institutions and the
keeping intact of a system of property and standing. Depending upon
the issue of the moment, or the state of alliance within the Sunni oligarchy, the Mufti sided with the (Sunni) prime minister of the country or sought to subvert his will by throwing his support to other
Sunni notables. The media reported his travels: Shaykh Hassan journeying to Cairo, or Baghdad, or making the pilgrimage to Mecca. In
the Sunni cities of Arab Islam, he found political patronage or financial support for Sunni endowments and institutions. The ease with
which Shaykh Hassan Khalid pronounced on social and political matters was rooted in that still unshakable Sunni sense of belonging to Islam's dominant culture and faith.

With Musa al Sadr and the Shia Council over which he presided,
the Shia of Lebanon were elaborating a religiopolitical culture of their
own, bringing it out of the hinterland into the center of things. Here,
too, the man and the institution expressed the historical situation of
the Shia subculture in Lebanon. Musa al Sadr and the Shia Council
were new phenomena: a man of Iranian birth bringing to a subdued
community some of the pride and skills of the larger Shia universe in
Iran and Iraq, in which he was steeped; an organization that gave
these changes official recognition. That the council was housed in a
predominantly Christian suburb overlooking Beirut pointed up the
dilemma of the Shia: they were new to the city. They had no elegant urban neighborhoods of their own in which they were supreme
and independent. The slums in which their shantytowns had been
erected over the preceding quarter-century were not places where
men anxious about their self-esteem could take a stand. Divided as
the Shia were into two noncontiguous parts of the country—the
south and the Bekaa Valley—their financiers and civil servants, to
find an appropriate building of their own, had to buy one on territory
which fell behind Christian lines. And that too was apt: now Shia
money was buying into the real estate of the city, even though that
money was still without commensurate political power or self-esteem.

In Musa al Sadr the Shia of Lebanon about this time discovered
their first Imam. Shia history, carried by the faithful, implanted as

well in the modern men who questioned the faith, assigned a central place to the extraordinary man—an Imam—and to the right moment. The title of Imam did not, as it were, come to Musa al Sadr with the council presidency. It was new, it just somehow emerged as the cleric's designation. Detractors of the man said that the new title was his own idea, that he had adopted it because he knew its evocative power and its hold. But this explanation is too simple. Had Musa al Sadr himself proposed the title, his ambition would have been transparent and the pious would have been scandalized. In most religious-political movements of this kind, a "pretender" lets other men who read into him their needs and stresses and ambitions assert his right to a title. This pretender was no exception. Others had to proclaim him their Imam; he himself was always scrupulous about the matter. He always referred to himself as Sayyid Musa, plain Sayyid Musa.

A Shia politician gives a subtle account of the emergence of the new title which takes in the pretender's ambition and the susceptibility of the faithful followers. Large crowds, says the politician, had been greeting Musa al Sadr whenever he turned up at religious and political gatherings. The momentum had been building up over a year or so. Whenever the striking-looking cleric made his dramatic appearance—and he was a master at staging an entrance—he was greeted with cries of *Allah-u-Akbar* (God is Great). Members of his own entourage, inspired by his leadership, determined to shore up his power, must have been the ones who led these chants and acclamations. The politician does not rule out the possibility that such events may have had an element of premeditation. But crude stage-management alone would not have worked. Spontaneity, too, had to be there and to play its part. The new title, suggested by the crowd, was accepted by the cleric. Musa al Sadr, says the politician, "did not mind" the new title; "he did not mind it at all." Older members of the clerical profession derided the change; politicians who had become increasingly troubled by his ambition noted the change as indisputable evidence of hubris. Even some early supporters winced. The editor of a Shia journal, *Al Irfan*—a forum where some of Musa al Sadr's first essays appeared—expressed an intellectual's cool and skeptical view. "Sayyid Musa," he said, "is our friend, and we have known him a long time." The Imamate, however was a "special designation. . . . The Imamate among the Shia is used to designate the twelve Imams, beginning with Imam Ali and culminating with *al Mahdi al Muntazar* (the awaited Imam). But as the Shia are prone to exaggeration—particularly after their contact with the Persians—the title is now used to refer to anyone with a turban who may even lack any religious educa-

[120]

tion."[24] The Imams, the twelve Imams, noted the editor, were infallible men. And surely, said this critic who knew Sayyid Musa "back when," the followers of Musa al Sadr were not laying claim to his infallibility.

The new title carried, however. It was part of the mystique, part of the growing belief that this was a cleric unlike others. It made apparent a distinctly religiopolitical agenda, for the title was assailable if judged on strictly religious grounds. The finicky editor's objections were brushed aside by the zealous. And once the title emerged, its magic and power were obvious. It tapped the millenarian expectation already read into Musa al Sadr by some of his devoted followers. Two years before the establishment of the Higher Shia Council and his rise to be its preeminent cleric, a biographer of Musa al Sadr had written of his subject with a note of expectation. The biographer quoted a hadith, a tradition of the Prophet Muhammad, that God sends to this *Umma* (the community of believers) a "man who will renew its faith once every one hundred years." Musa al Sadr, said the biographer, will be such a man in his time; he will remove from the Shia the dust of the ages. The skeptical, said the biographer, will live to see the fulfillment of this expectation.[25]

The cleric was without illusion about the council over which he presided. He knew and said of it that it was born amputated. After all, the nineteen Shia members of Parliament had cornered nineteen of the forty-three seats on the council's executive committee. These were, on the whole, men of the old order, who knew the country and its ways. They knew that the council could be controlled, and that their own judgments and predilections would carry more weight than those of others. Musa al Sadr could sway the masses, but these men were too stubborn to change. What the council did for Musa al Sadr was to provide him with a platform. In a country of sects he had become the preeminent cleric of one of the principal sects. The Shia patricians and professionals had sustained him during his first decade. The cleric with the good looks and eloquence had been made into an extension of their communal pride and ambition. The work of the second decade, the work of an "Imam," was a more populist endeavor. It required a different voice and a set of themes readily understood by the Shia masses. The office that Musa al Sadr had been elevated to was to be a vehicle. The men of means and influence who had thought that the cleric could be manipulated, that he would accept

---

[24]Nizar al Zayn, editorial, *Al Irfan*, 58 (July/August 1970), 279.
[25]Najib Jamal al Din, *Al Shia*, p. 155.

the rules of the game and know his limits, were in for a surprise. The new decade was one of great disorder in the country, and the disorder supplied the cleric with his material. He found a direct way to the Shia masses and their aspirations—and resentments.

[4]

Reinterpreting Shiism: Imam al Sadr and the Themes of Shia History

Musa al Sadr defined his task and agenda in an extremely ambitious way. A clue to what he expected of—and claimed for—himself is supplied by something he wrote about what an Imam had to be ready for. "The responsibility of an Imam of the Community (*Imam al Jama'a*), knew no limits," he wrote. "An Imam had to protect the interests of his flock; he had to be generous; he had to serve his community with advice and persistance; he had to be willing to undergo martyrdom on their behalf. No leader can claim Islam who ignores the daily affairs of the Community."[1] The term he chose, *Imam al Jama'a*, had a distinctly modern flavor: he was not using the title of Imam in its strict reference to the twelve Imams. He was endorsing the activist interpretation that a mujtahid could go beyond religious scholarship, could engage in worldly and political affairs, and could embody Shia Islam's expectation that a religious leader had political obligations and prerogatives as well. He made it clear from the outset that his was a political quest. The distinction between *din* (religion) and *dunya* (worldly affairs) would be obliterated in his pursuits. It was not religious ritual that men needed and that this cleric supplied over the course of the next seven years. His increasingly populist themes were elaborated against a background of mounting disorder in the country. The cleric's principal constituency, the Shia of the south, was caught in a crossfire between Palestinian guerrillas using the south as a sanc-

---

[1]Musa al Sadr, "Masuliyat al Imam al Qaid wa al Shihadah" (The Responsibility of the Leader-Imam and Martyrdom), in Musa al Sadr, *Nukhba Min al Muhadarat* (A Selection of Lectures) (Beirut, n.d.), pp. 3–4.

tuary and Israeli reprisals. The cycle of raids and reprisals hurled waves of refugees from southern villages into the city.

Musa al Sadr's emergence on the national scene began with a general strike that he declared on May 26, 1970, a day of "solidarity with the South." This was Lebanon's first general strike in two decades. And it was Musa al Sadr's first public act beyond the small circle of patricians and civil servants, an appeal to the country's better self, and a warning of things to come. He issued a manifesto to the country. It had the themes that were to become the standard ones of his appeals: It had his political language and symbolism.

My sons the students, my brothers the workers, the intelligentsia.

To the men of living sensibility and conscience, to men of the professions, to the sons of the threatened South;

To the Muslims who cannot accept as one of them he who does not care for the problems of others; To the Christians who bear the cross of the poor:

For over a year and a half, in hundreds of meetings, studies, declarations, official meetings, in countless lectures and statements, we have been asking, in the name of the Higher Shia Council, in the name of the violated rights of the South, for justice for the South, for attention to its problems, for serious effort to provide for its fortification.

Then the tragedy in the South began to unfold in a surprising kind of vacuum, under the eyes of everyone.

What do the ruling authorities expect? Do they want the people in the South to suffer in silence, to bear tragedies, death, and destruction in silence?

The people of the South do not want or expect charities and contributions and tents and medicine and canned food that would make them feel that they are strangers without dignity.

The state, he said, had to care for the south, and for its refugees. Otherwise, the refugees would occupy the "villas and the palaces" in Beirut. He called for "calm and discipline." A strike, he said, was the "lowest common denominator, an expression of our rage and our concern. . . . Be with what is right. . . ."[2]

On the day of the strike, Musa al Sadr made an appearance before more than a thousand students of the American University of Beirut. He went to the campus of the university at the invitation of its stu-

---

[2]See *An Nahar*, May 27, 1970; leaflet in author's possession; U.S. Embassy Dispatch 4108, Beirut, May 26, 1970; and U.S. Embassy Dispatch 4166, Beirut, May 27, 1970.

dents. In a country which then exalted things modern and Western, the campus of the AUB in the Western enclave of Beirut had the prestige and the aura of the distant American society that had built and sustained the university. Established in the 1860s, the American University of Beirut had trained generations of Lebanese and Arabs, given its graduates its discipline and skills—and authority. Its students—at first predominantly Christian, then more affluent (Sunni) Muslims, and Palestinians anxious for educational skills to compensate for their territorial dispossession in 1948—were sure of their own distinction, sure that they were light years ahead of the traditional Arab order around them. Men not quite "in" approached the campus of the university with awe. This was not a place where turbaned Shia mullahs had ventured before.

In 1970, the dominant political culture at the University was a mix of radical Palestinian politics and Marxism, or what passed for it in Lebanon. Of a student population of four thousand, there were two hundred Shia students. They could not have been particularly important in its politics. To the extent that a few of them concerned themselves with political causes, they must have been avid supporters of the Palestinian movement, young men eager to belong to a wider Arab cause.

The Shia cleric gave a memorable performance on that day. He spoke in the university chapel; in deference to him and to the occasion, hundreds of emancipated young women covered their hair with scarves. He must have known that he was setting a precedent, that clerics of his faith had never had the daring and the opportunity to reach an audience of this kind. He gave what was to become his usual brief on behalf of the neglected south. The men in power, he said, did not care what befell the south. He talked of villages without schools, of hospitals that were promised but never materialized, of idle talk about irrigation schemes. All these, he said, were "lies," premised on the belief that men were obedient "mules." He himself, he said, had given "sixty lectures" about the south, "ten manifestoes, four press conferences." But no one in power had cared to listen.

What of the militias now beginning to appear in Lebanon, Sayyid Musa was asked, and what of the armed Palestinian presence? He knew the appeal of the Palestinian cause, he knew his audience too and he fudged his answer. It was imperative, he said, for the Palestinians to bear arms and to train. But such things should be done in coordination with the Lebanese state lest chaos spread. He split hairs: Israel, he said, had no right to retaliate against the villages of southern Lebanon because Palestinian incursions into Israel are not launched from villages. At any rate, he said, Lebanon could not be Israel's policeman. Since Israel itself was unable to prevent Palestinian attacks, it surely could not expect the Lebanese government to be able to do so. As for the armed militias of political parties in Lebanon—his answer was that he was not an "expert in political matters." The burden of defending the country, he thought, rested with the state. The aim of his strike, he said, was to awaken and educate the state.

The call for a strike, according to a diplomatic report, was "heeded throughout the country."[3] The ineffective Lebanese government chose to view the strike in enlightened terms. Charles Helou, the weak president of the republic, saw the strike as a way of "preempting the Palestinians and the left, of preventing them from exploiting the frustration and bitterness of the predominantly Shia Southerners."[4] The government gave what help it could afford to give. It authorized the allocation of nearly ten million dollars for the south; it established a "Council for the South"; it made more of its promises and said it would search for more funds.

An American diplomatic report offers a fairly accurate summation of what was achieved in that strike—and of its limits: "Danger persists that he [Musa al Sadr] may unwittingly be creating a situation which ultimately he may not be able to control. . . . It is difficult to see where the Government is going to raise the money, and beyond that how it could even begin to meet the Southerners' demand for protection."[5]

The cleric, though, had found his voice. The learned lectures of the 1960s in which he quoted Orientalists and displayed his own erudition were now decidedly discarded in favor of a more passionate discourse. In part, this was because his relation to the Arabic language had changed. He had come to Lebanon with the formal Arabic of the Quran, of the religious sciences. Farsi, we must remember, was the language of his home and childhood and youth. Like other mullahs of Iranian birth and culture, he had known the Arabic of religious texts; Farsi, the language of Iran, was to a mullah of his background the medium of self-expression. (In an Iranian proverb, Arabic is learning, but Persian is sugar.)[6] The Arabic of Sayyid Musa was changed by Lebanon. Little more than a decade after his arrival, his Arabic was

---

[3]U.S. Embassy Dispatch 4108.
[4]Ibid.
[5]Ibid., p. 3.
[6]Roy Mottahedeh, *The Mantle of the Prophet: Learning and Power in Modern Iran* (New York: Simon & Schuster, 1985), p. 227.

freer and more evocative, the language of daily life and sentiments. The stilted language of formal discourse was replaced by the passionate speech of the pulpit and the crowd.

Beyond his relation to the language lay the increasing radicalization of the country: the early 1970s brought great changes to Lebanon. Strikes were becoming a way of life among the students, among laborers newly awakening to their rights. New demands—for reform of the educational system, for minimum wages, for medical insurance, for rent control, for higher prices for the tobacco crop grown by southerners—were put forward in a society that was simultaneously losing its tolerance for old inequalities and the traditional networks that once cushioned those inequalities. The country's political order remained its old self. It could not respond to change, did not know how to change. Its apologists insisted that the country's system was "subtle," that its free-wheeling ways could not be tinkered with. Young people were throwing their support to radical politics. The politically sensitive cleric had been appealing to the state. Increasingly the state was being demonstrated, in his words, to be a scarecrow. He had to compete with the radical spectrum in the country, to preempt its symbols and appeal.

Musa al Sadr did his work without illusions. He knew, and at times openly acknowledged, the weight of Shia history in Lebanon, its mixture of defeatism and opportunism. He referred to the Shia dilemma in his own way; he called it the "psychological and moral outlook" of the Shia community.[7] A Shia academic from the Gulf who observed Sayyid Musa noted the cleric's frustration and discomfort with the men of means in Shia Lebanon, with their political timidity, with their feuds.

He had two radically different parts of the country to work with: the south and the Bekaa Valley in the east. He had to bring these two communities together. Historically the two realms had been separated from each other by deep differences in temperament. They grew (licensed) tobacco in the south and (contraband) hashish in the Bekaa: this summed up the difference. The people of the south were patient, subdued peasants, their villages within the reach of authority. The Shia of the Bekaa Valley were wild and assertive clansmen who resisted the encroachment of outside power. A few gendarmes could terrorize entire villages in the south; the Bekaa was a place into which government troops ventured with great reluctance. The beys

[7]See Musa al Sadr's statement on the "psychological complex" of the Shia in *Al Irfan*, 54 (September 1966), 404–410.

of the south lorded it over cowed men. The beys of the Bekaa operated in a more egalitarian world. When the daughter of Ahmad Bey al Assad (a southerner) married Sabri Bey Hamade (the Bekaa's big man), she taunted Sabri Bey about the difference between the uncontested authority of her father and his frustrations with his more unwieldy followers. "I am a horse among other horses," Sabri Hamade is reported to have answered her. "Your father is a horse among mules."

Even matters of religious ritual were celebrated in markedly different ways by the two communities. *Ashura*, the days of mourning for the third Imam, were days of wailing and self-flagellation among the people of the south. The people of the Bekaa celebrated Kerbala with quiet readings of the Quran and of *marathi* (lamentation poetry), with considerable restraint.

If the men of the Bekaa saw the men of the south as unusually timid and squeamish, the south, the more settled of the two communities, the more learned and tamed, had its own view of the men of the Bekaa. It saw them as roughnecks, as wild men of an area beyond accepted ways. Musa al Sadr went a long way toward bridging the gap between the two communities or at least suppressing the differences. He was ideally suited for the task. He claimed descent from the south; he had had his start there, he could appeal to the new Shia money which was mostly based in the south and in the hands of urban newcomers who hailed from there. But he was a daring man, he was courageous. And this was a quality that the men of the Bekaa valued in other men.

The shrewd cleric had his own sense of the two regions that made up his domain. He wanted the southerners to be more daring and defiant. And he wanted to harness the energy of the wild men of the Bekaa, to channel it into politically and socially useful endeavors. He was appalled by the blood feuds of the Bekaa which often went on for generations. He needed the martial vigor of its men. On many an occasion armed men from the Bekaa were brought to political gatherings in the south; they were the ones who openly challenged the units of the Lebanese army and the gendarmes. It was all part of "educating" the men of the south, of putting the weakness of the Lebanese state on display, of enabling the people of the south to stand up to their beys and to the authority of the state that the beys often brought in on their side.

An Imam, a man who led, he had proclaimed, concerned himself with the "daily affairs" of men. Musa al Sadr was as good as his word. He ventured into matters of social and economic concern without

Reinterpreting Shiism

apology or hesitation. In early 1973, he took part in a confrontation between the tobacco planters and the security forces. The planters wanted higher prices for their crops and the right to unionize. A clash between the planters and the forces of the state in the southern town of Nabatiyya resulted in the death of two planters and the injury of fifteen.[8]

Tobacco was the perennial problem of Musa al Sadr's constituency. The cause of the tobacco growers and sharecroppers had been there waiting to be picked up. It had been there since the tobacco monopoly, the *Régie des Tabacs et Tombacs*, had been reconstituted in 1935. Large-scale disturbances over the policies of the Regie had erupted as early as 1936. A foreign diplomatic dispatch of May of that year noted the small growers' dissatisfaction with the monopoly's policies, which decreased the acreage of tobacco under cultivation and put men out of work.[9] Troubles had erupted now and then in the intervening years. The pressure on men and the land had increased the bitterness.

The political economy of tobacco was a fair reflection of the country's larger inequities. It reflected, above all, the structural imbalance between the agricultural and service sectors of the economy. The average annual income for the twenty-five thousand small growers for 1972–1973 was around three hundred dollars: the annual income of heads of households in the service sector in the city was about nine times larger. Then there was the gap between the growers and the large landholders. The average acreage per grower in the early 1970s was less than two *dunams* (a dunam was a quarter of an acre). The small growers were perennially in debt, constantly the prey for the loan sharks.[10]

None of the leading politicians of the south had paid much attention to the problems of the small growers. They themselves owned large chunks of land; more than that, they had the licenses that specified the numbers of dunams of tobacco that could be planted. For the

[8]*An Nahar*, January 25, 1973; and U.S. Embassy Dispatch, Beirut, January 26, 1973, Department of State telegram 1003. See also for a background essay Thom Sicking and Shereen Khairallah, "The Shia Awakening in Lebanon," CEMAM Reports (Beirut: Saint Joseph University; vol. 2, 1974), pp. 97–130.

[9]U.S. Consulate General, Beirut, Report of May 1936; Michel Morcos, *La culture du tabac au Liban* (Beirut: Centre de Recherches, Université Libanaise, 1974), offers a thorough history and analysis of the political economy of tobacco.

[10]See Morcos, *Culture du tabac*; for a more general assessment, Paul Saba, "The Creation of the Lebanese Economy: Economic Growth in the Nineteenth and Early Twentieth Century," in Roger Owen, ed., *Essays on the Crisis in Lebanon* (London: Ithaca Press, 1976), pp. 1–22; and a very good report in *Al Irfan*, 57 (September 1969), 738–744.

beys of the south, as for the other large growers, tobacco was one source of income among others, money to be spent in the city. Their tobacco crops were worked by sharecroppers and *wakils*, agents. Besides, when the inspectors of the tobacco monopoly showed up at the estates and villages of the powerful to estimate and price the crops, they took care not to offend. The tobacco story was a microcosm of the country. In the words of a small grower, it was "law for the weak, liberty for the strong."[11] The inspectors turned up in the downtrodden villages with bulldozers to smash excess crops. But they were timid when they approached the estates of the beys and the notables. A 1971 list of tobacco growers in the south was a veritable "who's who" in the country.[12] "Prince" Majid Arslan, a powerful Druze chieftain, a frequent minister of defense, appears on the list with holdings in the village of Ansar in the district of Nabatiyya. So do the daughters of a former prime minister, a Sunni politician by the name of Riad al Sulh, and his widow as well. Riad al Sulh was one of the founders of the republic; he was the Muslim party to the "National Pact" that had put the republic together in 1943. He had been struck down by an assassin in July 1951. His vast tobacco holdings had been passed on to his widow and his daughters, Alia, Muna, Lamya, Bahija, and Leila. One of the daughters was married to the king of Morocco's brother, Prince Abdullah. It is hard to imagine her worrying over the price of tobacco in southern Lebanon as she divided her time between Rabat and Paris.

Other "great families" were absentee landlords of the south's tobacco acreage. They did not need the help of Musa al Sadr. The twenty-five thousand small growers did, though, and they were inspired by his concern. Tobacco, he said, was *Qadiyyat al Qadaya*, the problem of all problems. The politically sophisticated cleric knew that men were waiting to be led, that the religious message had to be modernized, had to be linked to material concerns and issues of fairness and deprivation. He was, as an American diplomatic dispatch put it, "acutely aware of political inroads being made . . . by leftist (primarily Baathist and Communist) proselytizers."[13] He could choose to pick up the issue of the tobacco, or he could leave it to the radical parties.

In walking into the fight between the tobacco *régie* and the growers in 1973, Musa al Sadr must have grasped a historical parallel lost on

[11]The tobacco grower is quoted in *Al Irfan*, 57 (September 1969), 742.
[12]The list in Morcos, *Culture du tabac*, pp. 87–91.
[13]This was reported in an unusually thorough American diplomatic dispatch, eleven pages long, of April 3, 1974, number E–011652, by political officer Thomas Carolan; the quotation is on p.8.

his Lebanese followers and rivals alike. A large, ulama-led revolt had broken out against the Persian tobacco administration, the British-owned Imperial Tobacco Corporation, in Iran in 1891. The tobacco revolt of 1891–1892 had become part of the folklore of Iranian nationalism.[14] A concession had been granted to a British monopoly by the Iranian monarch Nasiruddin Shah. The rebellion against the concession brought together the opposition of "liberal" nationalists and mullahs "preaching everywhere against the surrender of the faithful into the hands of the infidels." Upheaval had erupted in the major cities of Iran. The ulama had given the grievances of tobacco growers and merchants religious sanction. Tobacco handled by foreigners was declared *haram*, impermissible and defiled. The ruling against the use of tobacco was made by the leading Shia cleric of the time, Mirza Hassan Shirazi. Shirazi lived in Samarra, one of the shrine towns of Iraq. After petitions came to him from the ulama of Iran, Shirazi first, in September 1891, sent a telegram to the Shah speaking against the concession. "The entry of foreigners," said the religious leader to the Shah, "into the affairs of the country, their relations and trade with Muslims, the concessions such as the bank, tobacco regie, railroads, and others are, for many reasons, against the exact sense of the Koran and God's orders. These acts weaken the power of the government and are the cause of the ruin of order in the country." Then in December came Shirazi's ruling: "In the name of God, the Merciful, the Forgiving, today the use of *tonbaku* and tobacco in any form is reckoned as war against the Imam of the age (may God hasten his glad advent!)."[15] The tobacco concession could not be saved and had to be canceled. The last throw of the dice was a government attempt to break the will of the leader of Teheran's ulama. He was given an ultimatum: he could break the boycott by smoking or leave the country. When he opted for the latter course, Teheranis, lead by their ulama, took to the streets. The ulama and their allies had formed an effective national movement which fused socioeconomic resentments and religious feelings.

For Musa al Sadr, this modern quarrel of growers and a tobacco *régie* must have seemed like the reenactment of an old tale one had heard and read about. The history of his birthplace, the deeds of its politically activist clerics, gave him wider horizons than those of his

[14]See Nikki Keddie's *Religion and Rebellion in Iran: The Tobacco Protest of 1891–1892* (London: Frank Cass, 1966).
[15]Nikki Keddie, *Sayyid Jamal ad-Din al-Afghani: A Political Biography* (Berkeley: University of California Press, 1972), quotations from pp. 399, 352, and 353–354.

politically cowed clerical rivals in Lebanon. He had a large history to draw upon and to live up to.

He also had sensitive antennae; he appropriated prevalent themes. At a time when Lebanon was beginning to wonder about its direction, he voiced what was on the minds of others. This was his great advantage at a time of drift in the country—the outsider grasping the issues, seeing and defining things clearly. In *Lord Jim*, Conrad had described that ability as the stranger's remarkable instinct. "He had proved his grasp of the unfamiliar situation, his intellectual alertness in that field of thought. There was his readiness, too. Amazing. And all this had come to him in a manner like keen scent to a well-bred hound."[16] This stranger too had a "keen scent" for the issues. In the escalating disorder that plunged Lebanon into civil war by 1975, Musa al Sadr was to become the country's most compelling figure. The years 1974 and 1975 were his. He was the Beiruti media's star attraction. He was, it was said of him, the hope of a "white revolution" in the country. As it turned out, no such hope existed; carnage was to become a way of life. But over the course of these two years, Shia history in Lebanon was changed for good, its symbols and heritage reinterpreted by the cleric and given an activist bent. It was not that Musa al Sadr was more "original" than others in the country. In general men who come to stamp particular epochs and times of transition with their own temperament and ideas are not necessarily more original than others. It is less originality that distinguishes them than an acute degree of sensitivity to their environment, to the mood of a particular situation.[17]

As Musa al Sadr emerged as one of Lebanon's most compelling

<hr />

[16]Joseph Conrad, *Lord Jim* (Harmondsworth: Penguin, 1980), p. 189.

[17]There are many parallels between Musa al Sadr's ability to express Lebanon's dilemmas and that of the radical monk Giraloma Savonarola and his brief moment of ascendancy (1494–1498) in Florence, as a "Prophet" of Florence's republican spirit. For those years, it was Savonarola, the "foreigner" who had come to Florence from Ferrara with his strange Ferrarese speech, who became "the outstanding advocate of the Florentine myth." Savonarola had first come to Florence at age thirty, stayed for a few years, failed as a preacher, and left, to return in 1490 with the blessing of the ruler Lorenzo de Medici. The Medici regime had invited the monk because of his learning; his presence, it was thought, would be to the credit of Florence and its rule. But the Ferrarese monk soon disappointed his patrons and began to speak against tyranny and corruption. And when the regime collapsed, Savonarola emerged as Florence's soothsayer and savior from a French invasion, an embodiment of her republican aspirations and virtues. During that brief moment of glory, before Savonarola was put to death by the papal authorities, his Ferrarese origins and speech no longer mattered. Florence made him its own and he adopted it as the "New Jerusalem." See Donald Weinstein, *Savonarola and Florence* (Princeton: Princeton University Press, 1970), p. 77. Also useful was Ralph Roeder, *Savonarola: A Study in Conscience* (New York: Brentano, 1930).

voices in 1974–1975, he was to display an amazing feel for the media, for getting his message across. Though born and raised in a Shia country, he showed a striking capacity to cross into the world of other men and sects. He knew how to reach an audience. No two speeches were alike. An address to an entirely Shia audience had one set of themes, a particular cadence; it drew on the private language and symbols of Shiism. A sermon at a church—and he delivered several —drew on the common themes of the martyrdom of the third Imam, Imam Hussein, and the crucifixion of Christ. On those occasions when he appeared with Sunni ulama, he said that there was no difference between his own black turban and the white turbans of his Sunni counterparts.

His people, the Shia, had long been known for their fear of defilement, their fear of what was morally polluted, *najas*, impure. It was a fear noted by travelers who ventured into their midst, a nervousness that extended from dietary matters to friendships. The fear had survived into the modern age. Like so many such tendencies that survive in our times, it had been concealed or given new names. But its core, a fear of venturing beyond the world of one's kinsmen, had survived. Musa al Sadr, a cleric, was remarkably free of this kind of timidity. An incident that took place in the city of Tyre was recounted by his followers, told by Shia men trying to break with the taboos of their world. There was a Christian in Tyre who owned a small ice cream stand. Tyre had a Shia majority, and the majority of them would not patronize his stand. Food handled by a Christian was pronounced *najas*, impure and defiled. The frustrated ice cream vendor took his case to the Imam of the Shia, to Musa al Sadr himself. And the cleric was sympathetic. On a Friday, after Musa al Sadr delivered his *khutba*, his sermon in the mosque of Tyre, he said that he felt like going for a walk. The usual crowd that was always there, pleased to be in his presence, followed him through the market and the streets of Tyre. Sayyid Musa and his entourage came upon the Christian ice cream man. The cleric stopped by the stand. "What sort of ice cream are you willing to give us today?" he asked. He then proceeded to accept from the man the ice cream he was offered. The lesson was not lost on the crowd. Things hitherto impermissible were declared acceptable by a man of religion and a sayyid, a descendant of the Prophet. The gates of a world closed unto itself were being forced open by a "man of God."

Sayyid Musa's daring in the face of old rituals and prohibitions went beyond dietary matters. On a Shia occasion honoring the sixth Imam, Jafar al Sadiq, Musa al Sadr appeared with a Catholic priest,

[133]

Bishop George Haddad by his side. Another Christian and admirer, the Maronite intellectual Michel al Asmar, joined him during a fast staged in a Beirut mosque to protest the violence in the country. He was a master of such gestures. A Lenten sermon that he delivered at a Catholic church became one of the country's special moments in early 1975. The Catholic hierarchy was there to receive him, as was one of Lebanon's former presidents and a cast of the country's political elite. A reporter who covered the episode for his daily paper wrote of the event with awe, in a nearly breathless way. He described the arrival of the Shia Imam and the large crowd of priests and nuns who were there to listen to him. "When Imam al Sadr entered the main hall of the church, faces of the audience showed a mixture of awe and delight. . . . The Imam nodded to the crowd that stood up to greet him; he sat down and they followed suit." He was introduced by the former president of the republic in the following words: "The believers are here to hear the word of God from a non-Catholic religious guide. It is only natural that Lebanon is the country in which this deed is taking place."

A reader encountering the sermon the cleric gave is struck with what must be called its Christian tone: the homage to Christ as an apostle of the weak and the oppressed, the preaching against "love of the self." It has that tone of deliberation and calm that is so much a mark of Catholicism and its ritual:

> Oh, our God, the God of Moses and Jesus and Muhammad, the God of the weak and of all creatures, we thank you for sheltering us, for uniting our hearts with your love and mercy. We are assembled here today in a house of yours, at a time of fasting. . . .
>
> Our hearts yearn for you; our minds derive light and guidance from you. . . . We have come to your door, we have gathered together to serve man. It is man that all religions aspire to serve. . . . All religions were once united; they anticipated one another; they validated one another. They called man to God and they served man. Then the different religions diverged when each sought to serve itself, to pay excessive attention to itself to the point that each religion forgot the original purpose— the service of man. Then discord and strife were born, and the crisis of man deepened.

Religions, he said, sought to liberate men from "the lords of the earth and the tyrants," to provide sustenance to the weak and the oppressed. But when the religious orders triumphed, the weak found that "the tyrants had changed their garb, that they now wielded power in the name of religion, brandishing its sword." The sermon continued in the same vein: It condemned the "narcissism of man," and the tyranny of wealth, man's "biggest idol." And there were some parting words about Lebanon—its tormented classes, its neglected districts.

"The Imam then stopped," we are told by the reporter covering the sermon, "bowed his head, moved from behind the pulpit to his place in the front row. The crowd wished that it was not in a house of God and worship so that they might be able to applaud. Before sitting down the Imam turned to the audience, bent his head in a greeting. . . . The archbishop asked the Imam al Sadr to proceed to the reception hall. . . . Then the crowd of worshipers began vying with one another to shake hands with the Imam who prayed and preached in the church of Christ."[18]

It was not the austere voice of Islam that spoke on that day. It was a more tender one—and a familiar one at that—that the Catholic audience responded to. In part, Musa al Sadr's ability to sway this particular audience must have owed something to the cult of sorrow and lament to be found at the heart of both Christianity and Shia Islam. But it was really his own style—the gentle demeanor, the melancholy, the tenderness he brought to his encounters with others—that endeared him to these hearers.

Lebanon was a county of deep religious antagonisms. Its people knew this even as they tried their best to hide their hostility and suspicions. The audience that left the Catholic church and those who read about the episode the next day knew the phobias and divisions of the country in which they lived. And they were flattered and touched by the cleric's performance all the more because of the stubborn divisions and feuds of the country.

Lebanon's elite press was receptive to him. He relied on two newspapers in Beirut, *Al Hayat* and *An Nahar*, both of which had conservative agendas. *Al Hayat*, launched in the mid-1940s, was owned by the Marwah family, a Shia family from the southern part of country. Kamel Marwah, the newspaper's founder who was assassinated by Nasserite operatives in 1966, had been a man light years ahead of the Shia world from which he hailed. He had known Musa al Sadr and had admired him; Kamel Marwah, too, had been one of the rare breed of men seeking to "modernize" the Shia outlook, to break with the taboos and the shackles of Shia history. His special bond with the

[18]The report on Musa al Sadr's Lenten sermon appeared in *An Nahar*, February 20, 1975. The full text is in Musa al Sadr, *Al Islam: Aqida Rasikha wa Manhaj Hayat* (Islam: A Firm Ideology and a Way of Life) (Beirut, 1979), pp. 9–18. Sayyid Hussein Husseini, who accompanied the Imam to the church, gave his own remembrance of the event.

cleric was honored after his death by his family. *Al Hayat*, I was told by Kamel Marwah's son, was Sayyid Musa's. The cleric needed to make no special effort to woo *Al Hayat* or to gain its attention.

But it was *An Nahar* that was Musa al Sadr's principal vehicle in 1974 and 1975. *An Nahar* was Lebanon's most enlightened and influential paper. It had a tradition of critical inquiry and social concern. Ideologically, it was a centrist paper. Its publisher, Ghassan Tueni, an American-educated Greek Orthodox, was a man who sat astride the two worlds of journalism and politics. In a land of clans and fractured politics, *An Nahar* stood for the city, for trade, for reform politics, for an enlightened kind of pro-Westernism. The man at the helm of *An Nahar* was sophisticated enough to know that the narrow base of Lebanon's ruling circle had to expand if its political system were to survive.

Musa al Sadr was good copy for Tueni's *An Nahar*. He was photogenic, he was good with words and crowds. He was becoming a mass preacher. It was of a better Lebanon that Musa al Sadr spoke, of the responsibility of the state toward the deprived. The Shia cleric appearing at a church, journeying to remote villages without amenities, staging a general strike, speaking out on behalf of the press against a government trying to clip its wings: such were the actions that endeared him to *An Nahar* and its brand of journalism. He was constantly on the move. For some, power flourishes in silence; for Musa al Sadr, tumult was an important source of power.

Acceptance encouraged him, seemed to sharpen his sense of the issues. He introduced a language that became his trademark; it revolved around the themes of "disinheritance" and "deprivation." The man of religion, he said, had to be on the side of the "wretched of the earth," of the "disinherited." He claimed that his movement, the "movement of the disinherited," went beyond the confines of his own sect. And he saw himself—as he put it in a letter to a sympathetic group in Parliament—as the "symbol," and the "rallying point" of the cause of the disinherited.[19]

The new language of disinheritance and deprivation was more subtle and more inclusionary than the language of class conflict that the Lebanese left had used with such dismal results. Musa al Sadr's language fitted the place. It appealed to the newly rich among the Shia as it did to the poor; the new language circumvented the Muslim (and Lebanese) phobia about "social classes" and "exploitation." The old

[19]Unpublished letter of Musa al Sadr, July 14, 1975, addressed to Hussein Husseini, Albert Mansur, and eleven other members of Parliament; made available by Hussein Husseini.

Marxian language was easily dismissed as the language of unbelief, as something ruinous to the Muslim faith; it was also, in a land of unbridled capitalism, dismissed as an attack on Lebanon's free-wheeling ways. A new language had to be introduced if the issues of equity and fairness were to be addressed without setting off the old sirens. Musa al Sadr found it in the popular feelings about fairness and disinheritance. He spoke in a native idiom; his words could not be dismissed as a heretical attack on age-old ways. At its roots, the language was deeply Shia. But it was suffused with a "Third-World" dimension; and it claimed to take in all the "deprived" in the country, all its "disinherited regions" and "sons."

Shia history in Lebanon taught that success in the modern city of Beirut required a break with the world of shabby elders—with the religion, the attire, the dialect, even the food of the hinterland. The charismatic cleric was imparting a different lesson: men could be themselves, yet still be successful and excel in the world beyond the faith. And he was doing it at mass rallies. As he broke out of hemmed-in elite politics, he found a direct line to the emotions and language of the masses. This happened in a dramatic way in early 1974. The preceding year had been a turning point for the country's fragile political balance. Full-scale fighting had erupted between the Lebanese army and the Palestinian organizations in May 1973. The basic understanding between the Maronite establishment and its Sunni counterpart had come unstuck as a result of the fighting. The Maronites wanted to assert the will of the state and the army; the Sunni establishment would not go along. The Lebanese state had never seemed as unsure of itself as it did after mid-1973. An increasing number of Shia youth were prey for the leftist parties. And this was to force Musa al Sadr's hand, and give him his opportunity; he had to speak to the poorer of the Shia classes, voice their resentments, or risk being pushed aside in a situation of increasing radicalization and disorder.

As he descended to the depths of society, to its lower strata and began to mine religious scripture and tradition for modern meaning and relevance, Imam Musa's vocation was transformed into that of a savior.[20] There was nothing rigged about this. The "savior" themes

[20]The great sociologist of religion Max Weber has written of the change that overcomes a religiopolitical movement when it reaches into the poor strata of society, when it connects with their yearning and resentments: "A salvationist kind of religion can very well originate in socially privileged strata. The charisma of the prophet . . . is normally associated with a certain minimum of intellectual culture. . . . But it regularly changes its character . . . when it penetrates to under-privileged strata. And one can

The Vanished Imam

were to be found in the Shia heritage itself, in its rich reservoirs of tales of martyrdom and persecution. Hitherto the Shia tradition had either been accepted as it had been received—as a tradition of defeat and worldly dispossession—or completely ignored, driven underground, if you will, by "modern" men and women trying to venture into the world beyond the faith. Musa al Sadr offered a new alternative: Shia history with its tales of defeat would neither be accepted as it had been received, nor apologized for and denied. The tradition would be reworked, cast in a new light.

Inevitably, it was with Kerbala, the seventh-century tale of Imam Hussein's martyrdom, that Musa al Sadr began when he went to the Shia masses in a direct way in 1974 and 1975. The "Kerbala paradigm" lay at the core of Shia history.[21] Kerbala "branded" the Shia. It set them apart. Kerbala cast a long shadow; for the faithful it annulled time and distance. Succeeding generations had told and embellished the tale, given it their sense of separateness and political dispossession. A gripping passion play, staged every year, reenacted the searing tale which culminated in the killing of the Prophet's grandson, Imam Hussein, and a band of zealous followers and in the captivity of the women of *ahl al bayt*. The tale of Kerbala is related here, in very brief fashion, so that the reader can best appreciate what Musa al Sadr made of it and how neo-Shiism worked with, manipulated and, in time, overthrew the dominant Shia tradition of political quietism and withdrawal.[22]

---

point to at least one feature that normally accompanies this shift; one result of the unavoidable adaptation to the needs of the masses. This is the appearance of a personal saviour, whether wholly divine or a mixture of human and divine; and of the religious relationship to that saviour as the precondition for salvation. The further one descends the ladder of social stratification, the more radical the ways in which this need for a saviour is wont to express itself." Quoted in Norman Cohn, *The Pursuit of the Millennium* (New York: Oxford University Press, 1970), p. 51.

[21]The "Kerbala paradigm" is Michael Fischer's term in his book *Iran: From Religious Dispute to Revolution* (Cambridge: Harvard University Press, 1980), pp. 13–21.

[22]For the tale of Kerbala and the larger history around it I have relied on a number of disparate sources. Muhammad Mahdi Shams al Din, a Shia cleric in southern Lebanon, wrote a book entitled *Ansar al Hussein* (The Companions of Hussein) (Beirut: Dar al Fikr, 1975). Habat al Din al Shahrastani (1883–1967), a distinguished Shia cleric who lived in Iran and Iraq, wrote *Nahdat al Hussein* (The Revolt of Hussein) (Baghdad, 1925). Abu al Faraj al Isfahani (897–966) wrote a sympathetic and vivid classic, *Maqatil al Talibiyyun* (The Martyrdom of the Talibids); the copy I worked with was published in Najaf, Iraq, in 1934. *Sawt al Hussein* (The Voice of Hussein) by Ahmad Ish, an Egyptian, tells the story of Hussein in the form of a historical novel (Cairo, 1963). So does the work of the Lebanese Shia, Raif Fadlallah, *Al Malhama al Ilhya* (The Divine Epic) (Beirut, 1933). Sir Lewis Pelly, a British diplomat in Persia in the 1860s, made a first-rate translation of the Persian passion play under the title *The Miracle Play of Hasan and Husain*, 2 vols. (London: William H. Allen, 1879). The multivolume work of the great Muslim his-

The central actor in the tale of Kerbala is the third Shia Imam, Hussein. Hussein is the beloved and revered figure of Shia Islam. Its history exalts him; it is silent about his older brother, the second Imam, Hassan. Hassan had inherited his father's mantle, after his father, Ali, the first Shia Imam and the fourth caliph of Islam, was assassinated in A.D. 661. But in the grim struggle for power which erupted in the new Muslim polity and claimed Imam Ali as its victim, Hassan had abdicated in favor of his father's rival, the governor of the province of Syria, Muawiyah, the founder of the Umayyad dynasty. It had been a struggle between two ideas of succession: a religious one, claiming rule through descent from the Prophet, and a worldly one, resting on the power and wealth of the expanding Muslim state and its formidable troops in the province of Syria. The birthplace of Islam, the Hijaz, had been dwarfed by the wealth of the newly conquered realms. Two provinces of the state, Syria and Iraq, battled for ascendancy. The men of Iraq had proclaimed their allegiance to Ali and, after him, to his son. But the Iraqis, and their Imam Hassan, were no match for the tribes and soldiers of Syria. Hassan had understood the harsh balance of force. The might of the Syrians was irresistible. This was the Muslim empire's most formidable center of power. Hassan abdicated; he was no martyr; he was bought off by the ruler of Damascus. The terms of the abdication called on Muawiyah to rule according to the "Book of God," and to refrain from appointing a successor to the Caliphate after him, leaving the choice of caliph to the Muslim community. After his abdication, Hassan retired to the city of Medina, led a quiet life, and died several years later. According to the Shia historical sources, he was poisoned by one of his wives, who was promised money and marriage to Muawiyah's son Yazid. The money was delivered. But the marriage was not to be: to the treacherous woman, Muawiyah said that he valued the life of his own son.[23]

It fell to Hassan's younger brother, Hussein, to supply Shia history with its pathos and its current of martyrology. In 680, Hussein rose in rebellion. The founder of the Umayyad dynasty had died, and Hus-

torian Ibn al Jarir al Tabari (838–923), *Tarikh al Rusul wa'l-Muluk*, ed. Muhammad Abu al-Fadl Ibrahim, 10 vols. (Cairo, 1961), gave a classical narrative of Kerbala in vol. 5. For English readers Edward Gibbon, *The Decline and Fall of the Roman Empire* (Philadelphia: Claxton, Remsen, and Haffelfinger, 1868), vol. 5, pp. 162–166, has a vivid account of the events of Kerbala.

[23]Shia history has always found it particularly problematic to deal with the abdication of Imam Hassan. Ali Zayn, a Shia Lebanese writer of some distinction, incurred the wrath of true believers when he probed the event's less-than-heroic dimensions; see his *Lil Bahth an Tarikhna Fi Lubnan* (In Search of Our History in Lebanon) (Beirut, 1973), pp. 90–116.

sein felt released from the pledge Hassan had given. The notion of a Muslim community ruled by God's law was becoming pure fiction. Muawiyah had designated his son Yazid as his successor. Opposition to the kingship of Muawiyah's son rallied under the banner of the Alids (the descendants of Imam Ali and his wife Fatima), with Hussein as the legitimate inheritor of religious authority. Piety on one side, worldly power on the other: such was the way Hussein's struggle against the ruler Yazid evolved.

Hussein's journey to Iraq, which ended in his death at Kerbala, in southern Iraq, was triggered by Yazid. Orders came from Damascus that Hussein should offer a pledge of allegiance, *baya*, to Yazid. He could and would do no such thing. He escaped from his home in Medina to the city of Mecca, with his family. Trouble shadowed him to Mecca. Assassins sent from Damascus were on his trail.

Emissaries came, Shia historical sources relate, from the city of Kufa in Iraq asking Hussein to go there: "We invite you to come to Kufa as we have no Imam to guide us." With a small band of followers and members of his family, Hussein undertook the doomed mission in the face of strong advice against it. Shia *marathi* (set pieces of lamentation for Hussein and his companions) are rich and evocative in their recounting of the martyred Imam's mission. A poet who loved the Imam is reported to have told him that the people of Kufa were hopeless, that their hearts were with the kindhearted Imam and their swords with his enemies. In the marathi, Hussein is turned into a willing martyr; he is made to say that he had washed his hands of life, that he had girded himself to do the will of God.

On his way to Kufa, Hussein arrived at the plains of Kerbala on the second day of the Muslim month of Muharram. Five thousand of the ruler's troops cut him off from the water of the Euphrates. The Imam who had come to this land of sorrow—the literal meaning of Kerbala—reminded the troops that he had come to Iraq upon the invitation of its people: "Did you not write to me that the fruit is ripe and that the garden is ready and that I would arrive in the midst of loyal troops?"[24] It was a dance of death. The Prophet's grandson reminded the large force that surrounded him of the "blood in his veins": "I am the grandson of your Prophet, my grandmother is his wife Khadija, the first woman to embrace Islam, my mother is his daughter Fatima." He was, the troops were told, carrying with him the Prophet's own sword: "Think who I am. . . . Search your hearts. Consider whether it is lawful to kill me."

[24]Fadlallah, *Al Malhama*, p. 277.

It was all to no avail. There were orders from the caliph in Damascus and strict orders from the caliph's governor in Kufa, and there were promises of treasure. One by one Hussein's followers and relatives fell before the army of the ruler; or they perished of thirst. The women and the children wailed. Hussein held an infant of his and asked the ruler's troops for some water for it; an archer's arrow slew the child.

Finally, on the tenth of Muharram, the day of Ashura, it was the aging Imam's turn to die. He was fifty-six years old; he bade farewell to the women in his entourage and asked them to meet the humiliations that attended them with dignity and belief. He then prayed to God to "withhold rain from this treacherous lot, to deny them the blessings of the earth, to disperse them after their moment of triumph."

Hussein was beheaded. On his body were found thirty-three strokes of lance and sword. The troops then looted his camp and his possessions, even his sandals. His body was trampled by the horses.

Shia legends and history and mourning recitals have told in endless variations how the heads of Hussein's band and his own were taken from Kerbala, to the governor in Kufa, then to the caliph's seat in Damascus. Along the way from Iraq to Damascus, the severed heads and the shackled women were exhibited as a warning to others: submit, for rebellion does not pay.

Unsentimental historians wrote off Kerbala as a wild venture that ended in defeat and failure. But the bearers of the Kerbala legacy drew from the tale a different lesson. The late seventh-century event marked with its themes of righteous defeat an entire branch of Islam. Kerbala, as it were, insisted on its permanent relevance. "Every day is Ashura, and every place is Kerbala," Shia history taught. The episode at Kerbala was turned into a warrant for political quietism and submission. Men commemorating Kerbala were invited to contemplate the capricious nature of power, the arbitrary way in which the unscrupulous prevailed.

Men and women grieved for the fallen Imam. They saw in his renunciation of worldly things and his martyrdom their own dispossession. The split between the *Shia*, the partisans, of Hussein, and those who accepted the dominant order that slew him would, in time, deepen into a psychological and political chasm. Lamenting Hussein's fate, the Shia exalted the third Imam into a tragic figure. The act of mourning Hussein and his equally ill-starred successors brought great religious merit and furthered a central religious function: the Imams' intercession, *Shafa'ah*, with God. The Imams were mediators between men and God: those who mourned *ahl al bayt* acquired standing and credit in God's eyes.

Musa al Sadr brought to the old tale of Kerbala a new reading, which stripped it of its sorrow and lament and made of it an episode of political choice and courage on the part of Imam Hussein and the band of followers who fought by his side. The annual occasion of mourning Imam Hussein, hitherto a reminder to the Shia of their solitude and defeat, was to become under Musa al Sadr a celebration of defiance on the part of an "elite minority"—the Shia—that had refused to submit to injustice.

Here, too, it was not so much Musa al Sadr's originality that carried the day and that made the Shia masses of Lebanon see old symbols and traditions in a new light. Sayyid Musa was a well-traveled man, for a Shia mullah, and he was well read. He took some ideas and conceptions that were dimly perceived, or that existed on paper, and translated them into accessible language and imagery.

To begin with, we know that Sayyid Musa had been deeply influenced by a book on Imam Hussein written by Abbas Mahmud Al Aqqad (1889–1964), one of the celebrated writers of Egypt's "liberal period," prior to the revolution of 1952 that brought Gamal Abdul Nasser and his fellow officers to power. Aqqad's book *Al Hussein: Abu al Shuhada* (Hussein: The Father of Martyrs), published in 1944, had depicted the struggle between Imam Hussein and his rival Yazid as the clash of "two temperaments," two radically different "moral outlooks." Hussein, in Aqqad's reverential treatment, represents everything noble in *Banu Hashim*, the Prophet Muhammad's family; He knew literature, was a man of eloquence, spontaneity, and gentleness, accepted the "cruel turns of fate," and was pious and benevolent toward those less privileged than himself. Yazid, on the other hand, said Aqqad, had in him all the "negative traits of his family" (the Umayyads, a clan that had opposed the Prophet Muhammad and had fought Muslims during their early years of adversity) and none of the merits that clan may have possessed. Yazid had the roughness of his family; he loved his drinking bouts, his horses, and his hounds. Yazid stood for power and its prerogatives, whereas Hussein represented Islam's emphasis on justice and equality of the believers. Aqqad had rejected the notion that the fight between Hussein and Yazid was over *mulk*, kingship. A struggle, he said, had been imposed on Hussein; martyrdom was the last resort to save Islam from becoming the dominion of *ahl al mal wa al sultan*, the men of wealth and power. Yazid had prevailed at Kerbala. But his was a temporary victory; in the end, history vindicated Hussein and what he stood for.

Closer to home than Aqqad's book, by the late 1960s and early 1970s, modernist Shia Iranians had begun to reinterpret Imam Hussein's legacy. And in the new Iranian discourse the Shia folk conception of Hussein as a willing martyr who rides to a sure death—a death foretold, according to folklore, when he was born—was set aside in favor of the idea of a political man who weighs his choices, and embarks on the best course left to him. Gradually Imam Hussein emerged as a precursor of political men who choose to rebel against overwhelming odds, and do so with open eyes.

The turning of old religious ritual into a radical politics of praxis in Shia Lebanon was evident in Musa al Sadr's Ashura oration of 1974. It was a dark time, said the cleric, when Imam Hussein rose in rebellion: "The *Umma* was silent, free men were fugitives; fear reduced men to silence. Islam was threatened." Hussein, a free man, made a choice of his own:

A great sacrifice was needed to . . . stir feelings. The event of Kerbala was that sacrifice. Imam Hussein put his family, his forces, and even his life, in the balance against tyranny and corruption. Then the Islamic world burst forth with this revolution.

This revolution did not die in the sands of Kerbala; it flowed into the life stream of the Islamic world, and passed from generation to generation, even to our day. It is a deposit placed in our hands so that we may profit from it, that we draw out of it a new source of reform, a new position, a new movement, a new revolution, to repel the darkness, to stop tyranny and to pulverize evil.[25]

The cleric acknowledged the sad history of the Shia: he knew its depth. "The record of our tears fills the cloud that follows us," he told his followers on another religious occasion. But history could offer something more than the spectacle of Shia defeat. Imam Hussein, he said, faced the enemy with seventy men, and "today we are more than seventy, and our enemy is not a quarter of the whole world."[26] A hundred million people throughout the world, a hundred million Shia, now celebrated the memory of Hussein. The men who claimed Hussein no longer needed to be frightened or silent.

It was political daring that the activist cleric was trying to teach.

[25]*Al Hayat*, February 1, 1974.
[26]*An Nahar*, February 18, 1974.

Exalting Hussein, he was attacking the dominant Shia tradition of mourning and quiescence. "Hussein," he said in another religious discourse, "had three kinds of enemies: Those who killed him—and they were tyrants; those who tried to obliterate his memory, like the men who plowed the earth and covered the spot where he was buried or like the Ottomans who prevented any remembrance of him. The third kind of enemies are those who wanted to ossify the example of Hussein, to restrict the meaning of his life and martyrdom to tears and lamentations. The third kind of enemies are the most dangerous for they threaten to destroy the living roots of Hussein's memory."[27] The third kind of enemies were the Shia themselves: Hussein had to be rescued from what the bearers of his legacy had made of his rebellion and his death. A cleric celebrating a tradition several centuries old was grafting onto it new themes of concern and activism.

On yet another religious occasion, Musa al Sadr read into the seventh-century tale the issue of women's rights and the place of women in Muslim society. He spoke of Imam Hussein's sister Zainab, who was with her brother on his doomed mission. She survived him, spent years grieving for him, and was turned by the faithful into a saintly figure of sorrow and grief. Zainab's shrine on the outskirts of Damascus was a place to which the defeated seeking solace journeyed. Of her, the cleric said: "Zainab went with the caravan of prisoners to Kufa; she had been the one who lifted Hussein's body, who presented it to God and said 'Oh God, accept from us our sacrifice.' She spread the message of Hussein. She took his message from the desert of Kerbala to the capitals of the Islamic world. . . . The woman in Kerbala carried on the work and the struggle. The woman can't just be an instrument of pleasure and procreation. Thus treated, she will be stripped of her potential and her dignity." Zainab, he reminded his audience, was the one who covered the body of Hussein's ailing son, Zayn al Abidin, with hers, who begged the ruler's troops at Kerbala to spare the young man's life. It was thus that Hussein's Imamate had been rescued, that he was left with an heir who inherited his mantle.[28]

In believers' minds, the time and distance separating present-day reality from that of Kerbala were nullified and overcome with remarkable ease. An enemy in daily life—a policeman, a landlord, an oppressive father-in-law—was dubbed a Yazid, the ruler who had ordered the killing of Hussein. A particularly cruel figure was referred to as Shimr—in the Shia literature and passion plays, the man who

[27]*An Nahar*, January 23, 1975.
[28]*An Nahar*, January 21, 1975.

beheaded Hussein. Musa al Sadr made the same kind of historical leap. The contemporary civil disorder became the "Kerbala of Lebanon." Imam Hussein was connected right to the present.

Others in Shia Lebanon had flirted with this kind of thing earlier, had tried to manipulate the old Shia histories. Some two decades before Musa al Sadr reread Shia history and symbolism, radicalized youth in the southern Lebanon town of Bint Jbail had attempted to make the fight between Imam Hussein and the Umayyad ruler Yazid a metaphor of their own. A group of Arab nationalists belonging to the Baath party, they made an attempt that was clumsy and contrived. In their reconstruction of Kerbala, Hussein was no longer a special individual, an Imam, but the "Arab nation" as a whole, and Yazid stood for the "nation's enemies." The role of the Hidden Imam, *al Mahdi al Muntazar*, was assigned to a "revolutionary cadre" that would appear and bring about a reign of justice.[29] Stretched that far, the tradition wilted and did not work. The Shia tale of sorrow and solitude could not be claimed by young secularists. But it belonged in a natural way to the cleric relating it in the mid-1970s: after all, he was a descendant of the twelve Imams. In the popular imagination, Musa al Sadr's title and attire were of a piece with the inherited history.

Religious occasions were becoming armed rallies. A special bond was being forged between men awakening to a sense of their own power—and violation—and an extraordinary figure. Seventy-five thousand men turned out in the eastern town of Baalbek to hear him in March 1974. The occasion was a religious one honoring Imam Hussein. Thousands of armed men were on hand, and Musa al Sadr, the "rebel Imam," was acclaimed by the masses. (His connection with the seventh-century Imam who fell in rebellion was left to their imagination.) The crowd closed in on the cleric: he had trouble reaching the platform; men reached out to touch his gown; he lost his turban and it had to be retrieved for him. He was unable to start his oration for twenty minutes. Men firing into the air had to be silenced. "I have words harsher than bullets," the cleric said. "So spare your bullets." "The town of Baalbek," he said, "is without a secondary school. There was a school under French rule. Two thousand years ago Baalbek was irrigated through a network of dams. Today its water is wasted. And the government still wants to know why we despair of it. . . ."[30]

[29]Waddah Chrara, *Transformations d'une manifestation religieuse dans un village du Liban sud* (Beirut: Publications du Centre de Recherches, Université Libanaise, 1968).

[30]*An Nahar*, March 18, 1974; for an analysis of the events surrounding the Baalbek appearance, see the American diplomatic dispatch of April 3, 1974, E-011652.

In this oration, he spoke of the plight of the south, working to bridge the gap between his two realms, the Bekaa and the south. To his more militant followers in the Bekaa he said: "You are the brothers of the sons of the south, a source of strength for them." He then spoke of the ruling authorities in the country, of what they had done to the south, of the diversion of the waters of the Litani River from the south to Beirut: "They have stolen three hundred million cubic meters from the waters of the south. They now want another sixty million cubic meters. They want to shatter the last remaining hope of the people of the south for a share in their own water." He ticked off the budget figures for the last four years—figures showing the south receiving only some 20 percent of its legitimate share. He ranged over other grievances. The Shia, he said, were underrepresented at the heights of the civil service. He noted that there were no Shia deans at the universities, that "Shia ambassadors are appointed to backward countries. . . . A meter of land in Beirut is worth more than ten thousand Lebanese pounds, a meter of land in the Bekaa is worth less than ten piasters. . . . Let us look at the ghettoes of Beirut: Oh men in power, do you not feel ashamed that a few kilometers away from your homes are houses that are not fit for human habitation? . . . If there are twelve hundred homeless children in the streets of Beirut, eleven hundred of them are sure to be Shia. Does Imam Hussein accept this for his children? Does Imam Ali?"

The wrongs had been there. They were now being tallied up. New grievances were dressed in old historic garb. The budget figures and the old Shia symbols the cleric mixed together. There was something here for men impressed by modern standards and budget figures, for the ambitious dreaming of ambassadorships to countries which mattered, and for ordinary people who understood and internalized the old Shia tales of persecution and defeat. And there was also a defense and justification by the cleric of his own worldly ambitions: he had been accused of ambition, of wanting the chairmanship of the Higher Shia Council for life (which he did want and which he secured). He linked his own dreams to those of the revered Imams: "The commander of the faithful, Imam Ali, was denounced from the pulpit for eight years and accused of unbelief. A judge in Kufa said that Imam Hussein had strayed from his grandfather's path. Now they say that I have abandoned my grandfather's way, that I should observe religious ritual and be satisfied." Musa al Sadr's worldliness and political ambition were far removed from the old tradition of clerical conservatism. A man of the religious institution, he was breaking with the role assigned men of the religious institution by those who possessed political power.

> The rulers say that the men of religion must only pray and not meddle in other things. They exhort us to fast and to pray for them so that the foundations of their reign will not be shaken, while they move away from religion and exploit it to hold on to their seats of power. Do not think that men in power who proclaim their opposition to communism are opposed to atheism. . . . They are the most infidel of the infidels and the most atheist of the atheists. They want us to give ourselves up to them.[31]

For all the standard assertions, Islam had known no distinction between God's realm and Caesar's. Caesar, the man of the sword, had triumphed in Islamic history. Kings and dynasties, and lesser men in power, had turned religion and the men of religion into instruments of their power. The man of God—pious, left behind by modernity, by modern schools, by foreign trade and great wealth—had become an adornment in the court of the bey, the *wazir*, and the ruler. The radical potential of the religion lay dormant. The triumph of this cleric over the men of conventional politics was an inversion of familiar things. It was not a predestined outcome; it had to be willed and organized. For it to happen, history had to be turned around. The revolutionary man of religion had to reinterpret the functions and the obligations of the religious institution and its custodians.

The idea expounded before the crowd in the Bekaa was to become a recurrent theme: the man of religion had to be at odds with the men in power. Not long after the rally in Baalbek, Musa al Sadr propounded the same theme to a group of fellow clerics: "The moment you find that you have incurred the ruler's wrath is the time to realize that you are on the right path. You should refuse to succumb to the lords of this earth, to the oppressors. You should stand on the side of the people, on the side of the wretched of the earth."[32]

Nearly fifty days after the armed rally in the Bekaa, there was another occasion, an ostensibly religious one that obliterated the line between the realm of religion and that of politics. This time, the gathering was in Musa al Sadr's old base in the city of Tyre; the purpose was to celebrate the memory of Fatima al Zahra, the Prophet's daughter and the mother of the two Imams, Hassan and Hussein. A crowd as large as the one that had turned out in Baalbek came to hear the cleric.

[31]*An Nahar*, March 18, 1974.
[32]*An Nahar*, May 6, 1974.

There were armed men from the Bekaa Valley, who arrived with their antitank weapons, with their sticks of dynamite and machine guns. The patricians of the Shia community who followed Musa al Sadr were there as well. Musa al Sadr arrived to shouts of *Allah-u-Akbar* (God is Great), to the sounds of rifles and machine guns and the ululation of women. He started off with a few words about Fatima, "the pure," the virtuous, the believing woman who was told by her father the Prophet Muhammad that he could not spare her on the day of judgment, that she would have to earn God's grace and mercy by her own merits. This said, he made the predictable leap from the old heritage to worldly and political matters. "For us today, we see, oh Fatima, daughter of the messenger of God, we are now beyond the stage of childhood and helplessness. We have come of age. We need no trustees. We have emancipated ourselves despite all the means adopted to keep us from learning and enlightenment. We have gathered in large numbers to say that we need no trusteeship. Oh Fatima, we are on your path; and our path will lead us to martyrdom."

He was becoming a "warner" of dangers to come—a role as old as messianic preachers. The warnings were put forth in an open statement to "the rulers" and the powers:

> Oh rulers, the lessons of history are within your grasp. All human societies have exploded at one time or another. We have asked you to deal with the problem. We have submitted to you studies and applications. There are ten billion cubic meters of water in Lebanon; only four hundred and fifty million cubic meters are exploited while the rest finds its way to the sea. Most parts of the country are thirsty and deprived. Is there anyone who cares for the plight of the citizenry. . . ? There are those who want to rule and oppress without giving anything in return; those who ruled us for years without building a school or a hospital. We are with the deprived of all communities, with all those whose dignity has been violated.

Musa al Sadr then asked for an oath and the crowd repeated after him that they would stay together until Lebanon had been rid of "deprivation" and "disinheritance." The oath was vintage Musa al Sadr, an evocative vow "in the name of the blood of the martyrs, the wailing of mothers, the anxiety of the students and the intelligentsia. . . ."[33]

An oath never overturns the world. Oaths can be made and broken. Men have never lacked ways of releasing themselves from the

[33]Ibid.

most sacred of obligations. But oaths have been important rituals and instruments in the formation of social movements—a process in which form has been as important as content.[34] In Muslim history oaths have been particularly important vehicles for men's commitment of themselves to one another and to a common endeavor. There were, as Roy Mottahedeh shows in a perceptive work on bonds of loyalty in Muslim society, costs to breaking oaths. Men took oaths with sufficient seriousness that they tended to avoid those they "knew they might have to repudiate."[35]

The cleric asking for the oath knew the place and the men: it was a hard place. Men saw social life as a realm of feuds and betrayals. It was accepted that the big fish ate the small one, that men, as the peasant sayings of the country had it, pulled their own thorns with their own hands. In asking for the oath, he sought to create a semblance of commitment to a common endeavor. The hope of such oaths—and such dramatic moments—is that men will be moved enough to make minor sacrifices or to feel slightly more courageous in facing their adversaries or to know that they are not entirely alone. Musa al Sadr led a community without a history of cohesion and solidarity. Pushed off the land, forced to scramble, men crowed about small achievements and wished ill for others. Men competed for the small crumbs that were available in the country, for the few prestigious civil service appointments open to the Shia. He could not annul that kind of situation. He knew it all too well. The most he could hope for through these dramatic gestures and moments was to create a fragile sense of fellowship, to "exploit" a common history of grief and to bring men together. In such a context, there is justification for the skeptic's argument that leaders trying to bind men together are ploughing the sea, that men separate and return to their familiar enmities as soon as the bubble bursts, as soon as the trance subsides. But something *does* happen when such oaths and obligations are made. Men—if only for a moment, and if only a handful of men—do give of themselves. Atomized men are brought together. In the face of the struggle of each against each, men hold up another vision of things: a more hopeful vision that enables them to act without second-guessing one another, without the conviction that the ruin of one man is to the other's advantage.

Religious oaths were a way of forging new bonds. The old tales of

[34]On form and ritual in social movements see ch. 6 in E. J. Hobsbawm, *Primitive Rebels* (New York: Norton, 1965).

[35]Roy Mottahedeh, *Loyalty and Leadership in an Early Islamic Society* (Princeton: Princeton University Press, 1980), p. 49.

Shia solitude and martydom were called on to instill courage in men who had no history of political concern and responsibility: this was Musa al Sadr's innovation. The men he led lived in the shadow of Kerbala and bore its burden. The tradition of Kerbala, and the larger Shia universe spun around it, had to be faced and reformed.

Kerbala was a tapestry of many threads. No tale of such great pathos and tragedy could have left men with a single unambiguous message. Stood on one end, Kerbala was a tale of choice and principle, the story of a man standing up when he could have groveled and acquiesced. Stood on the other end, it was a tale of doom and defeat. Kerbala celebrated the grandson of the Prophet who fell in battle. But in the dark recesses of the mind, Kerbala and the reiteration of its grim happenings could be an invitation to submission to powers that could not be defeated, to odds that could not be overcome.

The tale of Kerbala and the multitude of other Shia tales of dispossession and defeat worked the only way they could have: they twisted and turned and they made surreptitious suggestions. Those searing Shia tales had assumed that weakness would have clean hands, that men would not, as modern jargon has it, "identify with the aggressor." But in a harsh world where the outcome mattered more than the journey, where results vindicated the deeds of men, a certain measure of ambivalence, of dissonance, if you will, was inevitable. The caliphs who beheaded the just Imams were men of means and power. The world offered itself to them, they had prevailed, they had not been encumbered by scruples. Were the young in this Shia world to be the successors of those who died of thirst and hunger in doomed battles, or were they to prevail in their duels? Cut it as one might, men were told to exalt grief and martyrdom and lamentation but also to pursue success relentlessly and to pursue it wherever it might lead.

Martyrology lived in close proximity to crass self-preservation and easily spilled into it. Men extolled martyrdom, but they lived cautiously. They knew that men full of applause would fall away just when they were needed, that the zealous would be left alone to twist in the wind: the men promising to be there (like the men of Kufa promising to meet Hussein), the tales suggested, would scurry home to their wives and their children. And the men who risked, who really went out to change things, would reap the whirlwind. Women accompanied their sons to the Ashura celebrations and the passion play. But the lamenting mothers asked that young men refrain from playing with fire: heroism was delusion, sons were taught. The crafty inherited the earth; the daring were beheaded or poisoned. No one wanted his head to be thrown into his mother's lap.

Shia defeatism had worn a righteous mask, had consoled itself. This was what Shia history had to do to cope with worldly dispossession, with a seemingly endless trail of sorrow and defeat. The "Saintly Imams" (the words are Matthew Arnold's in a moving essay on Kerbala), "resigned sufferers" as they were, supplied a "tender and pathetic side" to Islam. The Imams lost. But the believers, Arnold writes, who themselves could "attain to so little" loved the Imams "all the better on that account, loved them for their abnegation and mildness, felt that they were dear to God, that God loved them, that they and their lives filled a void in the severe religion of Mohamet."[36] Matthew Arnold caught the vibrancy of Kerbala. Islam, mainstream Islam, had been a triumphant affair. The Prophet had died at the helm of a successful polity. But the tale of triumph could not be everyone's. There had to be pathos and defeat as well, sorrow and a measure of consolation. Kerbala had supplied what was most "tender" and pathetic to those who partook of it.

But men are not angels; they covet power and they admire winners. Men carry their oppressors within them. There was, to borrow the Shia metaphor, the danger of a Yazid lurking in every man. This is the underside of Kerbala; and a preacher like Musa al Sadr, disentangling a complex Shia history, had to confront it. The bearers of Kerbala wailed for their martyrs. But the laments provided a kind of moral absolution for what men did and did not do, for their abdication in social and political matters.[37]

There was darkness in Kerbala. A great tale of betrayal could hardly instill in the men who bore its chains and memorized its lines the con-

---

[36]Matthew Arnold, "A Persian Passion Play," in *Essays in Criticism* (London: Macmillan, 1937), p. 262.

[37]Elias Canetti's *Crowds and Power* describes Shiism as a quintessential "religion of lament" and probes what a "lamenting pack" finds in its grief for a martyred figure. Men are hunters, says Canetti. And so long as they continue to be hunters, they seek in a martyred figure a way of exorcising their guilt: "Why is it that so many join the lament? What is its attraction? What does it give people? To all those who join it the same thing happens: the hunting or baiting pack expiates its guilt by becoming a lamenting pack. Men lived as pursuers and as such, in their own fashion, they continue to live. They seek alien flesh, and cut into it, feeding on the torment of weaker creatures; the glazing eye of the victim is mirrored in their eyes, and that last cry they delight in is indelibly recorded in their soul. Most of them perhaps do not divine that, while they feed their bodies, they also feed the darkness within themselves. But their guilt and fear grow ceaselessly, and, without knowing it, they long for deliverance. Thus they attach themselves to one who will die for them and, in lamenting him, they feel *themselves* as persecuted. Whatever they have done, however they have raged, for this moment they are aligned with suffering. It is a sudden change of side with far-reaching consequences. It frees them from the accumulated guilt of killing and from the fear that death will strike at them too. All that they have done to others, another now takes on himself; by attaching themselves to him, faithfully and without reserve, they hope to escape vengeance": *Crowds and Power* (New York: Continuum, 1978), p. 145.

fidence in themselves and in others to go beyond fear and greed. Kerbala taught a distrust of political power. But more: along with this distrust another sensibility was imparted, a sense that the world offered no redemption and that every path led to a blind alley of fear and betrayal. Exaltation and all the frenzied politics that come with it were checked, driven underground. But the price was a deep-seated sense of despair. This was true of Shia history everywhere, but particularly true in a hinterland like the world of the Shia of Lebanon. Men here were always at the receiving end of someone else's power. They developed all the attributes that go with a long history of political dispossession: they propitiated power; they coped with it as best they could; they obeyed without being convinced; they rebelled in small ways or sulked and waited for a better day.

Tradition had provided shelter, had confirmed the futility of political life and the inevitability of betrayal. Now tradition—the same body of tales and myths and icons—was being mined for symbols of revolt, for new forms of solidarity. The left in Lebanon had talked of class and the "injuries of class." But ordinary men and women had not responded with great zeal. A religious reformer was succeeding where the left had failed. There was no need to borrow alien words and categories. The sad history of Kerbala was what men and women in Shia Lebanon had known. They had grown up with the Shia tales. A revolutionary figure working with the familiar history—subverting it as he went along—tapped something vital in those who rallied to him.

Something in Musa al Sadr's style and personal demeanor was particularly helpful to him: a gentleness in his dealings with others, a touch of reticence that attracted people. Authority and leadership in this culture were like a straitjacket: men who possessed authority strutted around, bullied other men, stared them down, and frightened them. Authority had what was called a *wahra*, an ability to intimidate, nearly to paralyze those at the receiving end of power. (One thinks of Saddam Hussein, the president of Iraq, frightening and forbidding, as the quintessential man with *wahra*; indeed, among the titles he possesses, there is one, *Al Muheeb*, which literally means the awesome, or the awe-inspiring.) But this was not Musa al Sadr's style. Men, regardless how young or unimportant, were treated with tenderness. The wife of one of his associates, who for a while lived with her husband in Musa al Sadr's home, said that she does not recall an incident in which the cleric berated another man or was severe or overbearing in the way he dealt with those around him. His style had its spell. And no doubt its power came from the melancholy that lay at the core of Shiism. The world of power had had no room for the

Shia. Their revered Imams had fallen in battle, had been deprived of what the righteous felt to be their due: the right of succession to the Prophet's political and religious kingdom, to the wealth, the taxes, and the power that Islam's dominion brought to its beneficiaries. A leader summoning the Shia masses had to have in him some of the sorrow of Shia history, its sense that the ways of the world were harsh and unpredictable, that the believers should come together without undue claims to rank and prerogative. That large Shia complex of sentiments was there in Musa al Sadr's demeanor: what Matthew Arnold described as the "abnegation and mildness" of the Imams, the Alids, was present in this claimant of the Shia tradition.

The notion that men rebel to set themselves free is illusion. More to the point, they rebel to create more tolerable relations with authority, to submit to newer men, to different men. There are relations of command and obedience that sully those who submit to them, and others that don't. The classes of men responding to Musa al Sadr in the mid-1970s had gone beyond the old bosses in the country. The "rebel Imam" offered a new relationship of authority and submission. The old bosses had in effect said, "Submit, for I am your better." The activist cleric made no such (explicit) demand. He did not have to: he had in his favor the Mahdist element, the repressed messianic yearning in his people's history; he was, after all, presented to the crowd as a descendent of the seventh Imam. Men offering him obedience felt that they were paying homage to their own Shia tradition and history. A new relation of authority and command was presented as something very old and reassuring. This was not exactly the "end of time." But it was an unusual historical moment, ripe for a pretender. The Lebanese state was caving in; a familiar world was coming unstuck. A familiar system of authority no longer awed men, or sustained them. People denied the strength of age-old ways and were ready to follow, to be instructed, to be led.[38]

---

[38]Norman Cohn's *Pursuit of the Millennium* (New York: Oxford University Press, 1970), provides a relevant description of the "disoriented, the perplexed, and the frightened" who made up the followers of messianic pretenders in medieval European society. The world Cohn depicts comes close to the kind of world that gave Musa al Sadr his material and role: the great mass of the disoriented, the perplexed, and the frightened, rural or urban or both, turning to a millenarian Propheta: "Revolutionary millenarianism drew its strength from a population living on the margin of society— peasants without land or with too little land for subsistence; journeymen and unskilled workers living under the continuous threat of unemployment. . . . These people lacked the material and emotional support afforded by traditional social groups; their kinship-groups had disintegrated and they were not effectively organized in village communities or in guilds; for them there existed no regular, institutionalized methods of voicing their grievances or pressing their claims. Instead they waited for a *Propheta* to bind them together in a group of their own" (p. 282).

[153]

The "traditional" world was being shoveled under. The crowds that came to hear Musa al Sadr in the towns of the Bekaa or in Tyre were made up of day laborers who lived in Beirut, of tobacco planters engaged in a doomed battle with economics, of schoolteachers with grievances against the "system" that employed them, of newly urbanized men forced out of the south into Beirut by an Israeli-Palestinian war over which they had no control. For those who needed it, Musa al Sadr played the part of that extraordinary figure essential to a situation of breakdown and redemption. In him, men possessed an Imam. Shia history was open-ended. Each generation could see itself as the repository of the Shia vision of breakdown and redemption, as the group destined to live through the foretold events—the wars, the ruins, the moral upheaval, then the coming of a day when the world is set right and history is brought to its legitimate conclusion.

The dominant Shia reality always coexisted with the promise of a hazy millennium. The promise provided consolation; it made social and political arrangements seem transient and precarious. It left men ready for extraordinary figures. The Islamicist Marshall Hodgson has sketched the Shia temperament with its penchant for a messianic figure and for a band of followers coming together in anticipation of great changes:

> It was always possible that the foreordained leader (the Mahdi) might appear and test the faithful by summoning them, just as they were to launch the great social transformation themselves under his command, with the promise of divine succour when it would be needed. But even before he appeared, the social role of the various elements in the population took on a changed air for those who knew what was to happen. Every mundane historical event might presage or prepare the Mahdi's coming. The faithful were always on the alert, ready to take their part in the final acts. In this way, a chiliastic vision dramatized all history, in the present as well as the future.[39]

In the Lebanon of Musa al Sadr, as in Khomeini's Iran several years later, the ambiguity of the situation was respected. No one stood up and violated the scripture by proclaiming either of the two clerics the anticipated Imam. Men were left to their most powerful possession —their imagination. The line between the "Imam" in their midst and the Imam of the scripture and the faith was blurred.

If the past was being undermined, if men were being recruited and

[39]Marshall Hodgson, *The Venture of Islam*, vol. 1 (Chicago: University of Chicago Press, 1974), p. 374.

brought together for a new understanding in their history, it was important to provide them with a dramatic sense of change in their fortunes, in their ability to alter their situation. Musa al Sadr began with a simple and profound thing: the name of the Shia in Lebanon. Hitherto they had gone by the name of *Matawlah* or *Metoualis*. He broke with the old name. "Our name is not *Matawlah*. Our name is men of refusal (*rafidun*), men of vengeance, men who revolt against all tyranny . . . even though this may cost our blood and our lives."[40] The Matawlah of Lebanon became the Shia of Lebanon, *Shia-t-Lubnan*. The old name was a product of Lebanon's history. It carried with it the old patterns of dispossession and the old associations; it set the Shia of Lebanon apart, marked them as a distinctive group. On levels both conscious and subliminal, the new Shia identity linked men, through time and space, with other Shia in larger realms. Musa al Sadr's break with the name came in a speech in mid-February 1974, before a large rally in Bidnayil, a town in the Bekaa Valley, on an occasion commemorating the death of Zayn al Abidin, the fourth of the twelve Imams. Of all his speeches, it remained the one best remembered by those who followed him. This was an indication of the burden of the old name.

Etymologically the origins of the word *Matawlah* or *Metoualis* were obscure. But the origins were not so important. It was the weight of the word and its history that made it a label of defeat and humiliation. Travelers had spoken of the persecuted Matawlah. Sunnis of the city had derided the dirty Matawlah. Even sophisticated, upwardly mobile young men of the Shia community had mocked their elders, the hopeless Matawlah. The Matawlah were the sweeper, the porter, the pregnant woman with two or three children tugging on her dress. There was a Matawlah form of speech, a particular intonation that gave the Shia away. And, above all, there were taunting words flung in the face of an uppity Shia in the city, *Matwali Abu Thanab*, "a Matwali with a tail," an expression that city men had tagged onto the people of the hinterland. The old name had to be left behind. A man summoning men to rebellion and defiance had to provide them with a new identity. The new politics required a new name. Men don't unfailingly rebuild the world and conquer old fears and temptations when they set aside old names and identities. The old always lurks underneath what is new. New names are statements of intention. They lend some courage, some evidence that men are determined to break old chains. The men told by Musa al Sadr to cast aside the old

[40]*An Nahar*, February 18, 1974.

name were assured on another occasion that there were "one hundred million Shia in the world," that this large mass of humanity was to be found in "Iran, Iraq, the Soviet Union, Afghanistan, India, Pakistan, China, Turkey, Syria, Lebanon, the Gulf, the eastern provinces of Saudi Arabia, Yemen, and Oman."[41] There was something intended in the way the distinct Shia realms were specified: the range and the prestige of far-off places. It was an effort to rid men of their provincialism and their sense of their separateness.

And along with this, Shiism itself was endowed with an explicit political meaning. Shiism, said Musa al Sadr in an important formulation, was not a *madhab* (a particular school of interpreting Islamic jurisprudence) but a "movement of reform led by an elite vanguard" that remained true to the spirit of Islam "in the face of oppressive authority." In other words Shiism could not be confined to ritual and scholastics. There were four recognized Sunni *madhabs*. The view of Shiism as yet another—hence a deviant—*madhab* had turned Shiism into an embattled ghetto in the Muslim world. That view corresponded to the social situation of the Shia in the largely Sunni world of Syria and Palestine. The cleric educated in Iran and Iraq put forth a different conception. He situated the Shia "movement" within the mainstream of Islamic society: "In all that has come to us . . . from the twelve Imams whose words and lives constitute the principal source of Shiism, there is a fundamental commitment to the general Islamic line. A man in pursuit of knowledge looking into the teachings of the twelve Imams is unable to come away with an impression of sectarianism, of any distance from the *Umma*, the Islamic community."[42]

If the distance between Shiism and the "general Islamic line" could not be traced to the realm of religious doctrine, it had to be located in the struggle going on in the Muslim world between unjust rule and legitimate rebellion: in other words, in this cleric's formulation, that "revolutionary elite" that embraced Shiism fought for Islam itself:

> The main reason for the official pressure against the Shia in history was the fact that they were an elite minority with a total view of an Islamic order that was at odds with the dominant regimes throughout Islamic history. This is why the writings of the Imams and the opinions (*fatwas*) of the jurists were replete with explicit positions against deviant rule, against unjust authority. . . .
> It was natural that this elite minority, fighting in the name of Islam,

[41]This was developed in a lecture entitled "Shiism: A Movement and Not an Institution," reprinted in Musa al Sadr, *Nukhba Min al Muhadart*, p. 2.
[42]Ibid., p. 1

was fought with all available means—ranging from murder to exile and imprisonments to charges of deviation. Throughout the Muslim world today could be found remnants of these old methods of dealing with Shiism.[43]

The Shia pain and solitude were given an ennobling reading. Men weighed down by a history of embattlement were given a new vision of the larger Muslim world and of their role in it. Hitherto Shia Lebanon was too small and too timid to produce a vision of its own. The cleric offered it the strength of a reinterpreted Shiism: a Shiism stripped of its sorrow and its sense of embarrassment and defeat.

As always with this supremely political man, the reinterpretation of the past was a political tool. Until the mid-1970s the Shia movement of Musa al Sadr straddled the fence between a Maronite domination of Lebanon and a growing Palestinian armed presence. The Maronites had at their disposal the ideology of Lebanon as a unique country in the Arab East and the legitimacy of what there was of the state. The Palestinians had the themes of Arab history and the primacy of the Palestinian cause over the other quests. Banished from Jordan in a grim civil war in 1970–1971, the Palestinians had set out to establish a state within a state in Lebanon. Lebanon, they said, was part of the "Arab homeland," and they could not accept restrictions on their right to strike into Israel from Lebanon. The Palestinian cause was an overriding Arab cause. And Lebanon was—in the honest retrospective statement of a Palestinian leader, Shafiq al Hut—a "garden without fences."[44] It had a weak state, a fractured social order, and its feuding sects. Musa al Sadr walked between raindrops; he was an agile man. But it was too grim a time and place for anyone really to direct events. In a situation of escalating disorder the line between agility and perceived "betrayal" can be very thin indeed. Lebanon was a country being claimed by two armed camps, two militant truths: a Maronite truth and a Palestinian one dressed in a Pan-Arabist garb. The cleric had learned the ropes of his adopted country. Sayyid Musa had set out to teach men to press their claims against the state, to shed their fear and acquiescence. Disorder gave him political space and material to work with. But the disorder of the civil war that was to erupt in the mid-1970s was to give rise to total claims—both Pales-

[43]Ibid.
[44]Shafiq al Hut's description of Lebanon as a "garden without fences" was made during the Palestine National Council meeting in Algiers, February 1983. I myself did not see the text of this speech; the description was related to me by Harvard University social psychologist Herbert Kelman, who attended the Algiers meeting as an outside observer.

tinian and Lebanese—that tested the agility of the man in the middle. He had adopted Lebanon; he had crossed the Arab-Persian divide. Over the course of the preceding decade suspicion and doubts had trailed him. Detractors had their methods of dismissing his new identity, of reminding him of his Persian origins. A time of civil war and totalism was to bring in its train greater stresses. To be Lebanese now required loyalty to a threatened, and inflexible, concept of Lebanon upheld by the Maronites. And for a man born in Iran, to be an Arab meant to be certified by the Palestinians, to accept the prerogatives asserted by armed Palestinian organizations, and to take in stride the reprisals launched by Israel into the ancestral Shia land in the south of Lebanon. The questions about the chameleonlike figure, about his "Arabism," about his loyalty to Lebanon were not only questions about himself; they were, in so many ways, questions about the problematic identity of the community he led.

[5]

The Tightrope Act

There was in Sayyid Musa al Sadr an outsider's eagerness to please. This was an attribute of his personality that a sharp-eyed Christian admirer of his had referred to when he described the cleric's encounters with others as "rituals of seduction."[1] It was a quality that some in Lebanon who knew him associated with the land of his birth. (The image of a more subtle, more graceful, more ambiguous Iran had always been juxtaposed to a starker and harder Arab culture. Iranians, said a Lebanese referring to this dimension of the cleric's personality, could slit a man's throat with a piece of cotton.)

It was also a quality that raised questions about his sincerity. Sayyid Musa was a man who turned up at both churches and Palestinian refugee camps. He was a man who was careful to pay homage to the pieties of Arab nationalism, to refer to the Persian Gulf as the Arabian Gulf (a matter on which Pan-Arabists insisted). Yet Iranian bodyguards and plotters against the Shah of Iran were part of his entourage, and it was amid those Iranians, it was reported, that he really felt at home. He preached a gospel of peace and coexistence, but he presided over armed rallies and was the man who had declared to his followers that "arms were the adornment of men." The Lebanese establishment had made room for him, ministers and representatives of the president of the republic saw him off and received him at the airport on his frequent travels; yet there clung to him the air of conspiracy, the sense that he was a man with an agenda all his own.

For the larger world of (Sunni) Arab Islam, the ambiguity of the

[1]Ghassan Tueni, *Une guerre pour les autres* (Paris: J.C. Lattès, 1985), p. 98.

man was the ambiguity of his faith. In the development of Islamic civilization, there were two distinct cultural orientations: a *zahiri* orientation—literally meaning the external of things—that stressed the outward meaning of religious scripture, the apparent order of things, and a *batini* orientation that stressed the inward meaning of the faith, the esoteric, to which the majority was blind and which was only known to the initiated, to the ones who followed an Imam. The *zahiri* orientation was the one of mainstream Sunni Islam and its self-assured cities and institutions. The *batini* tradition became the culture of the disinherited Shia, of the underground. Here in Lebanon, in the persona of Musa al Sadr, was a quintessential embodiment of the *batini* tradition. No one quite knew what "the Imam" wanted and where he belonged. When things fell apart in Lebanon, when men took up arms and had to declare themselves and the country split into warring communities, the cleric of so many hints and messages who refused to be blown into the open was not quite Lebanese enough for those who had sponsored him in his early years or Arab enough for the Palestinians and their Lebanese allies.

In his rise to power Musa al Sadr had courted the Maronite elites. Their acceptance of him was crucial to his early endeavors. He and the Shia patricians around him shared with the Maronite custodians of power a common opposition to the Sunni susceptibility to Pan-Arabism. Both the Shia and the Maronites were bearers of traditions of insularity and separation from the Arab world around Lebanon. Musa al Sadr's case to the Maronites had been the standard one that reformers put forth on behalf of a disenfranchised population: the Shia, he had said, were men of Lebanon; given half a chance, given their decent share of the spoils, the patronage of the state, they would be "faithful sons" of that land.

But with the Palestinian push into Lebanon, the Maronites were in no mood to discuss reform and Sayyid Musa soon lost his Maronite pillar. The Maronites brooded about the country's purity, about their hold over their own world. For two decades luck together with the Levantine propensity for compromise, for looking beyond the passions of politics, had kept Lebanon out of the Arab-Israeli conflict. Luck was running out. Driven out of Amman by King Hussein's bedouin army, Palestinian pamphleteers had established a new base of power in Lebanon. Once-timid Palestinian refugees were making their camps into armed fortresses. The Maronite mountain watched the change with growing apprehension: new men with weapons, new sources of troubles, "strangers" multiplying and threatening a familiar world. It was no longer possible to retain the sense of security that had reconciled the Maronites to Greater Lebanon. Their beloved country was becoming an alien world. Panic pushed the Maronites behind their own line; they wanted to be on solid ground. The leading families among them, who knew the Arab world, who were once sure of their right to rule, of their ability to strike reasonable bargains with the other communities in the country, even with the Arab world beyond, were losing out to more purist men. As one observer put it, the change in the Maronite community that spawned militant militiamen was a "revenge of the 'small' Maronite, the hick, the red-neck over the typical figure of the entrepreneur."[2] The violated country had to be reclaimed. The Arab world indulged the turmoil in Lebanon, gave the Palestinians rope, made available money and weapons. Its irresponsibility bred an embittered sense of betrayal among the Maronites.

The Maronite sense of panic about a country adrift could be seen in a revealing issue that came up in 1972: discussion of a proposed law that would grant foreign heads of state the right to buy land in Lebanon without limits. The land of Lebanon, said the law's Maronite critics, would be bought up if the law was passed. The issue—at once tangible and a euphemism for broader concerns about the direction of the country—came up in the Maronite patriarch's pastoral letter of that year. The country, said the patriarch, was at a crossroads. "Plans have multiplied that would put Lebanese lands, Lebanese citizenship, as well as the resources of the country within the grasp of all, that would open wide its doors, plunge its politics into uncertainty, perturb its relations, and render obscure its options."[3]

Musa al Sadr's—and the larger Shia—relation to the Palestinians was more tangled and problematic still. The cleric had improvised and straddled the fence between the Palestinians and the Maronites when it was still possible to do so. He had made the standard statements of fidelity to the Palestinian cause required in Arab politics. Back in 1970 when the Palestinian presence in Lebanon was still reasonably modest and he himself still on the way up, he had offered the easy assurance that "the Palestinian resistance and Lebanese sovereignty are compatible," that the Palestinians could operate out of Lebanon and strike into Israel, and that such operations gave Israel no legitimate right of retaliation. Lebanon, he said, could not be a

[2]Tewfik Khalaf, "The Phalange and the Maronite Community: From Lebanonism to Maronitism," in Roger Owen, ed., *Essays on the Crisis in Lebanon* (London: Ithaca Press, 1976), p. 55.
[3]Patriarch Cardinal Paul-Pierre Meouchi's Pastoral Letter of 1972, reported with its complete text, in U.S. Embassy Dispatch, Beirut, January 12, 1972.

"policeman for Israel" and keep the Palestinians under control.[4] He positioned himself, or tried to, between the Maronites who opposed the Palestinian armed presence in the country and the Sunnis who offered the Palestinians their support.[5] Now and then he talked of the shared dilemma of the disinherited Palestinians and the Shia. But as the cycle of Palestinian incursion into Israel and Israel's reprisals into the south of Lebanon brought greater suffering in its train to his constituency, it was harder for him to offer a coherent response. The Shia, he told an American political officer, sympathized with the Palestinians, but "our sympathy no longer extends to actions which expose our people to additional misery and deprivation."[6]

Fate had played one of its cruel and ironic tricks. The Shia villages and towns passed over by history and large events were in the midst of a storm. The villages with unpaved roads had become, in the Palestinian scheme of things, a base for the "reconquest of Arab Palestine." The Palestinians offered no apology to the men and women of the south of Lebanon for the disruption of their lives. The place was made into a part of something larger than itself. And in the process the "mundane" claim of a rural people to its own land could be brushed aside. A still largely silent hinterland versus pamphleteers with stout lungs: it was an uneven match. Arab money came to the Palestinians from the Gulf states, from Libya. The nascent Shia movement led by the cleric was no match for the Palestinian organizations. The Shia were not as articulate and organized. The Palestinians belonged to the mainstream of Arab political life; they were men of the Arab urban order, the majority of them Sunni Muslims. When they had been dispossessed in 1948, they had found their way into Arab courts and nationalist movements alike. They knew the Arab world and its ways and its custodians of power; they participated in spinning the myths and symbols of Arab nationalism. The Arab world had not been able to retrieve for them what was lost in 1948 to the Zi-

[4]See *An Nahar*, May 27, 1970, and June 2, 1970.
[5]This was the way his course was seen as early as 1969, when the Palestinian presence was still under control in Lebanon. In his inaugural address as chairman of the Higher Shia Council, he spoke of the rights of the Palestinians, but he distanced himself from those in Lebanon who wanted greater Palestinian freedom of action. A diplomatic dispatch put it as follows: "In his approach to the question of *fedayeen* activity, Sadr continues to take a moderate position when he takes any position at all. By his public statements and in personal contacts, Sadr gives the impression of not wishing to become embroiled in an issue which can be of little direct benefit to his community and to himself as its leader." U.S. Embassy Dispatch, Beirut, October 10, 1969, State Department file A-414.
[6]This statement of September 1973, as reported in U.S. Embassy Dispatch, Beirut, April 3, 1974, State Department file A-65, p. 7

onists; it did the next best thing. It invited the Palestinians into the Arab councils of power. The Palestinian cause was far more compelling in the wider Arab world than that of a marginal Shia population. To that wider political and cultural order the Shia were strangers.

The Shia knew enough about Israel, their southern neighbor. They needed no elaborate education to tell them what would happen if and when Israel swept into Lebanon. They were sure that the Palestinians would be overwhelmed, that their own world would be trampled in the process. The Shia squatters in Beirut and in the southern part of the country lived in close proximity to Palestinian refugee camps. For the Shia, the Palestinian camps stood as a reminder of the ruin that befell men deprived of their land. The rage of the Palestinian camps and their political sensibility could not be that of the Shia. The Shia had the skepticism and the caution of their peasant culture. They had their land and their homes to lose. They wanted the Israeli-Palestinian fight to blow over, to spare them its fury. Like other Arabs far away from Israel's reach, they wanted to say that they stood by the Palestinians. But for them these Arab credentials could not be earned while life went on as usual. The Palestinian infrastructure in the south of Lebanon and in the Muslim sector of Beirut became a formidable dominion.

The people Musa al Sadr represented were between the rock and the hard place, between the claims of the Palestinians and the facts of Israeli power. Hell came to the quiet villages and towns of south Lebanon. The result was a virtual exodus from the south into the ghettoes of Beirut. The people in the middle of the Israeli-Palestinian war were in an untenable position. They were either "sympathizers with terrorists" or "collaborators with Israel." Palestinian incursions brought Israeli reprisals; at first a few homes were blown up; then entire villages were leveled—and deserted.

The tucked-away villages with unpaved roads may have once seemed like a prison; the demanding plots of land may have been worked and loathed at the same time. But when the forced departure had come, when the ghettoes of Beirut became a place where one had to settle rather than to visit every once in a while, nostalgia made of those villages pretty places of the imagination. The Shia who lost were asked to endure. Rage at the Palestinian anarchy and bravado had to be muzzled. Men who complained, who questioned the wisdom of the Palestinian course in Lebanon, could be charged with "treason." It was hard for the Shia, a community on the fringe of Arab history, to find the self-confidence to say that they could not accept the destruction of their own world.

Musa al Sadr himself was particularly ill equipped to deal with the Palestinians. He was anxious, excessively so at times, to assert his devotion to the Palestinian cause. He not only knew that he was watched and suspected; he had something of an urge to play the Pan-Islamic figure, to be true to a Pan-Arab cause—a response to the fact of his Iranian birth. Shiism, as the scholar Hamid Algar noted, had "effectively isolated Iran from the rest of the Muslim world, both in feeling and in action. . . . Traditions of Iranian cultural individualism increased the sense of separateness."[7] Iranians breaking out of that isolation have been prone to exaggerate their devotion to a wider Islamic truth beyond Iran.

In Sayyid Musa's Palestinian and Arab predicament were to be heard echoes of a somewhat similar tale: that of the great nineteenth-century publicist and ideologue Jamal al din al Afghani (1838–1897). Like Sayyid Musa, Jamal al din was born in Iran, the son of a sayyid. But Iran was too small for Sayyid Jamal al din—and its Shiism too much of a burden for a man who wanted to play Pan-Islamic politics. Jamal al din concealed his Iranian identity, claimed an ancestry in Sunni Afghanistan, and set out on a political career of pamphleteering and intrigue which took him to Afghanistan, India, Egypt, and Istanbul. He faked a more universal Islamic identity; the land of his birth, he said, was a "small narrow cage."[8] At its center, Sayyid Jamal al din's enterprise was a defense of what he saw as an Islamic world threatened by the West.

Musa al Sadr had not denied his birthplace or faked a new identity. He had crossed into his new country as a Shia cleric of Iranian birth, but Lebanese *asl*, origins. But the dilemma of his birth and the drive toward overcompensation that his Iranian and Shia identity engendered in him in an "Arab" setting should not be underestimated. Sayyid Musa was a compulsive traveler: his restlessness took him to the Arab states of the Gulf, to Kuwait and Saudi Arabia and Qatar, to Egypt, to Algeria. Acceptance in that Arab world which he courted and in which he remained a stranger could not come without Palestinian approval. Moreover, there was the harsh balance of military force: the Palestinians were armed and the Shia were not. Sayyid Musa and the men around him had to swallow the slights.

By mid-1975, Lebanon was in the throes of a full-scale civil war. To the extent that the war that became Lebanon's way of life for so many

[7]Hamid Algar, *Religion and State in Iran, 1785–1906* (Berkeley: University of California Press, 1969), p. 25.

[8]Nikki Keddie, *Sayyid Jamal ad-Din al-Afghani: A Political Biography* (Berkeley: University of California Press, 1972), p. 34.

years to come could be dated, it erupted in April 1975, in a fight between the Maronite Phalanges and the Palestinians. It was on a Sunday, April 13: twenty-one Palestinians were on a bus that went through Ain-al-Rummaneh, a Christian suburb of Beirut, a stronghold of the Phalange party. They were passing through the place right after the bodyguard of the patriarch of the Phalange, Pierre Gemayyel, was struck down by three unknown assailants. The bus was attacked; all its passengers were killed.

The episode at Ain-al-Rummaneh was the spark. The fight for the country had been in the making for the last four or five years. The militias, several of them, had been arming; the faith in the state and the fear of state power had been eroding. It was a free-for-all in the aftermath of Ain-al-Rummaneh. The killing began, and there was no likelihood that it would soon come to an end.

Ruinous new ideas began to emerge—half apologetically at first, then with abandon. In this climate Dar al Fatwa (the Sunni religious institution) issued a militant ruling with a theme new to this polity of sects: The "true Muslim" in Lebanon, read the text of the fatwa "could only be loyal to what Islam imposes on him, including the establishment of a Muslim state." The polity that had smothered differences was drawing fine lines.

In late June, Musa al Sadr took sanctuary in a Beirut mosque and began a fast as a gesture of protest against the violence in the country. He arrived at Al-Amiliyya mosque with four of his aides, his gown in one hand and a briefcase in the other. He sat in a corner of the mosque and dictated a message about the step he had embarked upon. "Violence," he said, "had defiled the country; I have come to the house of God, and my sustenance is the book of God (the Quran) and a few drops of water. I will stay here until death, or until the country is saved. I have bid farewell to my family, to my wife and children, and have come here to ask God to save this country."

His followers came in large numbers to the mosque, as he must have known they would. The event was staged with Musa al Sadr's usual flair for the media and for publicity. He was there to protest Lebanon's violence. But many of his followers came with weapons; he left instructions that no armed men be allowed to come close to the mosque. "Our movement," he said, "is a peaceful movement." Over the next several days, the country's elite flocked to see him. The press was on hand to report the comings and goings. Christian leaders and members of Parliament came; so did the representatives of Sunni Beirut's notables and his Sunni counterpart, the mufti of the republic. The Shia political and religious leadership was there as well. He would stay in the mosque, he announced, on his first day of fasting, until the country had a national unity cabinet, until men responsible for the kidnapings and the murders of the last two months were brought to justice. "I will be here," he said, "until the guns fall silent."

A delegation of women arrived on the next day and asked for permission to join the Imam in his sanctuary and his fast. He refused, but said that they could stay there for a while in a "symbolic fast" of their own. He had his blood pressure taken—he suffered from low blood pressure—drank a glass of salted water, then delivered the *khutba* (the sermon) of his second day: "Nonviolence is our way and our answer. Let anyone who comes to us with arms depart from us. I will not wield a sword. Our weapons are the words of God." A group of Christian clergymen joined the stream of visitors. "Lebanon was with him," he was told by a Catholic bishop. The Maronite patriarch called and said that his fast was a "blessed step." A Maronite priest sent word that he, too, was on a fast. In the city of Tyre, a group of Christian and Muslim women began a fast and said that they would break it only on instructions from Imam al Sadr.

More visitors came on the fourth day. Again, a large delegation of women appeared, women from the southern (Shia) slums of Beirut; they would stay with the Imam until his fast was over. He spoke to them about the role of women in Islam's struggle "since the dawn of Islamic history." He then explained what he was doing; he said he had sought sanctuary to save "the innocent who were dying, victims of barbarism and ignorance."[9]

Outside the mosque, in the city of Beirut and its suburbs, the violence continued. Snipers—a new phenomenon that came to epitomize Lebanon's dirty war—stalked the Beirut streets. On the fourth day of Musa al Sadr's fast, an eerie silence settled over the city. The streets were empty of pedestrians and of cars. In a sad and ironic piece of reporting, a journalist said that the empty streets of the city had frustrated the snipers: it was not a particularly good day for the snipers' work. The affair at the mosque may have been amateurish or hopeless. But it was better than the war that raged outside.

The fourth night of his fast was a gruesome one in Beirut—and in the rest of the country. An American dispatch described the chaos:

[9]My narrative of the fast relies on *An Nahar's* reportage, June 27–July 2, 1975. Also useful was a detailed American report, U.S. Embassy telegram 8335, Beirut, July 2, 1975.

The country in general and Beirut in particular suffered through another night as bad as any in recent memory. . . . Roving bands engaged armed residents in many parts of town. Night crawlers and other local low-life again made their rounds planting explosives all over Beirut. In Tripoli also more than twenty-five explosions were heard during hours of darkness. Zahle [a large town in the Bekaa Valley] was reported scene of clashes between rival factions. And Baalbek, Sidon, Tyre, and Nabatiyya are quite tense. Firing in Beirut itself was so heavy that fire engines were unable to reach several large fires and were forced to give up attempts to evacuate wounded. Casualties since afternoon June 30 may have run as high as 100 dead and several hundred wounded.[10]

Musa al Sadr's fast was broken on the fifth day, on July 1. He was visited on that day by Yasser Arafat of the Palestine Liberation Organization and by the Syrian foreign minister, Abdul Halim Khaddam, who was becoming Syria's broker and negotiator in Lebanon. The occasion for breaking the fast was provided by the formation of a national unity cabinet. A newly designated prime minister appealed to the Imam to break his fast and end his sanctuary. Promises were made that this particular cabinet would succeed where predecessor cabinets had failed, that calm would return. He thanked his visitors in the *khutba*, the sermon that he gave:

> I am honored that you came today despite the dangers that threaten anyone who comes here for we are surrounded by snipers, cowards who hide and cut down the innocent. We all believe in struggle; but weapons today are in the hands of merciless beasts. . . . Weapons are available to the few, also to the rulers. We could resort to force if we really wanted to. Our brothers in the Bekaa Valley and elsewhere wanted to come to Beirut with their weapons. We refused. Enough destruction and enough ruin have befallen this country. . . . All I want is Allah's blessing, and I know that His blessing comes from serving you.

The fast highlighted what Musa al Sadr took to be his advantage and that of the people who followed him. In the dirty war, he and his followers were saying that they had clean hands. The country needed an alternative to bloodshed, and he presented himself as the man who would provide that kind of peaceful alternative. Fresh from his fast, he set out for the Bekaa Valley, a part of the country with religiously mixed towns and villages. He toured some troubled towns in

[10]U.S. Embassy telegram 8335, p. 2.

the Bekaa with a Catholic bishop, and was mobbed in a Christian town by the townsmen who came to see and hear him. The town, Dir al Ahmar, had been the scene of Muslim-Christian clashes. It was his first stop after the breaking of his fast.

But Musa al Sadr was no Mahatma Gandhi, and Lebanon was not British India. Five days after he broke his fast, he had to make public the existence of a Shia militia, the nucleus of which he had established earlier. He had said of himself that he was a man who grew up in Iran without hearing the sound of a bullet; the Lebanese tradition of firing in the air during weddings and public gatherings had always confounded him. Yet in early July, he acknowledged that the diffuse Shia movement which rallied around him had an armed movement of its own. Hitherto, he had claimed for himself the high moral ground, and he had said that he stood outside the sordid game of militias and weapons. He had approached the question of weapons with ambivalence. On the one hand there was his proclamation that "arms were the adornment of men," that he was not a pacifist, and that violence was at times permissible to rectify injustice. On the other, he had preached against the cult of violence in Lebanon, and against the proliferation of armed groups.

Musa al Sadr acknowledged that he and his companions had a militia of their own only after an incident in the Bekaa Valley forced him to do so: twenty-seven of his young followers, Shia men from the Bekaa, the south, and the shantytowns of Beirut, were killed at a military training camp in the Bekaa when antitank explosives they were learning to use went off by accident. The name of the militia, Amal, was improvised in a hurry. (Amal, meaning "hope," was the acronym of *Afwaj al Muqawamah al Lubnanya*, the units of the Lebanese Resistance.) The training camp and the rudimentary military formation had to be explained. The men in the camp were being trained to go to the south and fight Israel; they were unlike other militias, he said. The movement to which they belonged would be an auxiliary to the Lebanese army in the south. And at a press conference, he held up a petition the wounded had written with their blood: "Let us be Husseini martyrs"—after the third Imam, Hussein, the symbol of martyrdom. For the first leader of Amal, he drafted one of his closest associates, Sayyid Hussein Husseini, a member of Parliament from the Bekaa Valley and a man of impeccable credentials within the Lebanese establishment.

With this public acknowledgment of a militia under his tutelage, Musa al Sadr had crossed the Rubicon; he accepted the verdict of the new era. His people needed an armed force of their own. The Palestinians had their fighters, as did the Maronites. The Druze in the Shuff Mountains were a clannish community with a long martial tradition behind them. Alone, the Shia were still unprepared for the new rules of the country. Sayyid Musa could deliver moving sermons and could stage general strikes or fast in protest against this or that injustice of the state. But these methods worked only so long as a measure of civil peace held. In a society at war, he had to play by new rules.

The performance and the tortured explanation could not hide his political troubles with the more conservative members of the Shia establishment. The Shia establishment was still caught between the emblems of state authority and the new politics of militias and arms. Its members were not ready to take the plunge into the new ways; they lacked the means and the self-confidence to declare that they, too—like the Maronites and the Palestinians—were free to resort to self-help and to establish a mini-army of their own. Besides, Sayyid Musa had many rivals in the Shia establishment, represented in full force in the Higher Shia Council. Many of them were anxious to set the cleric on the side of sedition, to claim for themselves what was left of the trappings of state authority. The man who had been close to the Maronite custodians of state power and to other members of the Christian elite in Lebanon was now venturing into a new territory beyond the security and the ordered world of legitimate politics. There was not much left of legitimacy to lean upon; yet the older members of the Shia establishment, for long quiescent, were still too timid to go their own way.

Musa al Sadr did the best he could under the circumstances. He exonerated the Higher Shia Council of any responsibility for the training camp. Amal, he said, had nothing to do with the council. He had given up on the council: this was his chance to say so in public. At a funeral for the "martyrs of Amal," which turned into a political rally, the chants for Musa al Sadr acclaimed him as the "Imam of the Disinherited" and the "Imam of the Mujhaddin" (those who struggle).

Into the ranks of Amal came a wide variety of politically active Shia youth. Some were *assimilés* formerly active in leftist and Palestinian groups; disillusioned with the Palestinians and the left, they now wanted to belong to a movement of their own sect. The country was giving up on universal and ideological pretensions; men were returning to the world of their kinsmen. A young lawyer from a noted Shia family who had thrown in his lot with the Palestinians back when he was a freshman at the American University of Beirut and who, in 1975–1976, was to break with the Palestinians and join the leadership of Amal, was illustrative of this trend. "My experience with the Palestinians," he said, "led me back to my Shia roots. The suffering of the Shia at the hands of the Palestinians made me see things with new eyes." It was a hard decision, says my informant of his break with the Palestinians; it was an "acrimonious divorce." The Palestinians, he says, had forgotten what they were supposed to be doing in Lebanon; the cause that had attracted him when he was eighteen could no longer sustain him seven years later. After several years of experience and fellowship with the Palestinians, he could see with greater clarity the "Sunni core" of their movement, he said. So after a difficult year of straddling the fence between Amal and the Palestinians, he opted for Amal. In earlier days, this young man had thought of himself as a "universal man, a cosmopolitan man." He was fluent in French and English and the son of an influential member of the Lebanese judiciary—a thoroughly modern young man of Beirut, well-traveled, well-read in Marxism, and quite enthralled with Marxist categories and ideas. In the Beirut of the mid-1970s, it was no longer embarrassing for a young man with this kind of outlook to find his way into a political movement inspired by a Shia cleric.

Others, also representative young men, who joined Amal were from a different social stratum. Some were newly urbanized youth, sons of peasants and small shopkeepers and artisans, who lacked the culture and education of my previous informant and who would have been reluctant to join leftist parties. A political activist, born in 1953, who was to join Amal and to become one of its principal leaders a decade later, was typical of his peers. He described himself as "the son of a small shopkeeper" from a village near Sidon; he was very specific about the size of the shop, wanting it noted that it sold just a few trinkets and basic commodities. He had a limited amount of schooling; he had not gone on to a university; he had no knowledge of foreign languages. He was religiously devout, a Shia who believed that Lebanon and its powers-that-be had not given the Shia a fair chance. My informant was a mere fifteen years old when he first saw Musa al Sadr. It was an occasion sometime in 1968 in my informant's village, a funeral, that brought Musa al Sadr there. Musa al Sadr's fame had, of course, preceded him. And after hearing his speech, this young man was convinced that the "Shia heritage" could be enlightened, that a man of religion could bring his religious learning to bear on social and political issues. My informant became part of Musa al Sadr's entourage, devoted to "the Imam" and his cause. It was only natural that he became one of the first members of Amal. In no other political movement would this man of humble origins have felt at home. His

Islamic devotion precluded a membership in the Communist party; he was too much a product of the Shia hinterland to believe that he could belong to the Palestinian movement. My informant had in him that combination of simplicity and cunning to be found in those who come of peasant stock. He accepted the sectarian nature of Lebanon; he accepted that the bearing of arms was a prerequisite of political power. For him, fidelity to Musa al Sadr was part religious devotion and part conviction that the cleric's way held out the only hope for simple men from the countryside such as himself. The social contract of the country had been violated; all Lebanon's principal communities were convinced that they had to fend for themselves. The new Shia militia was a piece with the new ways.

It was not within Musa al Sadr's power to call off the storm. The country's new realities sanctioned the use of weapons as a way of defending turf and the most elemental kind of rights. The Shia had a long history of submission: weapons had been denied them. Had the cleric chosen to repudiate weapons and self-defense, he would not have been followed. As it was, the best he could do was put together a makeshift armed movement with very limited means.

Over the horizon loomed a fight for the shantytowns of Beirut. Increasingly there was talk of "rounding out" military and geographic positions. The city of Beirut was a quilt of neighborhoods and sects: East Beirut was solidly Christian, West Beirut a Sunni stronghold; several Shia neighborhoods—slums in southern Beirut, an Armenian-Shia settlement north of the city—were vulnerable to the power of the Maronite militias. In a test of arms, these neighborhoods, and with them the place of the urban Shia in Lebanon, would be lost. Sayyid Musa toured these shantytowns in the summer of 1975. In them were to be found his most devoted followers. These neighborhoods, he said, built with toil and hard work, were here to stay. Those who talked about clearing them out, he warned, were laying the ground for partition of the country. Under these circumstances, the bearing of arms, was a "sacred duty."

But the militia notwithstanding, Sayyid Musa was no leader of men under arms. His gifts were those of the pulpit and the long-drawn-out meeting. Some Shia mullahs came to handle weapons and brandish rifles. Sayyid Musa never did. A young man who was the son of a family with close ties to Musa al Sadr remembers an outing in Baalbek sometime in the summer of 1975 which included, as well as Musa al Sadr, a rambunctious Iraqi cousin of his, Sayyid Hussein al Sadr, and a retinue of his friends. There were weapons in the hands of the group, and several began practicing and showing off their marksmanship. The cousin of the Imam then showed him some dum-dum bullets and explained that these were special bullets that exploded in the bodies of enemies who were hit. "It is strange," was Musa al Sadr's response, "that man not only kills other men, but perfects ways of doing it." Sayyid Musa did not possess the temperament of a warrior. He still pressed for a reform of the old status quo: he wanted state authority asserted in the south; he did not believe that a civil war could be fought and "won." And he knew all too well that his own community, just beginning to shed its quiescence and timidity, could not prevail in a test of arms. Military power and the funds to equip and pay for an armed militia were not easily available to it.

A painful proof of the weakness of his own position and of the desperate situation of the Shia was supplied in 1976, a year after the eruption of the civil war. The Maronite militiamen of the Phalange party, anxious to clear out a "canton" of their own, drove out a large Shia population—the estimates are somewhere from one hundred thousand to two hundred thousand inhabitants—from the Armenian-Shia squatter settlement northeast of Beirut. This settlement had been home for the Shia since the late 1940s, when they began to make their way from the villages of the south and the Bekaa into Beirut. West Beirut, the traditional home of the Sunni middle class, a sector of the city made up of houses with gardens, was still off limits to the majority of them. So they moved in next to the Armenians, into shantytowns that Armenian refugees had built when they came to Lebanon in the aftermath of World War I. It was there that a large Shia population had learned what it knew of the ways of the city.

That urban foothold was lost. Sayyid Musa railed against the Phalanges. Guarantees, he said, had been given to him by the leaders of the Phalanges that the Shia population in that part of Greater Beirut was safe. Partition of the country loomed on the horizon, he warned. He knew where de facto partition would lead: the Maronites would hold onto the portion of the country that was theirs, chaos would be let loose in the mixed areas, and he and his community would be left in a Palestinian-dominated territory.

Sayyid Musa did not share the revolutionary exuberance of those on the Lebanese left and among the Palestinians who believed that the political order of the country could be overthrown, that Lebanon could be turned into something new, into a secular republic, into some radical experiment. The first two years of the civil war (1975–1977) were a time of such illusions. They were held by the more extreme of the Palestinians; they were pursued as well by the enigmatic

Druze chieftain Kamal Junblatt, the Palestinians' principal Lebanese ally, who took the disorder as a chance to settle the old fight between the Druze and their Maronite rivals in Mount Lebanon. "We feel," said George Habash, the head of the Marxist-leaning Popular Front for the Liberation of Palestine, in a mid-1976 statement illustrative of his sensibility, "that the reactionary, bourgeois, confessional regime has collapsed and that the Lebanese National Movement would make a big mistake if it allowed this regime to be resurrected and reconstructed on a reformist basis. The Lebanese National Movement has a chance to insist on a new Lebanon—a democratic, nationalist, secular Lebanon."[11]

Musa al Sadr, the outsider who had learned the realities of the country, remained committed to the idea of a sectarian contract among the country's principal sects. He was suspicious of grand schemes put forth for Lebanon; he had a strong sense of pragmatism, of things that can and cannot be. Some parties on the Lebanese left, he noted in a mid-1976 discourse, want the Palestinian resistance to devote itself to overthrowing Arab regimes, beginning with Lebanon. This cannot be but a doomed path, he said: the Arab world was far too important in the global balance for such change to be permitted by outside forces. Nor could such a course, he added, be true to the Palestinian vocation. The Palestinians' cause was the pursuit of their own political salvation; anything else would be a betrayal of what the Palestinian issue was about. He was careful to hedge his bets: a distinction was made between "honorable" Palestinians and "extremists," between those who understood the limits of Lebanon and those who played with fire.[12]

He had helped to stir up a storm; he had been part of a revisionist coalition that had sought the redistribution of power in the country. But the storm that raged in 1976 was far mightier than he and others in Lebanon could handle. Like a magnet, the disorder pulled Syria across the border. Syria had fed the flames in Lebanon; it had armed the Palestinians and given support to the Palestinians' Lebanese allies. But when the actual fighting broke out in Lebanon, and when it appeared that a thwarted Maronite population would opt for partition of the country, the regime of Hafiz Assad, an officer from the Alawi hinterland of Syria, made an about-face, and Syria intervened

[11]George Habash, quoted in Fouad Ajami, *The Arab Predicament* (New York: Cambridge University Press, 1981), p. 146.
[12]This was the position he took in a public statement on May 4, 1976; leaflet in author's possession. The text can be found in Musa al Sadr, *Nukhba Min al Muhadarat* (A Selection of Lectures) (Beirut, no date), p. 25.

[173]

The Vanished Imam

on the side of the status quo. There would be no revenge against the Maronites, the Syrian ruler declared; and there would be no Palestinian and leftist republic on his borders. The shrewd Syrian ruler assigned roles in what was left of the Lebanese state. The Lebanese would tend to their own internal concerns, and he would bring the rebellious and difficult Palestinians under control.[13]

The Syrian intervention on the side of a slightly altered status quo —such then was Syria's course in the summer of 1976—was to be Musa al Sadr's raft. He had been cultivating the regime of Hafiz Assad for some time. Back in 1973, Sayyid Musa had rendered the Syrian minority regime an important service. Hafiz Assad had risen to power in a coup d'etat of 1970; in February 1971 he had become Syria's first Alawi president. The Syrian hinterland—rural, impoverished, religiously heterodox—had subdued the Sunni cities and had done it through the instrument of the military. But the Sunni majority could not accept the change with equanimity. The Alawis were the bearers of an esoteric faith which Muslims, both Sunni and Shia, put beyond the pale of Islam. Rebellions broke out in early 1973 in the principal cities of Syria when the regime released a draft constitution that omitted the standard reference to Islam as the religion of the state. Taken aback by the depth of the disaffection, the Syrian regime sought religious sanction, a ruling that the Alawis were a legitimate branch of Islam. This was where Sayyid Musa, then head of the Higher Shia Council in Lebanon, stepped in and provided a fatwa that the Alawis were a community of Shia Islam. The fine points of scripture and doctrine, the fact that the Alawis carried the veneration of Ali, the first of the twelve Shia Imams, beyond the strictures of Islam, he set aside. In the words of a deft summation by political historian Martin Kramer, "the regime of Hafiz al Asad needed quick religious legitimacy; the Shi'is of Lebanon, Musa al Sadr had decided, needed a powerful patron. Interests busily converged from every direction."[14]

That the mysterious Shia cleric from Iran lent legitimacy to the Alawi soldier from the Syrian hinterland seemed to the urban centers of Sunni Islam, both in Beirut and Damascus, less a strategic alliance

[13]Itamar Rabinovich has covered the twists and turns of Syria's role in Lebanon in his book The War for Lebanon, 1970–1983 (Ithaca: Cornell University Press, 1984). I also found particularly useful for an understanding of this period an unpublished essay by a young Lebanese political scientist, Farid el Khazen, entitled: "Confessionalism and Coexistence: Lebanon's Arduous Mission." The Johns Hopkins University School of Advanced International Studies, Spring 1982.
[14]Martin Kramer, "Syria's Alawis and Shi'ism," unpublished paper, Conference on Shiism, Resistance, and Revolution, Tel Aviv University, December 1984, p. 18.

[174]

dictated by political necessities than a coming together of two mysterious underground communities. Sunni ascendancy had ended in Syria; it was in its waning years in Lebanon. Arab nationalism in the Fertile Crescent had not come to terms in an honest and clear way with the sectarianism of these fractured societies. It had not integrated the hinterland and heterodox; it had raised the banner of a secular ideology and refused to recognize that the disenfranchised and the marginal would see that ideology as a wrapping for Sunni domination. Now events moved with velocity, and no one could come up with a social contract among the Lebanese sects at a time of great upheaval.

Among the Palestinians and the parties of Sunni West Beirut, Musa al Sadr came to be seen as an enemy of everything "progressive." He had not shared in the exuberance of the left; he could no longer tolerate the Palestinian control in southern Lebanon or pass over it in silence. To the "black turban" with a "black heart"—as he was now described—were attributed all sorts of sordid deeds and conspiracies. At a rally of the Palestinians and their allies in the coastal city of Sidon in the summer of 1976, a speaker would say that "everyone knew" that the cleric had been "thrown into Lebanon" by American intelligence, that "the people" were keeping watch on what Musa al Sadr was doing. The "patriots" in this land, it was declared, did not need to import faith and patriotism from Iran. His dramatic periods of fasting were mocked at another rally: The land, said one of the orators, could not be liberated by fasting and prayer, but only through "armed struggle."[15]

For the preceding fifteen years the cleric had been concerned with teaching men to take on the "ruling powers," the "feudalists," the "oppressors." Now Musa al Sadr and his constituents faced a new situation. He himself described the Palestinian/leftist alliance as the "new feudalism." We fought, he told his followers, the old feudalists, we stood up to them only to face a new kind of hegemony. Over and over again, he reiterated what this "small noble" people in the south had done for the Palestinian cause, the ruin they had endured. He said in his own self-defense that he was no lackey of Syria, that he only sought to cap the volcano in the country, to restore a measure of sanity.

Lebanon's war was proving to be a war without a turning point. After a while, no one bothered to count the cease-fires anymore. Solu-

[15]See Adel Rida, *Ma'al I'tidar Lil Imam al Sadr* (With Apology to Imam al Sadr) (Cairo, 1981), pp. 152–154.

tions to the country's problems eluded the declarations, the Arab summits assembled in Arab capitals to resolve the crisis, and the "spiritual summits" of the religious leaders of the country's sects. Lebanon as a whole was venturing into a new world beyond the familiar incantations and cliches, discovering along the way, as it were, new levels of barbarism and cruelty. In March 1977, the preeminent figure in the revisionist coalition, the Druze chieftain Kamal Junblatt was assassinated. "I am told I am next in line," said the cleric; he was ready for martyrdom, he said. He quoted Zayn al Abidin, the son of Imam Hussein, who had inquired of his father if the line of Hussein was the right one. When told by his father that it was, the son had said that he welcomed death. "Such," said the cleric, "was our way."[16]

As the massacres and the sectarian warfare went on, it became harder and harder for Sayyid Musa to say those things about Lebanon's tolerance, about its genius for pluralism, that he had repeated in the years of relative civility. He seemed increasingly less sure of the country and of himself. The period of 1976–1978 was not a creative period for him. He never quite recovered from the expulsion of the Shia from northeast Beirut at the hands of the Phalange militiamen. When, in the midst of a raging war, he again drew on his repertoire of Shia history and symbols, he was no longer trying to teach a quiescent community the ways of rebellion. A few years earlier when silence and acquiescence were his targets, he had exalted the memory of Imam Hussein; he had made the man who fell in rebellion a contemporary example. Now, lacking sufficient armed power, and seeing a country disintegrate, he called forth from the Shia heritage another figure: that of Zayn al Abidin (d. 713), the fourth Imam. He turned to Zayn al Abidin's legacy for a lesson in patience and perseverence—and for consolation that his community was no military match for its Palestinian and Maronite counterparts. Zayn al Abidin had survived the massacre at Kerbala. He had been too ill to join in the fighting; his life had been spared by the ruler Yazid. He had returned from Damascus, where the surviving members of Hussein's family had been taken after the battle at Kerbala, to Medina in the Hijaz, where he lived for another three decades, staying away from politics and devoting himself to prayer and to scholarship. A year after the episode at Kerbala, Yazid's troops sacked and looted Medina, putting a large number of its inhabitants to death. Zayn al Abidin was spared; he differed with the militant partisans of his cause who be-

---

[16]This statement of April 1977 is reproduced in Musa al Sadr's *Al Islam: Aqida Rasikha wa Manhaj Hayat* (Islam: A Firm Ideology and a Way of Life) (Beirut, 1979), p. 190.

lieved that *Khuruj,* an armed rebellion, was the proper duty of an Imam.[17]

Zayn al Abidin, said Musa al Sadr in an oration in early January 1978, never acquiesced in oppression or strayed from his father's message. He had only changed the means; he chose a method that was in harmony with the conditions of his time. The fourth Imam became a noted scholar; he lamented the fate of his father and the fate of the Muslims of his time. Muslims who came to him drew strength from his strength and patience. By refusing to tilt against windmills, to take on impossible odds, Zayn al Abidin had kept alive the cause of *ahl al bayt;* he was willing and able to bide his time. He opposed oppression but held his ground, refusing to acquiesce in the oppression or to rise in a doomed rebellion. Zayn al Abidin knew the harsh balance of forces. The power and the wealth of the Muslim world had long shifted from Medina and Mecca to Damascus. *Jund al Sham,* the troops of Damascus, were then the terror of the Muslim world. To have risen in rebellion against such impossible odds would have meant a sure death for him and a setback for his cause. The "pragmatism" of Zayn al Abidin was the symbol the cleric held up during a time of carnage. The "game of nations" he said, was a harsh one. Enough blood had been shed in Lebanon; the "small country," he warned, was faced with the threat of dissolution; unless its citizens could do better, the country would become the plaything of others.[18]

Lebanon's war, increasingly senseless and ferocious, snuffed out many lives—and reputations. Men saw conspiracies and betrayals in the deeds of anyone in the public eye. Musa al Sadr had always been a magnet for all sorts of speculations. There is, however, a portrait of him during this cruel time that gives a fair summation of what he was trying to do. It comes from what is surely the Lebanon war's best political memoir, a book entitled *Al Salam al Mafqud* (The Missing Peace), written by Karim Pakradouni. (Pakradouni, an influential member of the Politburo of the Phalange party, was throughout 1976–1982 an aide and confidant to Lebanese President Elias Sarkis, and an alter ego to the rising star in Maronite politics, Basheer Gemayyel. He was a liaison man between the Phalange party and the Syrian regime of Hafiz Assad.) Pakradouni, though a partisan, wrote his memoir with the flair of an artist, providing sharply etched portraits of the cast of characters, both Syrians and Lebanese, and the games they played. Here is his summation of Musa al Sadr:

[17]On the apolitical course of Zayn al Abidin's life, see ch. 9 in S. H. M. Jafri, *The Origins and Early Development of Shia Islam* (London: Longman, 1979).
[18]*An Nahar,* January 7, 1978.

A handsome man who cares about his attire, about his looks, about his image, and about his words. . . .

Stubborn, ambitious, courageous, a populist. He inspired in the Shia a belief in their demographic strength, in their historic heritage, in their Lebanese identity. Often did he say, for us Lebanon is a final homeland, *watan nihai.*

He was an enemy of communism. In particular, he was an enemy of Junblattism [after the Druze leader Kamal Junblatt, then head of the "National Movement" of leftist parties], to the extent that he became most hated by the Lebanese left. He accused the National Movement of wanting to exploit the Shia masses and use them as cannon fodder in its struggle against the Christians. He once said to me that the National Movement wanted to fight the Christians to the last Shia. In 1976, he put the blame for the drawn-out war on Kamal Junblatt. He said in front of me: "Had it not been for Kamal Junblatt, the war would have ended in two months. Now it has been raging for two years. And God knows when it will come to an end."

At the same time, the Imam was put off by the arrogance of the Lebanese Front [the Maronite-based group]. He told me in 1977: "It is intolerable for the Front to be so arrogant in its dealings with the Muslims, to treat them as though they are traitors. The ruling right bears responsibility because it ignored the Shia and the south since the dawn of independence. They are deprived. They have become the proletariat of Lebanon. Let no one fool himself. Every oppression leads to an explosion." This rebel condemned "the greed of the ruling right" as much as he did the "recklessness of the Palestinians and the progressives." He developed a political project independent of both. . . . He was the Khomeini of Lebanon. But he is an enlightened Khomeini.

As for his relations to Syria, they were erratic. He was a friend and confidant of Hafiz Assad. But he was wary of Syrian intentions. He did not hide his concern that Syria might partition Lebanon. Once in June 1977 he told me: "it is fortunate that Syria cannot digest Lebanon. . . ."

He became impatient with Palestinian provocations, so he took a decisive stand against the Palestine Liberation Organization. Shortly before his disappearance he said to me: "The Palestinian resistance is not a revolution. It does not seek martyrdom. It is a military machine that terrorizes the Arab world. With weapons, Arafat gets money; with money he can feed the press; and thanks to the press he can get a hearing before world public opinion." And he then added: "The PLO is an element of disorder in the south. The Shia have finally gotten over their inferiority complex vis-à-vis the Palestinian Organization."[19]

[19]Karim Pakradouni, *Al Salam al Mafqud* (The Missing Peace) (Beirut, 1984), pp. 117–118.

Pakradouni's account captures the man and his difficult position. For all the aura of mystery that surrounded Musa al Sadr—some of it cultivated, some owing to his being a foreigner—the essentials emerge in the Pakradouni account. This was a cleric at odds with the dominant order in the country because it was inflexible and closed; he wanted its gates open, and he wanted a place in it for the Shia and for himself. But at the same time he had no faith in the Lebanese left, not so much because its adherents were not "pious" believers, but because they had too many airy and abstract doctrines and because they were his rivals for the allegiance of the Shia youth. He sympathized with the Palestinians; he had in him that Shia and Iranian need to demonstrate fidelity to their cause. But like the people he led, he was to break with the Palestinians; he grew tired of the polemics, and he came to remind the Palestinians in public that they must not seek a "substitute homeland," *watan badil*, in Lebanon. He had had his start in the city of Tyre, a few kilometers away from the Israeli border. He knew, and repeatedly said, that Israel was bound to sweep into Lebanon, in a major way, if Palestinian incursions continued.

In mid-march 1978, Israel sent its army into southern Lebanon, in a large-scale drive against the Palestinians. The invasion was triggered by a Palestinian raid into Israel which had ended in the death of thirty Israeli civilians. More than ten thousand Israeli soldiers crossed into Lebanon. The aim of this invasion—the "Litani Operation"—was to destroy PLO bases in the south and to widen a buffer zone on the Israeli-Lebanese border under the control of a renegade Lebanese officer, Major Saad Haddad, who was Israel's surrogate in southern Lebanon. Israel had a new and tougher government, the Likud regime of Menachem Begin, which had broken the hold of Labor party Zionism over Israeli politics. Begin vowed to "cut off the evil arm" of the Palestinian guerrillas in Lebanon; henceforth the Israeli response to Palestinian provocations from Lebanon would be more severe than it had been over the preceding decade.

But Israel's military campaign was inconclusive. To no one's great surprise, the Palestinian forces in the south of Lebanon retreated with the civilians. It had never been their intention, the leaders of the Palestinian guerrillas said, to fight Israel in a conventional war. The "tactical withdrawal" was easy to pass off as a wise Palestinian decision. The Palestinians were dealt a heavy blow, but their sanctuary in Lebanon was not destroyed. The principal victims of the invasion turned out to be the Shia population of the south. They were the ones who bore the brunt of that war. "Hardly a house remains intact in

Nabatiye. There are only 25 to 30 families left in the once prosperous farm center of 40,000 inhabitants," reported an American correspondent on March 20.[20]

Inconclusive as it was, however, the invasion of March 1978 and its staggering human costs made it easier for Musa al Sadr to speak with greater candor about the Palestinian presence in the south and the dilemma of his people. In late March he made a speech in the form of an "open message" to the Arab world about the ordeal of the south. It was clear, he said, what Israel was doing in the south, what it intended there. It was setting up a "security belt" in the south, "pitting groups against one another, arming some, exploiting the fears of others." But what of the Arabs, he asked. The Arabs have "great fortunes" and assets, but they seem to be "passive spectators" while Arab land is lost piece by piece. The land in the south, he said, could not be rescued by the Palestinians, for Israel would be sure to claim that the presence of "non-Lebanese" in the south gave it the right to intervene there. Only the people of south could defend their land.[21]

There were Israeli plans for "settling the land" of the south, he said in a sermon of March 21, in a Beirut mosque. But he added, in a clear reference to the Palestinians, there were "Arab settlement plans" as well that would give the land of the south to others. These latter plans were the product of "laziness and complacency, of the evasion of responsibility" on the part of the Arabs. The men and women of the south were being uprooted. All the ills of "exile and displacement from the land" threaten them.[22]

Sayyid Musa talked of a "general Arab strategy" to confront Israel, but he was under no illusions; he knew that no such strategy was in the offing. He put before the wider Arab world the dilemma of his people in the south, told of the sacrifices they had made over the course of a decade of Israeli-Palestinian fighting. But he knew that he and the men he led were on the fringe of Arab society.

Still, he remained addicted to journeys to Arab capitals, to the hectic motion, to the press coverage. He went on a new round of Arab excursions in the spring and summer of 1978. This was now the standard practice of political men in Lebanon: to search in other lands for the social contract that eluded them at home. The cleric's travels took him to Saudi Arabia, to Jordan, and then to Algeria. It was on his visit to Algeria that it was suggested to him by the Algerian authorities that he should visit Libya's leader, Muamar al Qaddafi. Qaddafi had

[20]*The New York Times*, March 21, 1978.
[21]See the text in *An Nahar al Arabi wa al Dawli*, March 26, 1978.
[22]Copy of this sermon provided to the author by Sayyid Hussein Husseini.

"ideas" for Lebanon, and Qaddafi had funds. Imam al Sadr had not been one of Libya's men in Lebanon. The Libyans had their Lebanese clients, the Nasserite parties and groups in West Beirut; and they had an erratic relation with the Palestinian groups in Lebanon. From the safe distance of Tripoli, Qaddafi urged a war across the Lebanese-Israeli border; he wanted the Palestinians and the Lebanese to live out his revolutionary fantasies.

Qaddafi and the cleric had met only once, in 1975, when Musa al Sadr had gone to Libya to attend a conference. The Libyan colonel and the cleric were men of radically different temperaments. The meeting, so the Shia sources report, had ended in disagreement. Qaddafi, not a particularly subtle man, had brought the meeting to an end by slouching in his chair and pretending to go to sleep. A year later, he had sent his prime minister to Lebanon to make the rounds and meet with all the principals in that country's feuds. The Libyan prime minister stayed two months in Lebanon and Syria; summoning a bit of tolerance he had even met with Pierre Gemayyel, the head of the Maronite-based Phalange party. Musa al Sadr was excluded from that round of meetings. But the Libyan invitation—solicited by the Imam according to the Libyans, suggested by the Algerian authorities according to the Shia sources—was accepted. The cleric, the Libyans were told, would come on August 25.[23]

Two days before the trip to Libya, an article of Musa al Sadr's on the struggle in Iran between the Shah and the religious opposition appeared in *Le Monde*. Iran was now consuming more of his attention. His birthplace, in rebellion since January of that year, had its claims on him. ("The Imam," as the Egyptian journalist Mohamed Heikal said of him, "had his fingers in too many pies.") The essay in *Le Monde* was tinged with the early liberal hopes pinned on the revolution. It was a plea for fairness to the opposition in Iran, for an understanding of the struggle in his birthplace. An "authentic revolution" was unfolding in Iran, he wrote. It was not a revolution of the right or the left, but of a people in all its diversity: "Students, workers, intellectuals, and men of religion participate in this revolution." The revolution's leader, "le grand Imam El Khomeini," has expressed the "national, cultural, libertarian dimensions of this revolution." The most

[23]There are two detailed memoranda by the Higher Shia Council that summarize the tangled set of events that began with Musa al Sadr's trip to Libya and document the search for him. One is entitled "A Summary of Initiatives and Efforts Connected with the Disappearance of Imam Al Sadr and His Two Companions." The other consists of a text of a communique about the disappearance of Musa al Sadr issued by Libya on September 17, 1978, and a point-by-point rebuttal of it by the Higher Shia Council. Both are official documents of the Higher Shia Council, published in Beirut, 1978.

heavily armed regime in the Third World, claiming to defend progress, is crumbling, he wrote, and "civilized men" everywhere could identify with Iran's struggle.[24]

The journey to Libya on August 25 was made with two companions—a younger cleric, Shaykh Muhammad Yaqub, who served as something like the Imam's cheerleader, and a journalist by the name of Abbas Badr al Din, who was to cover the trip, sending back items about Musa al Sadr's Libyan excursion to Beirut's papers. A handwritten letter from Sayyid Musa to a distinguished friend and supporter—a technocrat in Amman with close links to King Hussein—showed no great enthusiasm for the Libyan visit. Sayyid Musa would come to Amman soon, he said, as soon as the trip to Libya was over. The cleric inquired about the king of Jordan, wished him well, said he was looking forward to seeing the Jordanian monarch again.[25]

It was a journey made for greed, the cleric's detractors said: another political man of Lebanon going to Libya with a tin cup, asking for money. Worse still, those who suspected the cleric said that he was summoned to Libya to account for Libyan money he had already received. It was a journey of obligation, his supporters claim. A man had been invited to an Arab capital, through Algerian mediation, and was going to put before the Libyans the concerns of his people.

Lower-level officials received him in Libya. He was made to cool his heels and wait for Qaddafi. On August 30, he did what he was so good at: he gave another interview, this time to a Kuwaiti magazine, *Al Nahda*. In it he reiterated his standard themes; he spoke once again of the people of the south of Lebanon and their sacrifices on behalf of the Palestinians. The Shia, he said, have lost their homes and their land; some of these losses could have been avoided, had they chosen a safer course, had they chosen to accept collaboration with Israel. He was in a militantly anti-Israeli place, in a country which had suspected his motives, which was unyielding in what it expected of other Arabs, and the strain shows in his interview. "We have nothing left to lose in Lebanon. Let our Arab brothers with all their fortunes and their land realize that they too are threatened."[26] The Arabs far away from Israel's power were being asked to consider the crisis of those caught in the crossfire of the Israeli-Palestinian war.

The next day, August 31, was the last the cleric was seen in public. At midday Sayyid Musa and his two companions were seen leaving

[24]Musa al Sadr, "L'appel des Prophètes," *Le Monde*, August 23, 1978.
[25]Letter from Musa al Sadr, Beirut, August 24, 1978 to Ali Ghandour in Amman, Jordan. The letter was made available to me by Mr. Ghandour.
[26]Text is reproduced in *Nukhba Min al Muhadarat*, p. 109.

their hotel. He was on his way, he told a group of visiting Lebanese who encountered him, to a meeting with President Qaddafi. This was the day of the Imam's disappearance.

Six days of silence ensued. There were no further press items about Musa al Sadr, no statements from him to the press. On September 1 the Qaddafi regime celebrated the ninth anniversary of the military coup d'etat that had overthrown the Libyan monarchy and brought Qaddafi and his fellow officers to power. Musa al Sadr was not at the celebration, which he had been invited to attend. And in a break with the cleric's routine, no phone calls were made to his family or to any of his companions and confidants in Beirut.

The alarm bells went off on September 6. The Shia hierarchy in Beirut contacted the Libyan embassy and inquired as to the whereabouts of Musa al Sadr. The Libyan legation said that it would cable home—that is, it would get back in touch with the needed information—and that it saw no need for worry or alarm. When the promised information did not materialize, further inquiries were made to the Libyans by Musa al Sadr's companions in the Higher Shia Council, and by members of the Lebanese government. And on September 10, after an official inquiry from the Lebanese government, the Libyans said that the cleric and his companions had left Libya for Rome, on Alitalia flight 881 of August 31. Two days later, *As Safir*, a Lebanese daily paper financed by Qaddafi, said that perhaps Musa al Sadr's disappearance was connected to the "events in Iran"—the escalating struggle between the Shah and the broad religious-secular opposition arrayed against his regime.

Then on September 17, the Libyans provided what they intended to be their definitive statement on the matter. It was a statement issued by the Secretariat of Foreign Affairs. The Imam, the Libyans said, had been "warmly received" by Libyan officials. At his request, the Libyan authorities arranged for his flight to Rome, with his companions, on August 31. The rumors about his still being in Libya were being spread by "malicious circles" trying to "explode the situation in Lebanon, the last stronghold of the Palestinian Revolution."[27]

But the rumors continued. One rumor placed him in Amsterdam, a victim of kidnaping; another had him returning to his birthplace in Iran to participate in the final push against the Shah. On other days reports had him arriving in Syria, or in Iraq to visit with Ayatollah Khomeini, then still in exile in that country. In one diplomatic dis-

[27]The Libyan official text about Musa al Sadr's disappearance was provided, in its English version, to the U.S. Department of State on September 20, 1978; obtained from State Department documents declassified for the author on October 25, 1984.

patch, filed from Beirut, he was said to be "in Malta or near Lake Como": he was being kept there by Qaddafi's agents, who were "teaching him a lesson." "Keep an eye out for him," the dispatch added to those receiving it in Italy; he was "a tall man, wears a turban and long robe. Very attractive to women." Another diplomatic cable, this one filed from Teheran, said that the missing cleric was in Syria, a "guest of President Assad." The information was said to have come from the cleric's wife. Imam al Sadr, this cable reported, had gone to Damascus after spending "several days with Khomeini in Iraq."[28]

Then, inevitably, there were reports of his death—reports citing sources whose "credibility could not be established." In one such report, Imam al Sadr was said to have been killed on August 31, the last day he was seen in public. He had "gotten into a heated discussion with his Libyan hosts," this American cable reported. "The Libyans wished to intimidate the Imam and in the course of this intimidation, a Libyan struck the Imam a lethal blow." The whole thing was "an accident." There has been "no intention" of killing the Imam. The Libyans were "remorseful that the glove was not velvet enough."[29]

The Imam's followers wanted him back. His posters were everywhere in the Shia ghettoes of Greater Beirut and in the south of Lebanon and the Bekaa Valley. His followers read into his disappearance in that forbidding, faraway Libyan setting their own bitterness, their own sense of exclusion from the wider Arab society around them. The Shia *marathi* had mourned the beheading and the death by poisoning of so many of Imam Ali's descendants. The Shia literature of martyrology was rich in its depiction of the cruelty of the usurpers who killed the Shia leaders and pretenders; it made the rulers and soldiers who prevailed in their uneven fights with *ahl al bayt* embodiments of cruelty. And it grafted onto *ahl al bayt*—the doomed minority, the orphaned children, the wailing women—the popular yearning for virtuous martyrs. Muamar al Qaddafi and Musa al Sadr could have easily stepped out of the Shia literature and the Persian miniatures that reproduced scenes of struggle and defeat: a merciless soldier and an unsuspecting guest who had walked into a treacherous place. A Persian miniature of the kind hung in the homes of the peasants and the poorer classes of the Shia urban population depicting the poisoning of the eighth Imam, Ali al Rida (d. 818) by the ruler of the time, Al Mamun. Al Mamun, so the literature of martyrology maintained, had invited Ali al Rida to be his successor, and then, in a

[28]U.S. Embassy Dispatch, Beirut, September 1978; cable 05714–0107082. U.S. Embassy Dispatch, Teheran, November 1978; cable 078049–0390.
[29]U.S. Embassy Dispatch, Paris, November 1978; cable 0780489–0390.

change of heart, had him poisoned.[30] Rule was capricious: the Libyan ruler acted out the part that the imagination of a historically vanquished people expected men in power to play.

Nearly a month after Musa al Sadr's disappearance, Muamar al Qaddafi arrived in Damascus to attend a conference of the presidents of four radical Arab states—Syria, Libya, Algeria, and South Yemen —and Yasser Arafat, chairman of the Palestine Liberation Organization. It was one of the many summit meetings that brought together Arab states opposed to Egyptian President Anwar al Sadat's bid for peace with Israel. Four Shia clerics from Lebanon crossed into Syria to meet with Qaddafi and inquire about the missing Imam. They came to do what the Shia have been doing for so many centuries: to petition, to appear with a grievance before a man with power. But the four clerics did not come alone; they appeared at the head of some two hundred thousand protesters. A convoy some fifteen kilometers long—men in "cars and buses and tractors"—poured into Damascus. The placards and banners they carried were rich in meaning and insinuation: "Oh Arabs, where is the Imam?" read one placard. Another referred to one of Muslim society's sacred norms, that of hospitality and the pledge of safety any host extended and owed a guest: "Is this the way you treat your guests, oh Arabs?" A memorandum was submitted to the assembled heads of state and a meeting with Qaddafi was sought by the four clerics.[31] The meeting was granted. And the four of them were ushered into Qaddafi's hotel suite, at the Damascus Sheraton.

The Imam, the clerics said of the missing leader, was a mortal man. His people could understand and accept his death. But they could not accept that he could disappear, be "dissolved like some grain of salt." The clerics reminded the self-styled man of the desert of the strictures of Arab hospitality. Hospitality was owed one's enemies, let alone one's guests, they said. The four clerics were preservers of Shia history and orthodoxy. They knew by heart what befell the Alids down through the ages; the elegies and the history that the clerics had memorized and recounted told of the ease with which rulers devoid of scruples annulled the pledges of safety accorded to guests, rivals, and petitioners. The clerics knew that there were loopholes and ways around the pledges extended by rulers. In the searing history of Shiism and its struggle with the ruling powers in Muslim society, all sorts of atrocities were committed by the vassals of the rulers, with

[30]Abu al Faraj al Isfahani, *Maqatil al Talibiyyun* (The Martyrdom of the Talibids) (Najaf, Iraq, 1934), pp. 368–374.
[31]*An Nahar*, September 22, 1978.

the rulers feigning innocence. A tale from the reign of the Abbasid caliph Harun al Rashid (ruled 786–809) told of the murder of one of the Alids, one Abdullah Ibn Hassan, by Harun al Rashid's minister. The victim's severed head was presented to the ruler among the gifts given to him by the minister anxious to please. The ruler had wanted the deed done. But later, when the minister ran afoul of the ruler, the caliph reminded him of the blood of the murdered Abdullah Ibn Hassan, "whom you killed without my permission."[32] There were rumors and hints in the days that followed Musa al Sadr's disappearance that "zealous" aides of Qaddafi had assassinated Musa al Sadr without Qaddafi's permission. History sat in, as it were, on the meeting between Qaddafi and his four visitors.

The Libyan ruler offered no apologies. He brought up the matter of Musa al Sadr's origins. "I am told that Musa al Sadr is an Iranian; is he not?" he inquired. Lines were being drawn and the missing cleric was being placed beyond the bounds of the Arab world. The clerics in search of their leader went over Sayyid Musa's origins. They told of his Lebanese background, of the escape of Saleh Sharaf al Din, Sayyid Musa's ancestor, from Lebanon to Iraq. Then they related how Sayyid Musa's father had left Iraq in the 1920s; and they told in the way men careful about lineage and descent trace such matters, of the contribution that the Sadr family had made to the politics and culture of Iraq. The clerics' rendition put Sayyid Musa and his family on the *Arab* side of the great divide between Arabs and Persians. They then went on to something that must have been on Qaddafi's mind: the Imam's political "credentials" gained in the struggle in and over the south of Lebanon between Israel and the Palestinians. The Imam, the clerics explained, had fought for the people of the south, for their control over their land. The Imam had gone to a village that had been subjected to Israeli bombing; he had prayed in its mosque and advised the people to fight for their land. Sell your cow, he had said, your sheep, your bedding, but buy a weapon and hold onto the land. The Imam had warned that southern Lebanon alone could not bear the burden of the encounter with Israel. This was an Arab responsibility, he had said. The cause of Palestine was "dear to the Imam," the colonel was told. But the Imam did not believe that matters in the south could go on much longer as they had before. Sooner or later Israel was bound to strike. Was the Arab world ready to do much for these marginal men led by the Imam?

The clerics' meeting with Qaddafi was futile. Qaddafi promised to

[32]Isfahani, *Maqatil al Talibiyyun*, p. 329.

[186]

look into the matter; he talked about how much he had learned from and had enjoyed the writings of Sayyid Musa's cousin, Muhammad Baqir al Sadr. He said that he was working on bringing about the "doctrinal unity" of Sunni and Shia Islam, that the Islam that prevailed in Libya and North Africa was free of the kind of schisms present in Lebanon. He knew, he said, that the Shia of Lebanon were in the line of fire in the south and that they were the most oppressed community in Lebanon. Qaddafi reiterated that he made no distinction among Muslims and he told them of the contributions his regime had made to the Muslims in Malta and Africa and the United States. Libya's foreign minister, said Qaddafi, would be in touch with the clerics and with the Higher Shia Council in Lebanon should any information become available about the missing Imam.[33]

Others, outside Lebanon, called on Qaddafi to release his guest or, at least, to provide a credible explanation as to the whereabouts of Musa al Sadr. From the city of Qom, Ayatollah Muhammad Kazem Shariatmadari—probably Qom's most prominent marja, usually a cautious and apolitical man—sent the following cable to Qaddafi: "People in all lands know that Imam al Sadr was invited to your country and had gone there. . . . Thus all Muslims ask the Libyan government, whom they consider responsible for this disappearance, for information about the health and well-being of the Imam."[34] A more subtle letter, a private one, was sent to Qaddafi from King Hussein of Jordan. The wording had the care and reserve of the man who sent it, who spoke as one head of state to another. The "brother President" was reminded of the stature of his guest: Imam al Sadr was a "luminary of the Muslim world," Qaddafi was told. It was in the interest of all Arabs, observed the monarch, that this matter be brought to a quick end. The king, himself a Sunni Muslim from a family whose members are sayyids and Sharifs, descendants of the Prophet Muhammad, alluded to the "sectarian dimensions" of this case—a Shia man of religion coming to harm at the hands of a Sunni ruler. These are "sensitive and difficult times" for the Palestinians and for all Lebanese, the Jordanian monarch said. He put his good offices at the disposal of Qaddafi: "Help us so we can help you, with God's permission."[35]

[33]See Adel Rida, *Ma'al I'tidar*, p. 165.
[34]The text of Shariatmadari's cable is in the publication "A Summary of Initiatives and Efforts Connected with the Disappearance of Imam al Sadr," published by the Higher Shia Council.
[35]A copy of King Hussein's letter to Qaddafi, written on February 14, 1979, in Amman, was made available to me by one of the advisers of the Jordanian monarch.

[187]

Sayyid Musa had traveled to Libya with a Lebanese passport, and the Lebanese government went through the motions of inquiring about him. But the Lebanese government could not push Qaddafi too hard. Far too many Lebanese worked in Libya and depended on Qaddafi's good will for Lebanon to antagonize the Libyans. The country that lived off remittances and emigration could not antagonize the colonel with oil wealth. Besides, the Lebanese president, a technocrat with little power, felt no strong attachment to Musa al Sadr. "The Imam," said President Elias Sarkis to one of his aides, "hints more than he clarifies, disturbs more than he reassures."[36] It would be better, said the Lebanese president, for Syrian President Hafiz Assad and the Algerian authorities to use their influence with Qaddafi. There was not much he himself could do: he was a president without a state, and a technocrat in a land of rival militias. He had other things to worry about. He was caught between the growing militancy and panic of his own Maronite community and the Palestinian movement of Yasser Arafat. He had a large Syrian army that both sustained him as a client of Syria and diminished him. No particularly strong ties bound him to the Shia. And in the scheme of things, the Shia of Lebanon were still relatively quiescent. The man who had helped stir up a storm in Shia Lebanon was out of the way.

Lebanon still had its two principal warring camps: the Maronites with their sense that a country that was theirs had to be redeemed —or, failing that, partitioned—and the Palestinians and their cover, the militias of West Beirut that gained some power with Palestinian backing and support. In the long run the Palestinian position was untenable. In a world of states, the Palestinian case for the kind of presence and power they wielded in Lebanon could not be sustained. But precisely because their case was so problematic, it was imperative for the Palestinians to go on with what they were doing, to silence those who pointed out the dilemma of a Palestinian armed movement paying homage to the sovereignty of an Arab state and at the same time emasculating it. There was no Palestinian state to be had, no other political space outside Lebanon where Palestinian power could be exercised. The Palestinian leaders had two choices. They could break with an entire legacy of Palestinian history and come to terms with Israel, bid farewell to the "armed struggle," try to save what was left of Palestinian lands on the West Bank of the Jordan River. Or they could protect and hold onto what they had in Lebanon, the "substitute state," with all its illusions and consolations.

Somewhere between these two claims over Lebanon stood the

[36]Pakradouni, *Al Salam al Mafqud*, p. 118.

Shia. The third bid for the country, the Shia bid, had not yet been made. But its ingredients were there. They had been there for some-time. Lebanon's last official census, taken in 1932, had put the Shia population third in line behind the Maronites and the Sunnis. It had estimated that population at little more than a hundred and fifty thousand, mostly rural inhabitants, constituting some 18 or 19 per-cent of the country's population. By the mid-1970s it was known—in the way Lebanon knew things but never acknowledged them—that the Shia had become the country's largest sect. No one was sure of the exact numbers. A new census that would document the demo-graphic change was politically explosive, and therefore it was prohib-ited. But by 1978 there were figures that put the Shia population at something like nine hundred thousand inhabitants, approximating nearly 40 percent of the country's population.[37] And they were no longer a rural population, nor were they, for that matter, as econom-ically disadvantaged as the discourse about "disinheritance" and the stereotypes of the past made them out to be. Some of the great for-tunes in Beirut belonged to them—money made in West Africa, or in the Arab states of the Gulf, or in Lebanon's economy of speculation.

When the Shia bid for power was made, it would draw on Shia wealth seeking a political voice, on the ambition of a new Shia middle class created by education and some prosperity, and on the multitude of the urban poor, ready to bear arms in a place where arms were be-coming badges of self-worth and instruments with which turf was se-cured and protected. The truth and the claims of a sect were to be more important than the claims of socioeconomic categories. And in this Musa al Sadr was proved right: he had put forth an idea that claimed to encompass rich and poor, to smother the differences of class; he had said that there was something more to the making of history than economic forces. Deep within the men with some wealth and education, and more readily so in the case of the poor, Musa al Sadr had appealed to the pull and burden of Shia history. He had ap-pealed to the authority of the ancestors. Soon after his disappearance, the voice of the past pronounced on contemporary reality throughout the realm of Islam with new-found confidence and stridency.

Of heroes and men creating them and drawing on their myths, the psychiatrist John Mack has observed: "During his lifetime the hero has some, though often limited, control over what he would wish to

---

[37]Population figures are a matter that borders on the theological in Lebanon. This is not an issue that could be resolved here, but there is an attempt at something solid in a piece entitled "Demographic Developments in Lebanon," by Joseph A. Kechichian, *International Demographics*, 2, number 6 (1983), pp. 3 and 11.

represent. After his death he becomes public property and his meaning for history is determined by those of his works which endure and by the interpretations of his historical audience." The creation of a heroic myth, he writes, depends upon "the compliance of history, the coming together of special events and situations with unusual men and women who take hold of these circumstances."[38]

In his peculiar and powerful status—absent and thus above the fray, with no one quite willing to come out and announce his death —Musa al Sadr had become "public property" of Iran, of Shia Lebanon, of Shia Iraq. Many strands of Shia history were woven around him: the martyrdom of Imam Hussein; the mildness of many of Hussein's successors who saw the worldly struggles of men as things corrosive of the soul; then the obvious Shia themes of the Ghaiba of the Imam and his anticipated rujuh. What he represented was something very old, with a special sanctity of its own. Yet he was as trendy and new a man as the modern reality of Islam could call forth. Of the "compliance of history" there was aplenty in Musa al Sadr's life and work. Whoever removed him from the scene had been Shia history's unwitting tool.

[38]John E. Mack, *A Prince of Our Disorder: The Life of T. E. Lawrence* (Boston: Little, Brown, 1976), pp. 216–217.

[6]

The Legacy and Its Inheritors

Several months after Musa al Sadr's disappearance, the Iranian revolution pushed the Shah's regime over the brink. The once embarrassing symbols of Shia Islam were exalted. Men no longer awaited the millennium; they proclaimed that in Iran they had an answer for the ailments of the Muslim world. The Shia of Lebanon had become part of a larger story. And Musa al Sadr himself came to serve an entirely new function. He was a man of double identity, claimed by the Iranians and by the Shia in Lebanon; he embodied the bonds, both real and imagined, between the two.

The clerical revolution in Iran under the leadership of Ayatollah Khomeini brought a change in the relation of the Shia to the larger Arab world and its symbols. In times past, when Pan-Arabism was the strident faith of large Arab cities, and when men and women of the Shia hinterland were making their way to Beirut and its surroundings, the "Persian connection" of the Shia of Lebanon and other Arab realms was carried like some dubious and embarrassing baggage.[1] Now the Iranian revolution stood history on its head. A major revolt had succeeded in the name of Islam and cultural authenticity. A political tradition of submission gave way to a messianic movement; Shia clerics who once summoned men to worship, who monitored ritual, were summoning men to arms.

Iran's revolutionaries threw their weight into the search for Musa al

[1]See the essay by Abbas Kelidar, "The Shi'i Imami Community and Politics in the Arab East," *Middle Eastern Studies*, 19 (January 1983), for a perceptive analysis of the problematic relation of the Shia to Pan-Arab politics in Lebanon, Syria, and Iraq.

The Vanished Imam

Sadr. Years earlier, when Iran had seemed cut off from the Muslim world around it, Musa al Sadr had carried Iran's truth and education to a then-distant place. Now Iran's message seemed to cross borders with remarkable ease. Iranian clerical revolutionaries did not have to toil arduously to assert some community of faith and interest with the Shia of Lebanon. They appropriated and drew on that special Iranian personage who had lived and worked amid the Lebanese. Fidelity to the missing cleric was a potential bridge between Iran and Lebanon.

From exile—first from Iraq, where he had been living since 1965, then from France, to which he had gone in early October 1978—Ayatollah Khomeini had sent cables and emissaries to Muamar al Qaddafi in Libya, to Hafiz Assad in Syria, to Yasser Arafat in Beirut, urging that the matter of Musa al Sadr's disappearance be resolved. Khomeini's first communication concerning Musa al Sadr was made in September 1978, two weeks after the latter's disappearance; it was addressed to Yasser Arafat in Beirut, asking him to do what he could to "clarify the mystery" of Musa al Sadr's whereabouts. Ayatollah Khomeini was then still a figure of the Iranian opposition, an Ayatollah who had opposed the Shah and had been forced into exile. The power and the fame that were to make him a great historic personage were still a few months away.

An emissary of Khomeini was dispatched to Libya from France, three days after the Ayatollah himself had arrived in France. Then in late November, one of Musa al Sadr's principal associates in Lebanon went in the company of Musa al Sadr's oldest son, Sadr al Din, then twenty years of age, to the house in Nauphle-le-Château where Khomeini resided. The old cleric urged patience, said how much he cared about Sayyid Musa, and promised that he would continue to do what he could until Sayyid Musa's safe return.

In February, Khomeini himself returned to Iran. He now commanded the resources of a large state. A Shia delegation of clerics and politicians who had worked with Musa al Sadr arrived in Teheran three weeks after the revolution's triumph. They came to congratulate the cleric who had prevailed, to lay some claim to Iran's revolution, to ask Iran's leaders to pursue the case of Musa al Sadr. The Libyans were not far behind. In April 1979, Muamar al Qaddafi dispatched his prime minister to Iran. To the Libyans' discomfort, they found that the issue of Musa al Sadr's disappearance was one of great concern to the new regime. A heated exchange took place at the Teheran airport between Qaddafi's prime minister, Abdul Salam Jallud, and the Iranian foreign minister, Ibrahim Yazdi. Jallud repeated Libya's official line that Imam al Sadr was a "friend" of Libya.

[192]

Besides, said Jallud, Libya had already discussed Musa al Sadr with Lebanon because the missing man was a Lebanese citizen. Surely the Libyans, he said, could not be expected to answer to two governments for the fate of one individual. The Libyans, said Jallud, had aided the Shia of Lebanon, had "bought their olives and tobacco, dug wells for them." What mattered now was the unity of the "two revolutions" —the Libyan and the Iranian. And surely Iran's Islamic revolution should not become so "sectarian" and so divisive as to take up the problem of Musa al Sadr merely because he was a Shia. He was in Iran, Jallud said, to discuss the "strategic cooperation" of the two revolutions and not the issue of Musa al Sadr.[2] It took the intervention of Ahmad Khomeini, the Ayatollah's son, to bring the quarrel to an end and escort Jallud to his father. Then, in the presence of Ayatollah Khomeini, Jallud was again grilled about what had become of Musa al Sadr.

Sayyid Musa's birthplace claimed him. In the fantasy of his Shia followers in Lebanon, their Imam, Musa al Sadr, was destined to return to the land of his birth in the aftermath of the revolution's triumph. He would have risen to the top there, they were sure, and they were fond of saying so. Musa al Sadr had sheltered Iranian dissidents against the Shah. He had done so initially with caution: Lebanon was a cockpit for the intrigues of others, and the Shah did have Lebanese Shia clerics and politicians who reported to him, who sought his patronage. The complexity of Musa al Sadr's position here was apparent when, in 1970, a struggle erupted in the Shia world over the choice of Marja al Taqlid, following the death of Ayatollah Muhsin al Hakim, who was acknowledged to be the leading marja in Najaf, Iraq. Muhsin al Hakim, an Arab, had never been accepted by a sufficiently large number of clerics in Iran as their marja. The Shia center in Qom had come to think of itself as a more distinguished center of learning than Najaf. Thus the decade between the death of Ayatollah Hussein Borujerdi in 1961 and that of Muhsin al Hakim in 1970 had seen a degree of decentralization in the religious hierarchy, with Muhsin al Hakim being something of a first among equals, rather than the sole, undisputed marja. In addition to Muhsin al Hakim, there were other grand mujtahids; there was in Najaf the exile from Qom, the politi-

---

[2]U.S. Embassy, Teheran, report to State Department, E.O. 12065, April 25, 1979. This particular report was among American diplomatic documents pieced together by Islamic militants in Iran after their seizure of the American Embassy on November 4, 1979, and published under the title *The Spy Nest Documents*. The released documents were authenticated by the *New York Times* of July 18, 1984. For the report on Yazdi's encounter with the Libyan prime minister, see vol. 18, p. 129.

cally active Ruhollah Khomeini, the opponent of the Shah; in Najaf also, there was Ayatollah Abu al Qasim al Musawi al Kho'i, a much more cautious cleric than Khomeini, a scholar by temperament. In Iran itself there were two marjas with large followings, Ayatollah Ahmad Khunsari in Teheran and the relatively moderate Ayatollah Muhammad Kazem Shariatmadari in Qom. Following Muhsin al Hakim's death, the issue of religious leadership in the Shia world was again a matter of dispute. No one could anoint a single marja; nor was it a foregone conclusion that there would be one sole, undisputed marja as had been the case when Borujerdi was alive. As it turned out, events following Muhsin al Hakim's death revealed sharp political and doctrinal differences over the nature of the marja's role, over the balance between political activism and scholarly restraint to be found in the work and conduct of a particular marja.

Predictably, Ayatollah Ruhollah Khomeini, then a relative newcomer in Najaf, was the choice of the politically active clerics of Iran. Forty-eight of the ulama of Qom sent the exiled Khomeini a cable of condolences for the death of Muhsin al Hakim and pledged him their support. The Shah, who hoped for Khomeini's eclipse, had given his blessing for the choice of marja to either the relatively moderate Ayatollah Muhammad Kazem Shariatmadari or Ayatollah Ahmad Khunsari.[3] In the city of Najaf itself, there was a strong body of support for Ayatollah Abu al Qasim al Musawi al Kho'i. Al Kho'i had been Sayyid Musa's teacher and it was to him that Sayyid Musa pledged support in a public statement in July 1970.[4] More than political caution was at work here: in part, the Shia world in Lebanon had traditionally looked to Najaf as its religious center. And by the strictures of Najaf—the religious hierarchy, the scholarly seniority—the case for Ayatollah Kho'i was a good deal stronger than it was for Khomeini. In 1970, with Musa al Sadr still searching for a political role in Lebanon, it would have been hard for him to make the more radical choice of declaring himself in favor of Khomeini as marja.

By 1974, Sayyid Musa had thrown caution to the wind and had become a relentless critic of the Shah. (A fellow Iranian, Mustapha Chamran, an American-trained physicist who worked with the cleric in Lebanon for nearly a decade, later went back to postrevolutionary Iran to become a minister of defense in the new regime; he was killed on the Iraqi front in 1981.) Musa al Sadr had given of himself, of the

[3]See Hamid Algar, "The Oppositional Role of the Ulama in Twentieth Century Iran," in Nikki Keddie, ed., *Scholars, Saints, and Sufis* (Berkeley: University of California Press, 1972), pp. 251–252; *The Times* (London), June 24, 1970.
[4]American Embassy Dispatch, Beirut, cable 5974, July 20, 1970.

resources he commanded, to the fight against the Shah. He had taken what seemed like a hopeless band of conspirators against the Shah to the Syrians and had secured some Syrian help for them. For his followers he was a precursor of the revolution in Iran. Like Iran's revolutionary clerics, but several years before them, he had blurred the distinction between religion and politics, he had established a hitherto novel claim to the ascendancy of the religious over the political. But beyond the specific, he had belonged to the two radically different Shia realms in Lebanon and Iran. He had made the transition from one realm to the other. It then followed that the larger revolutionary society in Iran could somehow embrace the Shia of Lebanon. It was something that the Iranians wanted; and it was something that flattered a community in Lebanon that had always lacked a foreign patron. The difficulties of the transition, the suspicions that had surrounded the man himself, were forgotten. "Musa al Sadr held a great place in the hearts of the Persians," said Iran's prime minister, Mehdi Bazargan, shortly before he, an Islamic modernist, lost out to the hardline theocratic strand of Iran's revolution. "We have asked Libya to receive our inquiry commission and to help us in the search for Musa al Sadr. Nor will we establish relationships with that country until they do what we have asked."[5]

That the Imam's disappearance had become a *cause célèbre* was, in part, a measure of his standing. It was also what historical timing had made of him. Musa al Sadr had come into the world of insular men; he had walked with and for them out of their cloistered world. In the search for him, men in Shia Lebanon saw an affirmation of their own importance. And the clerics in Iran expressed, through their concern for him, their growing sense that their revolution belonged to the realm of Islam as a whole, their belief that Shiism had a center in Iran, that the Shia in Arab realms were tributaries of that center.

Sayyid Musa's concerns were essentially those of social change; his agenda was a thoroughly political one that accepted compromise— too much compromise, thought the purists. The cleric who emerged as Iran's prophet seemed obsessed with ritual, with purity. A quarter-century younger than Ayatollah Khomeini, Musa al Sadr had brokered rival truths, had worked side by side with Christian priests and bishops. Ayatollah Khomeini, a stern man whose vision left no room for compromise, thought of contact with men beyond the faith as polluting. Yet these differences were submerged. To the older cleric in

[5]Oriana Fallaci, "An Interview with Mehdi Bazargan, Prime Minister of Iran," *The New York Times Magazine*, October 28, 1979.

Iran, the missing man was a son and a disciple. "I can say that I nearly raised him," said Ayatollah Khomeini of Musa al Sadr on one occasion. His "detention," in Libya, he said, was "suffering in the cause of Islam." Sayyid Musa's "grandfather," the seventh Imam, Musa al Kazim, said Ayatollah Khomeini, was imprisoned "for seven years, fourteen years according to some sources." Sayyid Musa, too, so it was hinted, would return to his followers.[6]

Side by side in the Shia parts of Lebanon were posters of Ayatollah Khomeini and of the younger cleric. But though they were intended to demonstrate a community of faith, to link the leader of Iran's revolt and the cleric, the posters point up differences hard to miss. The picture of Khomeini are of a stern old man spared doubts and compromise; those of the cleric by Khomeini's side show a man with tousled hair barely covered by his turban—and a winning smile. The older man lived in a closed world—the religious city of Qom; the sanctity of Najaf, another city of learning; the cloistered world of his religious books. The world beyond the faith held no great interest for Khomeini. During his brief stay in France, members of his entourage took the old man on an outing to see Paris, took him on a visit to the Eiffel Tower. Khomeini stepped out of the car, took a look, and then got back into the car, bringing the tour to an end. He kept the defiling world at bay. Musa al Sadr was a man whose life was lived amid conflicting claims and truths. He had emerged in the Levantine city of Beirut with its Christian population, its Sunni core, its Palestinian refugees, its Western pretensions. The world of Beirut was a variegated, not a pure one. Whoever was to live and prevail in the Beirut of Musa al Sadr's time had to be good at walking in and out of different cultures and temperaments. Musa al Sadr was a product of more complex circumstances than those that formed the older Ayatollah. Two of Sayyid Musa's four children, his sons, were born in Iran; his two daughters were born in Lebanon. His household in Lebanon was a bilingual one; members of his family spoke both Arabic and Farsi. He remained through and through a man of two different societies: in the baggage of Sayyid Musa, which the Libyans dispatched to Rome in a clumsy cover-up attempt, were to be found fragments of both Iran and Lebanon, his native country and his adopted one: two books published in Iran in Iran's language, two cassettes of Iranian music, an unmailed letter, in Farsi, addressed to Ayatollah Khomeini in his Iraqi exile, a list of Iranians working with him which specifed their salaries, a similar list of his Lebanese militia, Amal.

[6]Adel Rida, *Ma'al I'tidar Lil Imam al Sadr* (With Apology to Imam al Sadr) (Cairo, 1981), p. 194.

In Iran, the theocratic imperative that a jurist, a *faqih*, not only serve the time-honored function of giving guidance and advice on matters of Islamic jurisprudence, but also govern asserted itself shortly after the revolution had triumphed.[7] Khomeini's Wilayat al Faqih prevailed in Iran. Its parody was quick to come to Lebanon. Iran had its purists, its *Hizbollah*, the Party of God—men bent upon imposing a strict order of zeal and conformity. Lebanon, too, was to have its Hizbollah, its religious warriors and devotees, who believed that Lebanon, the country of antagonistic sects, could be remade in Iran's image. In the words of a young cleric of the Hizbollah, Sayyid Ibrahim Amin: "The realm of the Faqih, the jurist, is not a specific geographical realm; it covers the entire world of Islam."[8] The case for the traditional restraints of Shiism was made in Lebanon, as it was in Iran. An older clerical and scholarly Shia tradition held that faith should be kept apart from grubby political struggle lest it be contaminated. It knew the history of Shiism; it knew that the embattled faith had survived because the Imams who elaborated it during times of adversity did so because they were able to check the unbridled enthusiasm of the extremists. The fourth Imam, Zayn al Abidin, survived because he kept apart from the intrigues of the time, because he accepted that his cause could not carry the day against the might of the Islamic state based in Damascus. The sixth Imam, Jafar al Sadiq, gave Shiism its scholarship, assured its continuity, by stripping the notion of the Imamate of the expectation that an Imam should rule. Shiism made its accommodation with the world as it was.[9] The cautious course of the main body of Shiism enabled it to escape both defeat in hopeless battles, and absorption, as one American Islamicist put it, "into the Sunni synthesis."[10]

One of Shia Lebanon's most outstanding jurists, Muhammad Jawad Maghniyya, issued a dissent from within that older tradition of Shiism against Khomeini's notion that a mujtahid had the right to rule. He did it in a reasoned book entitled *Khomeini wa al Dawla al*

---

[7]For one thoughtful interpretation of how Khomeini's new political notions reinterpreted the old Shia tradition, see the essay by the late Hamid Enayat "Iran— Khumayni's Concept of the 'Guardianship of the Juriconsult,'" in James Piscatori, ed., *Islam in the Political Process* (Cambridge: Cambridge University Press, 1983), pp. 160–180.

[8]Ibrahim al Amin's interview, and the interviews of other Muslims and clerics and activists, were put together by Dar al Shira' in a book entitled *Al Harakat al Islamiyya Fi Lubnan* (Islamic Movements in Lebanon) (Beirut, 1984).

[9]On the quiescent course of Twelver Shiism, see Marshall G. S. Hodgson, "How Did the Early Shia Become Sectarian?" *Journal of the American Oriental Society*, 5 (1955), 1–13.

[10]Ibid., p. 1.

Islamiyya (Khomeini and the Islamic state) published in 1979.[11] Maghniyya paid homage to Khomeini's piety and learning. Khomeini's triumph, he wrote with awe, was "one of the riddles of the twentieth century." Khomeini proved, he said, that "faith was stronger than missiles and tanks." He dismissed the Pan-Arab critique of Khomeini: Islam, wrote Maghniyya, was never based on race or territory or nationality. At any rate, he said, there was not much that Arabs could be proud of today: he noted the feuds of Arab society, the massacres, the humiliations at the hands of Israel and the West. Khomeini's triumph, he said, returned Islamic history back to where it had been wronged, to the rule of the first Imam, Imam Ali, the son-in-law of the Prophet. All this, however, could not be taken, said Maghniyya, as a basis for establishing a clerical polity. The realm of the infallible Imam could not be equated with a state led by the ulama, the custodians of the religious institution. The faqih was a mere mortal; he was "vulnerable to oblivion, to pride and vanity, to personal predilections, to the impact of environment and social standing and economic circumstances."[12] In other words, purity is not of this world; the men of religion could instruct men, could pronounce on what was permissible, *hallal,* and impermissible, but they could not lay claim to rule. Against the new Shia politics which gave clerics an ascendant political role, Maghniyya deployed the older Shia strictures. On one level the debate was a scholarly one between two mujtahids. But something else was illuminated in Maghniyya's dissent. Ayatollah Khomeini hailed from a land where Shiism was the dominant faith; in that large realm religion could be merged with the *raison d'être* of the state, could be made to buttress it. Maghniyya, the Lebanese scholar, lived in a small land of rival faiths. Restraint was a long-standing tradition for a minority community in a land that was not fully autonomous. The Shia of Lebanon had learned to live in the shadow of alien powers.

But there are historical moments and situations when restraint is easily dismissed as weakness and when men push caution aside. And the immediate aftermath of Iran's revolution was one such moment. Men in Lebanon were eager to be linked to a large realm of Islam and to a revolution of zeal—to the point of parody. Sayyid Musa al Sadr, coming as he had done into a Lebanon with a subdued Shia community, had tried to perfect his Arabic, to rid it, to the extent that he could, of his Persian accent. Now, clerics born in Lebanon affected a

---

[11]Muhammad Jawad Maghniyya, *Khomeini wa al Dawla al Islamiyya* (Beirut, 1979).
[12]Ibid., p. 59.

Persianized Arabic. Sayyid Musa was turned into an icon, made into the man of war and purity who was needed.

In Shia Lebanon, in the slums of Greater Beirut, in the villages of the Bekaa Valley, and in the south, posters bearing Imam al Sadr's picture were everywhere. He was claimed by sly politicians, by a new Shia middle class grasping for its own place, by starry-eyed young boys pushed out of the villages of the south into the anarchy and confusion of Beirut. The boys had not known the man. They had not been around when he cut deals and juggled different truths. They had his posters and his memory—and his words. They distilled his life into simple militant maxims. He had tried to teach men militancy when they were so quiescent. In the aftermath of his disappearance, younger men formed by a hellish decade of war in Lebanon, inspired by Iran's millenarian message, plunged into a whole new world of zeal and combat. A "suicide brigade" was named for the Imam who never quite felt comfortable with the violent ways of Lebanon. The anniversary of Musa al Sadr's disappearance became an occasion for deeds of daring and of anger. In Early September, 1979, a year after he vanished, a band of young men took control of an Alitalia airliner. They wanted it flown to Havana so that the case of the missing Imam could be put before the leaders of the nonaligned countries, then meeting in Cuba. They assumed that the leaders of the nonaligned countries—so many of whom ruled by terror—would be moved by a case of political foul play. It was not the first hijacking by young Shia, nor would it be the last. The hijackers wanted their Imam released and returned to his people. Otherwise, they said, "we shall overturn the entire world." But they were a gentle group, the Alitalia passengers said of the hijackers: they put flowers in the muzzles of their guns and offered chocolate candy to their hostages.[13] More violent deeds were to come. Events both in Lebanon and in the larger world of Islam beyond seemed to move with terrifying velocity. The Shia were to swing all the way from quietism to martyrology. Men needed "saints," and in Sayyid Musa they found the elements out of which militant sainthood could be constructed. His aura hovered over the ruined world of the Shia in Lebanon, and its politics became, in many ways, a fight over the realm of a vanished Imam.

From the eastern part of the country, in the Bekaa Valley, one Hussein Musawi, a former schoolteacher who became one of revolutionary Iran's operatives in Lebanon, offers his own version and remembrance of Musa al Sadr. He, Musawi, was in Tyre in 1976 with Imam

---

[13]*The New York Times*, September 8, 1979.

al Sadr, he says. There was a struggle in that year in the movement launched by Musa al Sadr between "Muslim elements" on the one hand and those who "grew up in the Western way, including Marxists." The Imam, says Musawi, settled the matter and declared that Amal, the militia launched the preceding year, was an "Islamic movement" and its political thought "Quranic Islam." In Musawi's account, the goal of these years was to realize "a Muslim society, and God willing, in time a Muslim state as well." The Musa al Sadr Musawi holds up is a "genuine son of the Islamic revolution."[14] The political cleric who courted the Christian custodians of power during a time of Shia quiescence, who went out of his way to show fidelity to the country he had adopted, becomes in this militant's vision a precursor of the politics of absolutes. In the Levantine polity that was Lebanon before the breakdown, with all its pretensions and hierarchies, men like Musawi, men of the countryside lacking the right background and education, were spectators. In a climate of breakdown and carnage, their chance had come. They cloaked their resentments and ambitions in the garb of a religious tradition; in that tradition and its symbols and custodians, they found the warrant they needed for merciless politics.

Sayyid Musa's followers had their Imam; in the ruined slums of Beirut, with so little else to draw upon, a community with a history of disinheritance held onto the legacy of the missing cleric. In the summer of 1982, four years after Musa al Sadr's disappearance, when Israel invaded Lebanon and shattered the Palestinian dominion in the south and in the Muslim parts of Beirut, a rumor swept through the Shia masses that the missing Imam had been found by the invading army. He had been in Lebanon all along, so the wild tale suggested, in captivity. It was not said who had kept him prisoner. But the Palestinian-Shia enmity in the south left little doubt as to the identity of the villains. The fantastic was given a semblance of precision: Musa al Sadr, it was said, had been found, his beard long, his attire unkempt. Only one of his two companions who had disappeared with him, the journalist Abbas Badr al Din, had turned up; the other, Shaykh Muhammad Yaqub had perished. A time of war and upheaval: the believers wanted the cleric returned to them.

The cleric's versatile legacy was apparent when Israel came to occupy the Shia towns and villages of southern Lebanon. By dismantling Palestinian power in the summer of 1982, Israel had done for the Shia what they had not been able to do for themselves. Initially the

[14]See *Al Harakat al Islamiyya Fi Lubnan*, pp. 221–222.

Shia gave the Israeli campaign of 1982 their silent approval. But, unlike the Lebanese Christians, they could not openly embrace Israel. They were not that kind of people: traffic with men beyond the faith was not part of their history. For centuries, the Maronites had played the game of inviting strangers and drawing on their resources. The Shia, on the other hand, carried with them a nervousness about encountering strangers, a fear of defilement. The peculiar Shia relationship to the larger Arab world—they were of it, but not fully—rendered them unable to come to terms with Israel. Like Caesar's wife, they had to be above suspicion. They were sure that they would not be forgiven a close association with Israel.

Israel's long-range designs in Lebanon were yet another problem for the Shia. Israel had come as a savior, but saviors could betray. There had always existed in Lebanon a suspicion that Israel coveted the lands of the south and the waters of the Litani River. A body of political literature had popularized that theme. There was enough Zionist scripture around, and enough Palestinian reiterations of it, to make men wonder and worry. Israel could never provide sufficient assurance that its presence would be temporary. And the longer Israeli troops stayed, the more credible the suspicions became.

The south was "being amputated from Lebanon's body": that was how Musa al Sadr's clerical deputy on the Higher Shia Council, Shaykh Muhammad Mahdi Shams al Din, put it in the religious celebration of Imam Hussein's death, Ashura, in late October 1982, some five months after Israel had entered Lebanon. Israel, he said, had come in to Lebanon under the pretext of protecting the security of Galilee. But, increasingly, the threat is clearer; that "Lebanon's identity would be erased, that its economy and waters would be exploited."[15]

The grace period extended to Israel lasted little more than a year. Israel had entered Lebanon with a flawed understanding of the country; Israeli decision-makers knew next to nothing about the Shia. Israel was, in effect, trying to impose Christian hegemony in a part of Lebanon which had very few Christians. On Israel's coattails rode the brigands of Major Saad Haddad, a renegade Christian officer from Lebanon's army who had been Israel's ally since 1976. Major Haddad's militia, a predominantly Christian force, moved from its strip on Israel's border farther north to the Awali River. Then came the zealous units of the Maronite "Lebanese Forces," the most extreme

[15]Shaykh Muhammad Mahdi Shams al Din, *Ashura: Mawkab al Shihada* (Ashura: The Caravan of Martyrdom) (Beirut, private publication of the cleric's office, of sermon delivered October 27, 1982).

[201]

among the Christian militias. Haddad and his men wanted power and spoils—those advantages, psychic and material, that checkpoints conferred on those who manned them in Lebanon. The Lebanese Forces wanted to impose their will on the south, a portion of the country where the Shia represent 80 percent of the population. Palestinian dominion in the south was replaced by a Christian regime of harassment and extortion.

Trouble between Israel and the Shia was waiting to happen. And it happened on a particularly symbolic day: October 16, 1983, the day of Ashura, the tenth of the Muslim month of Muharram, commemorating the martyrdom of Imam Hussein at Kerbala. An armed Israeli convoy coincidentally turned up in the Shia town of Nabatiyya on that day and tried to make its way through the procession of mourners and flagellants. Two people were killed, several wounded.

The die was cast in the south. The next day Shaykh Muhammad Mahdi Shams al Din, Musa al Sadr's designated clerical deputy and vice-chairman of the Higher Shia Council, issued a fatwa calling for "civil disobedience" and "resistance to occupation in the south." Dealing with Israel, he said was "absolutely impermissible." Of his "brothers and sons in the south," the cleric asked fidelity to the land, that they defend and hold it at any price. Every generation, the cleric said, has its own Kerbala; man makes his own choice; he can "soar and sacrifice" or he can "submit and betray."[16]

The discourse of Shams al Din echoed Musa al Sadr's. Shaykh Shams al Din, however, was a religious functionary who played by the conventional rules of the Lebanese political order. He was a man devoid of charisma, who had been selected for his post by Musa al Sadr. He was cut of more conventional material than Musa al Sadr: a conservative man, suspicious of popular passions. But he was being challenged from below by more zealous clerics. Shams al Din had issued his call for civil disobedience from Beirut. But there were other clerics and true believers in the south of Lebanon, under Israeli occupation, who believed in an entirely different kind of politics. The suicide drivers and the "martyrs" were not far behind. On November 4, a suicide driver struck the Israeli headquarters in Tyre. He was a young man, it was reported, around twenty years old. Sixty people were killed, including twenty-nine Israeli soldiers and security men. Israel responded by closing the bridge on the Awali River which connected the south to Beirut. Clinton Bailey, an Israeli academic who served as a liaison officer in southern Lebanon, summed up the im-

---

[16]See *An Nahar*, October 18, 1983.

pact: "The basis of the Southern economy collapsed. It was this event that finally smashed the last friendly sentiments toward Israel."[17] A relentless war erupted between the Shia and the Israeli occupiers. In 1984 alone, there were more than nine hundred attacks against Israeli soldiers in southern Lebanon.

Musa al Sadr had exalted martyred men; he had made the seventh-century tale of Kerbala into a contemporary one. Now young men willingly went to their deaths declaring fidelity to Musa al Sadr and saying that he had taught them martyrdom and love of the land. In the final testimonies of so many of them, there were parting words about Sayyid Musa, about the "absent Imam's return."

Stepchildren of the Arab world, the Shia fought Israel with zeal. In the fury with which they fought, they exorcised their historical sense of being excluded from the mainstream of Arab history. Untouched by the exalted doctrines of nationalism, they wanted to be admitted. The Arab world had invested some of itself and its wealth in the Palestinian cause; then in the aftermath of the war of 1982 the Shia turned out to be more formidable enemies of Israel than did the PLO. "A great Arab fortune was invested in the Palestinians," said Nabih Berri, the leader of Amal. "We showed the Arabs the lessons of martyrdom and courage."[18] Men from the fringe of a large society, "from its edges, the outer marches of it" were displaying their militancy on its behalf.[19] Nationalism—in an old and familiar twist—was finding its most fanatical adherents amid marginal communities and men. Like the Iranian-born cleric who had led them, who was desperate at times for Arab acceptance, Musa al Sadr's inheritors wanted to fight a large Arab fight. Their timing was off, but they did not know it. Pan-Arabism with its stout lungs and its slogans had passed them by when it was ascendant. Now that they exalted the fight against Israel, there was peace between Israel and Egypt, and the mainstream of Arab society had gone a long way toward shedding its Israeli obsession.

Sayyid Musa had labored among the Shia as they were leaving the hinterland villages in the south and the Bekaa and beginning to learn

[17]Clinton Bailey, "Lebanon's Shi'ites after the 1982 War," Tel Aviv University, December 1984, p. 18.

[18]See the proceedings of the Lausanne meeting of Lebanon's "warlords" in March 1984 in *Geneve—Lausanne: Al Mahadir al Siryya al Kamila* (Complete Secret Proceedings), published by the newspaper *As Safir* in a book released in 1984, p. 266.

[19]The tendency of "marginal" men and communities to embrace nationalism with a fury is elaborated by Isaiah Berlin, in his essay "Benjamin Disraeli, Karl Marx and the Search for Identity" in his book of essays *Against the Current* (New York: Penguin, 1982), p. 258.

city ways. They approached Beirut with the awe with which villagers look upon great cities. A character in a work of fiction, *Hikayat Zahra* (published in 1980), by the Shia novelist Hanan al Shaykh, said of the elegant parts of the city that they belonged to a "different breed of men."[20] The character was recalling the Beirut of the 1960s. In 1984, six years after Musa al Sadr's disappearance, West Beirut, the traditional haven of the more privileged Sunni community, fell to the Shia squatters and urban newcomers. Amal, since 1980 under the leadership of Berri, a lawyer in his mid-forties, and a man who came of a modest social background from the south, emerged as the dominant force in West Beirut. The world had been stood on its head: sons of villagers proclaimed their triumph over the city, over its ruins.

An outdated fantasy had continued to picture the Shia of Greater Beirut as intruders in the city, peasants who could be sent packing to their ancestral homelands in the south or the Bekaa Valley. Such was the apparent scheme entertained by the fragile Maronite-dominated regime that emerged (with brief American backing, from the fall of 1982 until the winter of 1984) from Israel's Lebanon war of 1982. It was in this vein that one militant young Maronite spoke to an American journalist of the Shia: "The Shia in Beirut are an unnatural concentration. They are refugees from the South and should return."[21] Boulos Nammaan, the influential head of the Maronite order of monks, put forth a similar view to a Shia journalist. In the vision of this thoroughly political priest, the urban Shia—some 700,000 inhabitants, perhaps more—would be sent back to the land. A large Shia population had been formed by the city, and much of the real estate in Greater Beirut belonged to them. Yet their right to a place there was not yet recognized.

The Shia had been through this before. Early in the civil war, they had lost one of their major footholds in the city, the Armenian-Shia settlement northeast of Beirut. They were expelled in 1976 when the suburb fell behind Maronite lines. It took no great imagination to see the new scheme: East Beirut would remain Christian; West Beirut would have come to terms with the Maronite-dominated order for it lacked the military means to defend itself. In the plan there was no room for the Shia of Greater Beirut. The arrangement was to be

---

[20]Hanan al Shaykh *Hikayat Zahra* (Zahra's Story) (Beirut, 1980), p. 80. This is a remarkable work of fiction by a young woman writer who knows the world of the Shia, with all its warts and pain; it is available in French under the title *Histoire de Zahra* (Paris: J.C. Lattès, 1985).
[21]Craig S. Karpel, "Onward Christian Diplomats," *The New Republic*, September 3, 1984, p. 23.

shored up by American support and power. Guilt for the terrible summer of 1982, for the green light the United States had given Israel's invasion of Lebanon, and for the carnage that took place had taken the U.S. Marines to Lebanon in the fall of 1982 on an undefined mission in a society that America did not fully understand. It was billed as a "peace-keeping mission"; the United States enlisted French, British, and Italian participation in its excursion. Once on the ground, the distant power became a party to the sectarian feuds of Lebanon. Behind the shield and prestige of a great power, the Maronite regime set out to subdue an unwieldy country. In times past, when France was a power to be reckoned with, the Maronites had made themselves part of France's mission in the Levant. And for a brief moment from the fall of 1982 until early 1984, history seemed to repeat itself for the Maronites. The United States was to do for them—so they hoped—what France once did. It was a time of great delusions: an American-trained army would hold the country together; the Shia "squatters" in the southern suburbs of Beirut were to be cleared out; the clannish Druze in the Shuff Mountains southeast of Beirut were to be defeated. A new order would be created.

But the Maronite bid for hegemony could not be sustained. And the United States, dragged into the sectarian feuds, could not make the Shia and the Druze submit to Maronite power, nor could it push Syria out of Lebanon. Revolutionary Iran, too, was now a party to the politics and the bloodletting of Lebanon. A trail led to Beirut from Teheran, through the Bekaa Valley in the eastern part of the country and through Syria. The trail brought to Lebanon pamphleteers, clerical "guides," and revolutionary guardsmen. Lebanon had been a "sideshow" for sometime; Iran's entry into Lebanese politics was a variation on an old theme. Lebanese had always invited outsiders to tip the scales against other Lebanese, to check the foreign patrons of rival sects. The Christian Maronites had drawn on the resources of Western powers and on those of Israel. The Pan-Arabists in Lebanon had ridden the coattails of larger Arab powers. Naturally there were anxious Shia recipients of Iran's patronage. Historically the Shia of Lebanon had lacked a foreign patron. In Iran the Lebanese Shia groups like Hizbollah (the Party of God) had now found one. For its part, Iran was anxious for converts, anxious to show that its revolt was a wider revolution of Islam as a whole. Iran was shedding that sense of separateness from the Muslim world that had been its fate since the passing of the high Persian medieval culture that was once the culture of Islam all the way from Turkey to Indonesia. The revolutionary leaders of Iran would not and could not fight American power in the Persian Gulf. In the anarchy of Lebanon, and in what American presence there was there, Iran's leaders found the opportunity they wanted.

On October 23, 1983, a year after the Western multinational force had come to Lebanon, two suicide drivers struck the U.S. Marine barracks and the headquarters of the French. Two-hundred-and-forty-one Americans and fifty-eight Frenchmen were killed. It had been a doomed American mission. Lebanon was not a vital American interest and there was no use pretending that it was. Under the fire of American warships in the Mediterranean, the United States began its retreat from Lebanon.[22] In early February 1984, the Shia and their Druze allies swept into West Beirut; the American-trained army of Lebanese President Amin Gemayyel collapsed and split along sectarian lines. (All along the army had had a rank-and-file Shia majority, men from the hinterland who had joined because it was their only chance of secure employment.) Nabih Berri called on the Shia units in the army to desert the regime and they did so. The battle in the south against Israel was being waged by militant clerics. The extremists of the Party of God in the Bekaa Valley were gaining ground. If the leaders of Amal in Beirut were to hold what was left of the Shia political center, this was their chance to do so, and they seized it.

The country had to be seen and apportioned in new ways. The hinterland had spilled into the city. The Shia festivities of the month of Muharram, the celebrations of Ashura commemorating the death of Imam Hussein—the mourners, the self-flagellation—which were once affairs of tucked-away towns and villages, were now celebrated in Beirut. In the new militancy with which a younger Shia generation flaunted its devotion to tradition could be seen the attempt of men to exorcise the embarrassments and the humiliations of the past. The Shia leaders who emerged as the masters of the ruins of Beirut recall a time not so long ago when Beirut was an alien place, and when the dead in the Shia community had to be taken to their ancestral villages for burial because there was no Shia cemetery in the city. Power had come to the Shia of Beirut. But it came during a time of calamity. Wrath had reduced the city to rubble.

Privilege had spawned its nemesis: wrath. There was no middle ground on which men could stand in Lebanon, or in much of the Muslim world around Lebanon for that matter. To use Victor Hugo's summation in *Les Misérables*, a war pitted the "egoists" against the

---

[22]The gifted *New York Times* correspondent Thomas L. Friedman covered this period with unusual depth and grace in his reportage from Beirut.

"outcasts." On their side the egoists had "the bemusement of prosperity which blunts the sense, the fear of suffering which in some cases goes so far as to hate all sufferers, and unshakable complacency, the ego so inflated that it stifles the soul." The outcasts came with what waiting and denial had hammered into their souls: "greed and envy, resentment at the happiness of others, the turmoil of the human element in search of personal fulfillment, hearts filled with fog, misery, needs, and fatalism, and simple, impure ignorance."[23]

A prophet of the outcasts had to be a vehicle for all their emotion. And Musa al Sadr had become a prophet of Lebanon's Shia outcasts. Young men carrying his posters, marching under banners of his pronouncements, shut down West Beirut—the Muslim part of the city, the former home of a "cosmopolitan" culture blown away by a drawn-out war—on August 31, 1984, the sixth anniversary of Musa al Sadr's disappearance. Were they really anticipating his return? Or was it an expression of gratitude for what a man born in a distant land and his myth had done for a community that had always waited and always obeyed? Or were the men displaying their fidelity to the missing cleric by performing a ritual repentance? A revolt of penitents broke out in the city of Kufa, in Iraq, four years after Imam Hussein's murder at Kerbala. The Kufans had not been there when they were needed: Hussein, the man the Kufans revered and had invited into their midst was cut down in a solitary and doomed battle. The Kufans sat out the battle. Four years later, they erupted in sorrow, honoring the memory of the man they had failed to support. Likewise, the Shia of Beirut loved the memory and the words of the Iranian-born cleric. They saw themselves in him. Now that he himself was no longer with them, men were willing to follow him and to obey and to give of themselves. Deep down, newly dedicated men must have remembered what the recent past was really like; they knew that the revered man did battle for their loyalty and the loyalty of their kinsmen against the normal range of human temptations: the desire for safety, the desire to be left alone, the tendency to see a scoundrel in every hero, the search for individual gratification. But imagination had worked wonders, had attributed to the missing cleric all sorts of powers he had not had.

No one wanted to remember that in a different political climate many of the cleric's associates and companions moved back and forth between his political movement and leadership and that of the authority of the old oligarchs. Money and followers and devotion had

[23]Victor Hugo, *Les Misérables* (Penguin Classics, vol. 2), p. 525.

never been easy for him to secure and command. The ambitious men—aspiring civil servants, younger men with university degrees trying to make their way into prestige government appointments, men with money dreaming of seats in Parliament—were behind the cleric when his political stock rose, when they thought that he could deliver favors from the state or enhance their careers. Conversely, they were nowhere to be found when the old notables and political bosses offered them patronage or made more extravagant promises. A journalist recalled an incident in 1972: he had gone to the headquarters of the Higher Shia Council to call on "the Imam," the chairman of the council. There in a large hall, in the building whose costs had to be secured from men who parted with money reluctantly (several of whom had given on condition that photos be released to the press of the Imam receiving their checks), the journalist found Musa al Sadr sitting alone. The two of them talked for a while. Then out of politeness, the journalist, a younger man and deferential to the cleric, said that he had taken enough of the Imam's time. But he was asked to stay. The cleric had time on his hands. He also had an errand to run, some meeting to go to. But although his chauffeur was there the cleric's car was without gasoline and neither the driver nor Sayyid Musa had money to buy any.

Another remembrance—a variation on the same theme—was offered by an observer who followed the career of Musa al Sadr, and whose family of financiers and bankers made early contributions to his work. In mid-June 1976, Palestinian gunmen attacked Musa al Sadr's home in West Beirut. His bodyguards came under fire. He and his guests were unharmed—but a warning was being delivered by the Palestine Liberation Organization's forces to Musa al Sadr. And there was no Shia answer to that slight. The Palestinians, refugees in Lebanon, had asserted and organized themselves; the Shia were still timid spectators of their country's politics. "Sayyid Musa," recalled this observer "had such difficult material to work with. The Shia leaders were still lackeys of the Maronites, fixated on the Maronites and afraid of the Palestinians. They put up with what was dished out to them, and Sayyid Musa knew this." Less then a decade later, a younger Shia generation had broken in a dramatic way with the timidity of their elders.

Whether they were repenting or demonstrating newly acquired power, the Shia had walked out of a sullen hinterland into the politics of a contested city. They were hurled into the city; its settled ways, its responses were alien to them. The ruined land in the countryside and a decade of Israeli-Palestinian war had brought them out of their co-

coon into a place that was not fully theirs. The frenzy of the Shia, so disturbing to men and women of long-standing residence in Beirut, was the response to a bewildering place. Urban life—in the greater entity of Syria out of which Lebanon was carved, and to which it historically belonged—was the life of Sunni Islam; the Sunnis had given the cities their rhythm and their politics. The hinterland and the remote mountains had been claimed by minorities: Alawis and Druze in today's Syria, Maronite, Druze, and Shia in today's Lebanon. Urban Sunni Islam in the greater entity of Syria established its nine-century hegemony in the final years of the eleventh century. It was the forces of urban Islam that repelled the attack of the crusaders against this region and took Syria into its urban age.[24] The Franks came to conquer Syria in 1097; the forces of the countryside and the local Christians offered token resistance or became outright collaborators. Alone, urban Islam stood in the way of the Crusades. It triumphed by making common cause with Kurdish and Turkish dynasties and soldiers and by drawing on the self-confidence that a revived international political order of urban Sunni Islam exhibited in both political and cultural realms in the twelfth and thirteenth centuries. This international political order survived a great disruption in the mid-thirteenth century when the Mongols overran the domain of Islam. Urban Islam was able to bounce back, absorbing the energies and enlisting the loyalties of Mamluk soldiers and then of the Ottomans, who served as the standard-bearers of orthodox Sunni Islam from the early sixteenth century until the collapse of the empire after World War I. Under the umbrella of the Ottoman order, urban notables had governed the city of Damascus, and its hinterland, as part of a larger political and cultural whole. Arab nationalism, under the French mandate and then after independence, had inherited the universalism of the Ottoman empire and its urban bases of political authority. All this was brought to an end when the Alawis of the countryside claimed power in Damascus in 1970–1971, using the military and the coup d'etat. In Beirut a decade later, other children of the countryside, the Shia in this case, were clamoring for a place in the sun. That it took a cleric, a man born in a distant Shia realm to bring this about is a statement of its own on the cunning of history.

Modern Beirut, a seaport, a city of trade and services, was created by international trade, by the ascendancy of the West in the Levant. It was only in the 1830s and 1840s that Beirut became the center of a

[24]The thesis about the ascendancy of urban Islam is developed by the able historian Kamal Salibi in his book *Syria under Islam* (Delmar, N.Y.: Caravan Books, 1977), pp. 166–167.

trading network, emerged as the most important trading city in the larger entity of Syria. A city of middlemen, Beirut had all the strengths and the weaknesses of seaports: it was both vibrant and superficial. It belonged both to its hinterland and to the Western world beyond the Mediterranean. In part, the city was undone by its own success. It had imparted to quiescent men, to insular men, urban skills and urban impatience.

The commercial prosperity of Beirut, the privileges of an administrative center, had pulled men from the mountain and the hinterland to the city. But the process brought what one historian called a "steady stream of unassimilated newcomers."[25] Maronites from Mount Lebanon, Shia from the south came to Beirut—the first in the nineteenth century, the second in the mid-twentieth. But the two communities were not, culturally, city people. Long before the civil war of the 1970s revealed it for everyone to see, Beirut was a city divided by sectarian lines. Two communities, the Greek Orthodox among the Christians and the Sunni Muslims of West Beirut, were the bearers of its culture and spirit. But these two communities were to be overwhelmed. The Maronite ascendancy among the Christians left very little room for the Greek Orthodox, and a civil war which exalted the soldier and the militiaman sealed the sect's fate. The Greek Orthodox were not soldiers and fighters, and power in Lebanon went to those who could bear arms. As for the Sunnis of West Beirut, their dominance was derived from the power of the larger Arab world beyond Lebanon and depended on the quiescence of the Shia. The Sunni merchants and oligarchs were part of urban Arab Islam. They partook of a culture and faith larger than Lebanon. At one time or another, the Sunnis of West Beirut could look for sustenance to Damascus, or to Gamal Abdul Nasser's Egypt in the 1950s and 1960s, or to the wealthy Arab states of the Gulf. The political demise of the Sunnis of Beirut was a reflection of profound changes in the Arab regional order. Damascus itself had fallen under the control of Alawi soldiers and officers from Syria's hinterland. Egypt had been diminished; it was no longer a power in the Fertile Crescent. The Arab states of the Gulf could offer financial support to the Sunnis of Beirut; but they could not reverse a historical verdict that issued from Lebanon's realities or turn demography around, nor could they, in the aftermath of Iran's revolt, offer an immediate response to the passion of that revolution, which seemed to release the Shia of Lebanon.

[25]Leila Tarazi Fawaz, *Merchants and Migrants in Nineteenth Century Beirut* (Cambridge: Harvard University Press, 1983), p. 124.

As late as 1982, Saeb Salam, a Sunni oligarch, a man born in 1905, spoke for Muslim Beirut, embodied its spirit. Saeb Bey, several times prime minister of Lebanon, was Beirut's quintessential patrician. He was the dominant figure in the Maqasid Benevolent Society, the leading educational, medical, and philanthropic body in Beirut, established in the 1870s. Saeb Salam's ancestors had risen to power and influence in mid-nineteenth-century Beiruti society, a family of merchants and notables. His grandfather, Ali Salam, was one of Beirut's leading citizens and merchants by the early 1870s. Saeb's father, Salim Ali Salam (1868–1938) inherited his father's commercial and political domain and expanded the power of the Salams; in 1909 he was elected president of the Maqasid Society. Hitherto the leading Muslim family of Beirut had been the Beyhums: Salim Ali Salam pulled off a coup of sorts within the Beirut oligarchy, surpassing the power and the prestige of the Beyhums. A Lebanese historian describes him as "personally uninhibited, full of self-confidence and daring, and though conventionally religious, completely unfanatical,"[26] a Sunni man of wealth and distinction who allowed his sons and daughters to be tutored in French and classical Arabic by a Greek Catholic priest and by an accomplished Maronite literary figure. Until his death in 1938, Salim Ali Salam had remained one of the great power brokers in the politics of the city, a notable of Beirut who threw his weight behind this or that particular candidate for mufti of the Sunni community. He had participated in the abortive effort in 1920 to declare the Hashemite Prince Faisal a king of Syria, and when that bid failed and Lebanon and Syria came under French control, Salim Ali Salam had opposed the French mandate and kept his distance from the French. In 1922, he had been imprisoned by the French and then briefly exiled. Salim Ali Salam's place in the Muslim politics and society of Beirut had been claimed by his son Saeb, and though he was not the oldest surviving son, he had become his father's political heir. In Saeb Bey's salon—in an imposing mansion that Saeb's grandfather had purchased in the late 1860s and his father had remodeled and enlarged—deals were sealed and political bargains over the direction of the country were made. In the 1950s, when Nasser's writ and word dominated the agenda of Arab politics, Saeb Bey Salam was Nasser's man. He journeyed to Cairo and returned with blessings and support. It was Saeb Bey who led the revolt of Muslim Beirut in

[26]Kamal Salibi, "Beirut under the Young Turks: As Depicted in the Political Memoirs of Salim Ali Salam," in *Colloques Internationaux du Centre National de la Recherche Scientifique*, no. 555 (Paris: Editions du Centre National de la Recherche Scientifique, 1976), p. 198.

the civil war of 1958 against the American-backed president of the time, the Maronite Camille Chamoun. After that Saeb Bey enjoyed a quarter-century of prominence. When the power of Cairo declined, he already had supporters and patrons in the Gulf. Money and help came to Saeb Bey from the regime of Saddam Hussein of Iraq and from the more conservative Arab states of the Gulf. And even when the Palestinians and the street gangs of West Beirut usurped his power in the mid-1970s, Saeb Bey remained a figure of authority. It was in his home in the grim summer of 1982, during Israel's long siege and heavy bombardment of West Beirut, that Beirut's notables made the final request to Yasser Arafat that the PLO quit the city and spare it further carnage. Throughout the Israeli siege, Saeb Bey was the liaison between Philip Habib, President Reagan's envoy and Arafat. Saeb Bey delivered the American assurances and concessions that Arafat sought as a price for leaving the city. Saeb Bey was the bearer of a proud tradition of urban notables who once dominated the politics of cities like Damascus and Beirut. In the summer of 1982, he did what little he could for his city.

Saeb Bey knew how to bend with the wind. He had opposed the election of the leader of the Phalange militiamen, the young Bashir Gemayyel, to the presidency of the country that August. Bashir Gemayyel was a "tough" who had no regard for the old political games of bargains and compromise which Saeb Bey knew and lived by. But Bashir Gemayyel had prevailed and had secured his election to the presidency with the help of the invading Israeli army. After a "decent interval" of two weeks, Saeb Bey accepted the new order of things. In his home in West Beirut, he gathered twenty-five of the country's Muslim leaders and offered an olive branch to the Phalange militiaman. Some Muslim leaders stayed away, declaring the newly elected man a puppet of Israel. But Saeb Bey read the balance of forces for what it was. He would accept Bashir Gemayyel's regime so long as the extremist militiaman did not push his triumph too far and too hard. And it was again Saeb Bey who walked by Amin Gemayyel's side when the latter was elected to the presidency after the assassination of his younger brother on September 14, before Bashir could assume the office he had secured. Saeb Bey, it was assumed, was Muslim Lebanon's most authoritative voice. The country had its old assumptions. A Maronite-Sunni pact had given it its previous stability. Clans and notables who knew one another and accepted one another had seen it through earlier crises. In the embrace of Saeb Bey and Amin Gemayyel, the country—a segment of it—yearned for simpler times.

Eighteen months later the country was without its illusions. At a conference of Lebanese "warlords" in Lausanne, Switzerland in March 1984, nine leading figures—two Sunnis, two Shia, a Druze, four Maronites—came together for yet another discussion of the country's troubles. Saeb Bey was there, a figure of the older order, a man in his late seventies. So was the lawyer Nabih Berri, three decades younger, one of Musa al Sadr's heirs, a man with roots in the countryside. Saeb Bey had come to this conference unable to do anything but plead for the security and safety of West Beirut. The younger man from the countryside had come to the table a month after the Shia militia, which he commanded and Musa al Sadr had launched, had prevailed in West Beirut.[27]

Another portion of Musa al Sadr's legacy was there to be picked up in the disorder of a ruined city: his politicoreligious mantle. Just as he had emerged on his own, a mullah making his way into the political world, there were inheritors of his role, fellow clerics, finding a new political role for themselves. There was the man he had handpicked to be vice-chairman of the Higher Shia Council, Shaykh Muhammad Mahdi Shams al Din. But Shams al Din, religiously learned as he was, had the makeup of a bureaucratic functionary: he was attached to his post and its prerogatives, more comfortable striking political deals than leading newly radicalized men. There was something in his personality—aloof and pedantic, distrustful of others—that made him unable to take up where Musa al Sadr had left off. The old clerical tradition that Musa al Sadr had assailed seemed to cling to his designated deputy. And he had, too, Lebanese ways and characteristics—the gossip and the bickering, the limited horizons—that doomed him in the eyes of those who had been enthralled by Musa al Sadr. Besides, the Higher Shia Council had collapsed in the mid-1970s along with the other institutions of the Lebanese state; it had turned into an empty shell, a high-sounding name and nothing more.

To the extent that any mujtahid inherited the radical religious mantle of Musa al Sadr—and no one after him in Lebanon was acclaimed as an Imam—it was Sayyid Muhammad Hussein Fadlallah to whom some power passed. It was Fadlallah, born in Najaf in 1934, the son of a mujtahid from the southern Shia town of Aynatha in the district of Bint Jbail, who became the "spiritual guide" of groups such as the Party of God, and whose sermons stirred the faithful. The "willing and the bewildered"—the words are those of a Lebanese journal-

[27]The proceedings of the Lausanne Conference are reported in *Al Mahadir Siryya al Kamila.*

ist—rallied around Fadlallah. His Ashura orations in a mosque of Greater Beirut served the same kind of function that Musa al Sadr's had done less than a decade earlier. Fadlallah, a shorter and stockier man than Musa al Sadr, more deliberate in his movements, more reserved and scholarly, had received his education in Najaf; he was a gifted poet and writer who showed an early flair for the language (a poem of his, written in 1954, was a moving eulogy of Sayyid Musa's father, Ayatollah Sadr al Din al Sadr). Throughout the 1950s and early 1960s, while he lived in Najaf, he remained in close touch with the Shia of Beirut and the south, spending stretches of time in Beirut and Bint Jbail, participating in the literary and social life of his community. Coming to Lebanon to stay in the mid-1960s, he settled in an Armenian-Shia settlement northeast of Beirut. Over the course of a decade there, he turned out a vast scholarly output of a specialized variety that had very few readers in the Beirut of those days. He had on his hands, as well, a constant battle with an older mullah, a shallow and conservative cleric who had preceded him to that squatter settlement, a man who, among other things, courted the Shah's regime in Iran and received some subsidies from the Shah's operatives in Lebanon. The two men had clashed; Shaykh Rida Farhat, the older man, was a man who loved his comforts and prerogatives, who acquired property, and who had a roving eye for the women in his neighborhood. Fadlallah was a more dedicated and serious cleric. Fadlallah's radicalization had come in 1976: that year, the neighborhood in which he lived and worked was to fall to the Maronite militias, and its Shia inhabitants were to be driven out. It was during that difficult summer that he put together a book that foreshadowed the militant thought of radicalized Shiism: *Al Islam wa Mantaq al Quwa* (Islam and the Logic of Force). Speaking of the harsh conditions under which he worked, he says, this book was written during "times of intermittent fighting in the part of the city where I lived . . . by candlelight, under heavy shelling. This is a word I record so that it may be remembered."

In Fadlallah's book can be seen the intellectual and psychological change which turned the familiar Shia history of political quietism and withdrawal into a doctrine of rebellion and confrontation. Passed on and elaborated by jurists, hammered into the psyche by a folklore of lament, Shiism had reconciled its adherents to worldly dispossession. With this tradition Fadlallah parts company. He exalts force and power. Force, he says, enables a man to be himself and not someone else, enables him to seize control of his life. "Force means that the world gives you its resources and its wealth; conversely, in conditions of weakness, a man's life degenerates, his energies are wasted; he becomes subject to something that resembles suffocation or paralysis. History, the history of war and peace, of science and wealth, is the history of the strong."

Since its inception, Shia thought had not seen the acquisition of power as a prerequisite of a good and pious life. But this is where Fadlallah's thought leads. Fadlallah gets there more by relying on the main body of Islamic doctrine than on the strictures of the narrower and politically worsted Shiism. As in Ayatollah Khomeini's thought, there is in Fadlallah's a curiously Sunni orientation—the sense that *taqiyya*, dissimulation, should be abandoned, that men should create a Muslim order and defend it. "Strength" and "force," he writes, are attributes beloved by God. The "pious strong" man is more meritorious in God's eyes than the "pious weak." The "truth of religion" is a "call to strength." Only a society on its feet could carry on its assigned mission as a just and pious society. Fadlallah quotes the Quranic verse: "Allah loves those who fight for his cause in ranks as firm as a mighty edifice" (61:4). "Muslim society" he writes, is compelled by its own teachings to stand up to those who would "threaten its unity and safety." From the Quran again, Fadlallah quotes God's call to his Prophet, Muhammad: "Prophet, make war on the unbelievers and the hypocrites and deal rigorously with them" (9:73).

The old stricture that had seen other clerics through periods of political withdrawal—that of "enjoining the good and forbidding evil"—acquires a new interpretation in Fadlallah's work: it is not only by words that men forbid evil, he writes, but through "armed power" as well. There is an erroneous assumption, he continues, that "the word is the weapon of religion, not the bullet," that the ulama "deviate from their religious mission when they interfere in politics, or resort to force to change social and political conditions, because their proper domain is thought to be the mosque and not life itself." Such a view, he says, is erroneous because "Islam is both a call and a state, *Dawa wa Dawla*." Religious ritual is not enough in Islam: The Prophet was both a ruler and a religious guide. And Imam Ali, the commander of the faithful, had fulfilled the same functions.

What of the Shia idea of the Hidden Imam, *al Mahdi al Muntazar*, Fadlallah asks? Does that idea mean men should abandon the political realm, does it rule out a just state in the absence of the Imam? "We reject this entirely," he says. "Society needs a state, needs to be organized. The issue is not the existence of an infallible Imam but society's innate need for a ruling order, to rescue men from confusion and chaos." Even during times of *al Ghaiba*, the Imam's absence, "society

[215]

has to be organized, men have to have the proper conditions that enable them to be pious believers and proper men."

Armed rebellion did not come to an end, Fadlallah says, with "Imam Hussein's revolution." The Shia of Hussein misinterpret his legacy when they assume that history after Hussein entered a "peaceful stage that avoided the ruler and submitted to him." It is true, he says, that *taqiyya*, dissimulation, became a practice during difficult times. But surely, the avoidance of struggle cannot be a permanent resort and a permanent response to injustice. It was true that the Imams who succeeded Hussein refrained from armed rebellions, counseled the believers against them, and tried to rein in extremist movements of their partisans. But they did so, in Fadlallah's interpretation, because they knew that such movements were doomed to failure or because such movements did not carry within them the seeds of a "just Islamic order, *Nizam Islami Haq*." The Imams, he says, could have had "information or prophecies that foretold the failure of such opposition movements."[28]

In Fadlallah's reading of what the legitimate Imams taught, silence and submission could be only "tactical and temporary." The Prophet's family could not have bequeathed a different message, he says. Shiism itself, he adds, knew the secret organization, the cell, the attempt to bring the faithful together against oppression. Shiism authorized violence in some historical circumstances, forbade it during others.

There is no evidence that Fadlallah's book attracted much attention when it was first released. The Iranian revolution was still two years away, and the kind of ideas that the book set out were still the thoughts of only a few religious professionals. The discourse about Shiism being a revolutionary philosophy must have seemed like a piece of wishful thinking. We have no way of knowing whether Musa al Sadr himself read Fadlallah's book. He, of course, knew its author, respected his scholarly output. Both had been students of the marja in Najaf, Abu al Qasim al Musawi al Kho'i; in 1976, Fadlallah had been designated a representative of Kho'i in Lebanon. A certain amount of tension must have been built into the relationship between Fadlallah and Musa al Sadr; some informants in Lebanon hint that the younger man might have resented the "star quality" of Musa al Sadr and his political preeminence. At any rate, 1976–1977 was a time when Musa al Sadr was busy fending off the charges of the Palestin-

[28]Muhammad Hussein Fadlallah, *Al Islam wa Mantaq al Quwa* (Islam and the Logic of Force), 3d. ed. (Beirut, 1985). Passages quoted from pages 17, 57–58, 92, 137–138, 236–237, 243–244.

ian organizations that he was a mere puppet of Syria, that he had sold
out the Palestinian-leftist camp and opted for an alliance with Syria
and for giving the status quo in Lebanon a chance. He also had on his
hands the staggering human problems of the Shia refugees who had
been forced out of northeastern Beirut. What resources and attention
he was able to muster must have been spent on trying to keep his
movement and program alive during a particularly critical period.

Fadlallah's book acquired a new kind of authority several years
later. Events had conspired to supply these militant words with con-
firmation. Fadlallah himself acknowledges this in a preface to the
third edition, written in November 1984—a year after Shia suicide
drivers had become worldwide news. "To speak of force today is not
an abstract, misty philosophical discussion. . . . It is the discussion of
the hour." There is an attempt, he says, to write off "Islamic resistance" to the West as terror, to strip it of any kind of legitimacy. But
this, he says, obscures the fact that the Great Powers in the world
"write the laws" and leave the weak with no other resort than obedience. In a world dominated by powerful states, Fadlallah concludes,
the weak do what they can. "Civilization does not mean that you face
a rocket with a stick or a jet-fighter with a kite, or a warship with a
sailboat. . . . One must face force with equal or superior force. If it is
legitimate to defend self and land and destiny, then all means of self-
defense are legitimate."[29]

The sense of siege, of being in the midst of a long battle, is all too
apparent. The book written in an embattled ghetto of Beirut speaks of
political life as nothing but a realm for vigilance and continuing enmity. Men no longer believed that peace was possible. They were left
with exalting war and those who waged it.

Two Shia revolts were rolled together in Lebanon: an extremist millenarian revolt and a reformist mainstream one. And both were
grafted onto the legacy of Musa al Sadr by their respective adherents.
The first revolt could go nowhere. It could rail against the world; it
could talk about the establishment of an "Islamic republic" in Lebanon. But it could not change the nature of that land of rival sects, nor
could it overcome the harsh economic limits of a small country that
has lived off trade and services. There is no viable agricultural hinterland in Lebanon to sustain a zealous state of the faithful. Unlike Iran,
Lebanon has no oil wealth that would accrue to those who fight their
way to political power. The space and resources for a utopia of any
kind do not exist. Pamphlets, icons, and "political money" could

[29]Ibid., preface to third edition.

bring to Lebanon the passion and the schemes of Iran. But men and women in Lebanon sharing Iran's Shia faith live in a world and a state of their own. Carried across frontiers—particularly across a tough, unsentimental state like Syria—the Shia truth of Iran runs into concrete social realities very different from those of its base. Beirut is a tough and cynical city; Lebanon itself is a country in the shadow of two larger powers, Syria and Israel. This is not exactly the ideal site for a great movement of redemption. Even Fadlallah dismisses the idea of an Islamic state in Lebanon. The "objective conditions," he says, are not there for "Islam to rule Lebanon." Such ideas, he says, are leaps into the void; one has to consider the "larger balance of forces," the limits and the makeup of the country.[30]

The larger revolt by Lebanon's Shia mainstream has familiar aspects. It wants for the Shia, the country's largest demographic group, pride of place in the distribution of power and spoils. History in Lebanon has again changed direction. The Druze of Mount Lebanon once governed the Lebanese heartland as feudal rulers and warlords. Then, in the mid-nineteenth century, the Maronites overtook them, found their way to the city of Beirut when it was becoming a thriving trade center, developed links to Europe through a vibrant silk industry, and learned the ways of the modern world. The Druze were too inflexible to change. The Maronites had something more substantial and viable to offer Lebanon—and even the Arab world beyond. It was on that reserve that the Maronites drew for a little more than a century.

In the aftermath of 1982, the Shia bid for power was made. The Shia had emerged as the country's principal sect. They and their leaders had not yet acquired the skills and attitudes which a long tradition of power imparts to men. They had their resentments about past grievances and humiliations, and they had the familiar assortment of ambitious and driven men who emerge in moments of social and political breakdown and push on to build small tyrannies and turfs of their own. Born of terrible times and circumstances—a sense of historical disinheritance and dispossession, a decade of Israeli-Palestinian war, an Israeli occupation of the south, a Syrian occupation in the Bekaa Valley—this Shia bid had typically Lebanese characteristics: the primacy of the religious sect and clan, the will of the "big man" leading a particular sect, the intensity and the passion of the feuds between men, between sects. This drive for change had the country's dust and limitations in its eyes. It had emerged out of Lebanon's own soil; it

---

[30]Muhammad Hussein Fadlallah in *Al Harakat al Islamiyya fi Lubnan*, pp. 259–265.

could not be disowned by those who lived to see it, to suffer at its hands. A mullah of foreign birth had given the movement his political skills and, then, his legacy. But countries and men turn strangers and legacies that they receive in their midst into familiar figures and themes, into extensions of themselves.

The story of Sayyid Musa's rise, of the devotion accorded him when he was on the scene, was embellished and reworked, made to serve the need of a people in distress for an Imam with remarkable authority and powers. But before the millenarian myth there was the man himself. A young Shia historian who knew him, who argued with him over the fine points of Marxism versus Islam whenever the restless cleric turned up in the historian's home, strips the tale of its triumphant note. He tells a simpler story of a time before the exaltation. He recalls the melancholy of the man, the suspicions that surrounded him, the difficulties he had enlisting money and support from reluctant men in a hard country. "He gave us more than we gave him," says the historian. "He groped for solid ground but it was denied him. Think of what befell him in Libya. Think of his Iranian-born wife waiting for him in Lebanon."

Then in a remarkable set of images, the young historian borrowed a figure from Greek tragedy which captured what he saw to be the tragedy of Musa al Sadr: that of Icarus, the son of Daedalus. In the myth, Daedalus, imprisoned in a tower by King Minos, came up with a plan to escape with his son. "Minos may control the land and the sea," he said, "but not the regions of the air. I will try that way." Daedalus then made wings for himself and for his young son Icarus. He put the wings together out of thread and wax. Icarus was instructed not to fly too low lest the damp clog his wings, or too high lest the heat of the sun melt them. Flying was thrilling, and Icarus soared upward as if to reach heaven. The blazing sun softened the wax; the feathers came off and Icarus plunged to the sea.

In the tale of the cleric who came to Lebanon from his Iranian homeland, there was an attempt to soar; there were times when it seemed possible that the old Shia tradition could be modernized without becoming merciless, when a mix of tradition and tolerance could be hoped for. But it was not to be: Sayyid Musa helped stir up a storm, and when the storm came, he was one of its victims.

Sayyid Musa had sought to change the stagnant Shia tradition, to strip it of its sorrow and quiescence, to make it come to terms with the world. But when the change came, it came with a vengeance. In the land of his birth and in the country he adopted, Shia clerics made of sterner stuff than he now threw themselves, in one historian's phrase, "from their shoes to their turbans into politics and into other people's business."[31] Sayyid Musa had been one of those who had rehabilitated the legacy of Imam Hussein, who had turned the tale of sorrow into one of political choice and daring. In the years that followed Musa al Sadr's disappearance, the Shia romance with Imam Hussein lost any sense of proportion and restraint. So many claiming Hussein as a contemporary and a guide got the legacy wrong: it was not to Kerbala, the site of his death, that he had been journeying; he was going to the city of Kufa on the invitation of men who promised to be on his side. Kerbala was where Hussein was trapped while on a mission of commitment and obligation. And his destination was far from a perfect realm of justice: he was journeying to a city whose wordly ways he knew all too well.

Men speaking of what they see as exemplary lives often speak of their own notions of themselves, of what they take to be the driving force of their own lives. In a eulogy of the Iranian radical sociologist Ali Shariati (1933–1977)—a pamphleteer who mixed the symbols of Shia Islam with the radical outlook of Frantz Fanon and Jean-Paul Sartre—Musa al Sadr said that men living through difficult times which fail to meet their aspirations split off into four categories. There are those who submit, become "pillars of society," become like the large unjust society around them. A second group rejects the standing order, but despairs of its ability to change it, and "migrates" in its mind and spirit. A third believes in the necessity of change, but believes as well in the "bankruptcy of its own heritage" and turns outside to foreign models of change and foreign ideologies. This group, he said, should not be judged too harshly: it sought the right thing even if its means were in error. The fourth group, to which Ali Shariati belonged, believed in change, but sought to bring about justice through an "authentic ideology that emerged out of the soil of Islamic society."[32]

What Musa al Sadr said of Shariati was a fair summation of where he himself stood, of what he had attempted to do. The Shia scholarly and political tradition was what he knew and worked with. The Shia worlds of Iran, where he was born, of Iraq, where he had studied in the religious city of Najaf, of Lebanon, where he had his "reign" as

[31]Roy Mottahedeh, *The Mantle of the Prophet* (New York: Simon & Schuster, 1985), p. 356.
[32]Musa al Sadr's statement on Ali Shariati delivered in the summer of 1977 is to be found in his collection of lectures, *Nukhba min al Muhadarat* (A Selection of Lectures) (Beirut, no date), p. 101.

Imam, were all difficult, in many ways merciless, societies. He made his way between the power of a status quo that he sought both to change and to appeal to and lower classes whose mood was a mixture of fatal resignation and wrath awaiting a chance to have their day against the mighty and the pampered. He gave some of his own courage and grace to men who had known only a sullen and resentful kind of quiescence. It was not his fault that power and privilege did not know how to share what they had, how to open the gates of the social order and let the excluded in. And, surely, it was no fault of his that when the excluded stormed the citadels many of them smashed through with little if any mercy for others, or any grace.

A deep chasm separates the dominant thought and institutions of majoritarian Sunni Islam from the rival culture of the Shia. In the Arab world, the split between Sunni wealth and political power and the Shia is made no less acute, no less problematic, by denying that it exists, by writing off the issue as one of "primitive sectarianism." Late in the twentieth century, that seventh-century battle of Kerbala is being refought: Shia quietism and submissiveness were their own hell. Traded in a hurry, they were traded for a politics of exaltation and martyrology. The Shia tradition had too much grief and pent-up resentment for it to be unleashed without a long season of anger and carnage. Sayyid Musa had wanted his clerical colleagues to oppose the rulers, the oppressors, to be on the side of the "wretched of the earth." He had been a precursor of activism during a time of submissiveness. But the fury that carried with it much of Shia tradition to which he was an heir went well beyond the limits he knew and lived by.

Lebanon, too, permitted no great flights and possibilities. Sayyid Musa tried to soften a hard country, to remind its people how small the country was, and thus how self-defeating were the dreams of purity and monopoly of power that seized its warring camps. He appealed to the country with its own claims—that it was a place where faiths embraced, where rival truths were made to coexist. But in the last years of his work in Lebanon, and then in the years that followed his disappearance, the country became a much harsher place. It bid farewell to the niceties and formalities that had both concealed and made more bearable its religious schisms. Lebanon had no patience for subtleties: all roads inevitably led men to the simple truth of the armed camp.

Musa al Sadr led his Lebanese followers at a time when they were beginning to make a claim on their country. He vanished and left them with a text and a memory and some institutions at a time when

[221]

the country as a whole had become a ruined place. Young men behind sandbags, with their Imam's posters, defend the ruins that are theirs and their sect's. A measure of equality has come to Lebanon. On the other side, too, in places once forbidden to the Shia, once vain and pompous, there is ruin as well.

Of the impossible history of Costaguana, the fictitious South American republic of plunder and cruelty that was the site of Joseph Conrad's *Nostromo*, Conrad wrote: "The cruel futility of things stood unveiled in the levity and sufferings of that incorrigible people; the cruel futility of lives and of deaths thrown away in the vain endeavor to attain an enduring solution of the problem."[33] The Lebanese had their history and their temperament: their history had failed them. But they could not and would not change. Men who labored to change them must have felt as though they were ploughing the seas.

[33]Joseph Conrad, *Nostromo* (New York: New American Library, 1960), p. 293.

Index

[223]

Index

[227]